Recent Investigations in the Puuc Region of Yucatán

edited by

Meghan Rubenstein

Archaeopress Pre-Columbian Archaeology 8

Archaeopress Publishing Ltd
Gordon House
276 Banbury Road
Oxford OX2 7ED

www.archaeopress.com

ISBN 978 1 78491 544 5
ISBN 978 1 78491 545 2 (e-Pdf)

© Archaeopress and the authors 2017

Cover image: Stucco fragment from Kiuic, Yucatán, Mexico.
© Melissa Galván Bernal and the Bolonchén Regional Archaeological Project

This book is available direct from Archaeopress or from our website www.archaeopress.com

Table of Contents

Introduction

The scholarship assembled in this volume was first presented at the 79th Annual Meeting of the Society for American Archaeology (SAA) in Austin, Texas, in April 2014. Some of the authors have chosen to publish their conference papers while others have expanded on their topics. As a collection, the papers demonstrate a myriad of approaches to the history of the Puuc region, incorporating archaeological, architectural, epigraphic, and iconographic studies. The geographic scope is also broad. Many of the recent and ongoing archaeological projects in the eastern Puuc region and its periphery are represented, including Dzehkabtún, H'wasil, Kabah, Kiuic, Labná, Sayil, Uxmal, and Xcoch, as well as the Chocholá ceramic tradition from the western Puuc. The projects are at various stages—some preliminary, others a portion of a larger investigation, while still others are revisiting older data—all with the aim to advance our field of study.

While this volume covers a wide range of topics, it is by no means an exhaustive view of the current state of the field nor does it include all the scholars involved in long term research in the Puuc region. Two additional papers from the SAA session were also left out of this publication, due to the authors' competing obligations. In Austin, Rebecca Hill presented her research on geochemical characterization of obsidian artifacts in the Bolonchén district and Maggie Morgan-Smith shared her work with archival documents and oral history from Rancho Kiuic. David Stuart was the session's discussant.

It has been many years since a volume dedicated solely to the Puuc region has been published. While Puuc research frequently appears in collected volumes on the Yucatán peninsula or the Terminal Classic period, we are pleased to have the opportunity to present this representative collection of ongoing work.

Meghan Rubenstein, editor

Part I: Archaeology

An Enigmatic Maya Center: Climate Change, Settlement Systems, and Water Adaptations at Xcoch, Puuc Region, Yucatán

Michael P. Smyth, Nicholas P. Dunning, Eric M. Weaver, Philip van Beynen,
and David Ortegón Zapata

Xcoch was a large Preclassic center that became even larger by the Late Classic period. Though water management and agricultural intensification were always critical in this drought prone hill region, the presence of a deep water cave near the site center, a massive central acropolis, and widespread Preclassic pyramid architecture render Xcoch rather unique in the settlement history of the region. This paper will discuss settlement and water features, cave research, and the cycles of drought recently reconstructed via speleothem analysis from the Vaca Perdida cave near Xcoch. The central architecture, the Xcoch cave, and other major settlement groups incorporate aguadas, reservoirs, and other water features to show that water management was highly developed and fundamental to site occupation. These findings begin to reveal a long developmental sequence, rapid declines, and human ecodynamics in a region once thought to be relatively late and short-lived in the prehistory of the Northern Maya Lowlands.

Xcoch fue un centro grande del preclásico que llegó a ser incluso más grande en el periodo clásico tardío. Aunque la administración de agua y la intensificación agrícola fueron siempre críticas en esta región de colinas que es propensa de la sequía, la presencia de una cueva de agua profunda cerca al centro del sitio, un acrópolis central masivo, y grupos de arquitectura numerosas con pirámides en el Preclásico hacen Xcoch algo único en la historia de la región. Este papel discutirá los elementos del asentamiento y del agua, la investigación de las cuevas, y los ciclos de la sequía reconstruidos recientemente vía análisis del espelotemos de la cueva de la Vaca Perdida cerca de Xcoch. La arquitectura central, la cueva de Xcoch, y otros grupos importantes del asentamiento incorporaron aguadas, los depósitos, y otras elementos del agua para demostrar que la administración del agua era altamente desarrollada y fundamental para la ocupación del sitio. Estos resultados comienzan a revelar una secuencia de desarrollo larga, deslaves rápidos, y los ecodinámicos humanos en una región de la cual se pensó de ser relativamente atrasada y de breve duración en la prehistoria de las tierras bajas Mayas norteñas.

At the site of Xcoch and grotto of the same name, an arduous subterranean journey took place on January 6, 1841 by John L. Stephens who remarked:

As a mere cave, this [Xcoch] was extraordinary; but as a well or watering-place for an ancient city, it was past belief, except for the proofs under our own eyes. Around were the ruins of a city without visible means of supply [water]...(Stephens 1963:217).

In 2006, the first systematic archaeological investigation at Xcoch began to determine the extent and composition of settlement features across a large urban center suspected to have begun in the Preclassic period. By 2009, interdisciplinary research expanded into a study of water management, climate change, and human ecodynamics. Indeed, results now show Xcoch to be one of the largest settlements in the Puuc region covering over 10 sq km with massive central architecture, huge water reservoirs, and diverse settlement features including numerous pyramid groups constructed during the Preclassic. Heavily populated during the Late Classic (c. A.D. 800), there is ceramic and stratigraphic evidence at Xcoch for a 'hiatus' period of site abandonment or site reduction between the Late Preclassic and Early Classic periods (A.D. 100-300; Smyth et al. 2014), though how widespread this phenomenon may have been across the Puuc region is not known. Paleoclimatic data from northern Yucatán and elsewhere in the Maya Lowlands, however, strongly suggest that recurring droughts may have dramatically affected the distribution of Maya settlement during the Preclassic to Classic transition (Brenner et al. 2000; Dunning, Wahl, et al. 2014; Gill 2000; Haug et al. 2003; Hodell et al. 2005; Medina-Elizade et al. 2010; Smyth et al. 2011).

Paleoenvironmental research now provides compelling evidence linking climate change, especially drought, to the 9th century Classic Maya collapse as well as previous and later Maya declines. These proxy data have identified either general trends or specific events within the paleoenvironmental record to draw questionable conclusions regarding the impacts on Maya civilization as a whole (Dunning et al. 2013). Our study focuses on one large community at Xcoch and its hinterland to suggest that although all Maya communities indeed shared a set of common vulnerabilities to environmental hazards, there were communities in some regions that were more resilient to changing environmental conditions than others; we need to know the range of variability in the kinds of human response. To understand these complex phenomena requires studies that target specific individual sites and their hinterlands that are representative of human ecodynamic variability and must include the reconstruction and the

Michael P. Smyth - Foundation for Americas Research, Inc. (mpsmyth@netzero.net); **Nicholas P. Dunning** - University of Cincinnati (dunninnp@ucmail.uc.edu); **Eric M. Weaver** - University of Cincinnati (weaverem@mail.uc.edu); **Philip van Beynen** - University of South Florida (vanbeyne@usf.edu); **David Ortegón Zapata** - Instituto Nacional de Antropología e Historia (INAH), Mérida, Yucatán (josegradena@yahoo.com.mx).

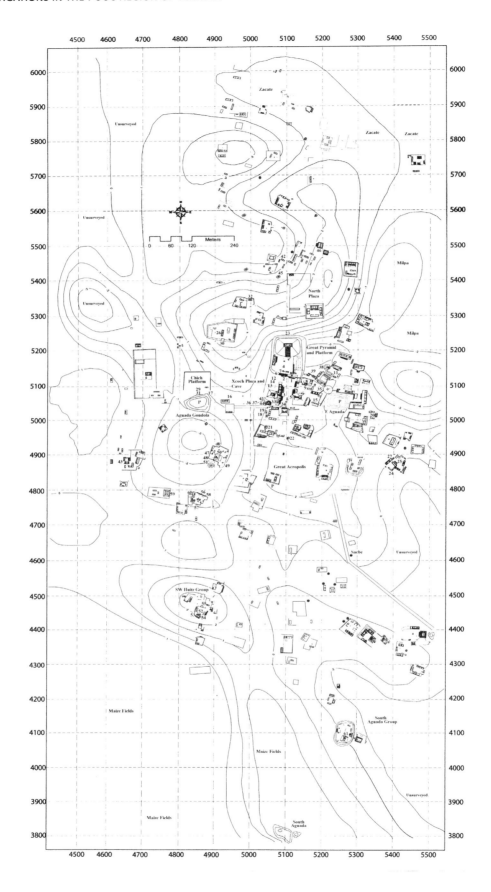

FIGURE 1. TOPOGRAPHIC AND PLANIMETRIC MAP OF XCOCH SHOWING THE MAJOR SETTLEMENT GROUPS, THE XCOCH CAVE, *AGUADAS* (WATER HOLDING PONDS), AND THE NUMBERED LOCATIONS OF TEST PITS AND OTHER EXCAVATIONS (P).

systematic linking of both the paleoenvironmental record of severe climate change and the archaeological record of the Maya response.

This paper discusses the results of settlement pattern research, including surface collection survey and architectural mapping, and a program of test excavation, ceramic analysis, and radiocarbon dating. In addition, we present data on water management practices such as *aguadas*, water tanks, and catchment systems at Xcoch as well as the related cave investigations and speleothem analyses carried out at the Xcoch and Vaca Perdida caves. These studies indicate that the site of Xcoch and vicinity were occupied at the beginning of Maya settlement in northern Yucatán and that drought cycles had significant impact on human adaptation and culture process in the Puuc hill region.

Xcoch Settlement

Xcoch is known for its deep water cave, a tall megalithic pyramid, and a giant platform covering about one hectare that together stand more than 42 m above the ground surface. The Great Pyramid is the highest point of a massive multi-level acropolis incorporating at least ten architectural groups covering ten hectares, representing one of the largest integrated constructions in the Puuc region (Figure 1). Much of the acropolis is constructed in the early megalithic style, characterized by large shaped boulders with abundant chinking stones, and believed to be an indicator of Preclassic to Early Classic occupation. On the south side of the Grand Platform leading to the Great Pyramid are two megalithic staircases with large treads and risers. The central megalithic staircase is virtually identical to one recently consolidated at Xocnaceh, a relatively small site approximately 20 km to the east of Xcoch containing an enormous Preclassic period platform (Bey 2006; Gallareta and Ringle 2004; Stanton and Gallareta 2002). Atop the megalithic staircase at Xcoch are three stone buildings, a three-room vaulted building on the west, a long rubble structure on the east, and the Great Pyramid of Xcoch, which towers over the north end of the Grand Platform. The lower sections of this enormous terraced pyramid show megalithic characteristics, but the uppermost reaches are clearly formed by multiple Classic period constructions, now badly fallen.

The megalithic 'Cave Pyramid' sits immediately adjacent to the sinkhole (Xcoch Grotto) and entrance to Xcoch Cave on southwest edge of Xcoch Plaza, the apparent central point of the ancient community. This long plaza measures approximately 100 m N-S by 50 m E-W, not including the megalithic staircases on the north and large pyramids on the east, west, and south sides each flanked by stone buildings. The East Pyramid also is in the megalithic style and contains recessed staircases with boulder-shaped treads and risers. These megalithic pyramids do not support vaulted buildings, however, but show summit foundations with perishable roofs and have been dated to the Middle Preclassic periods by excavations and C-14 dating (Table

1). Numerous altars and platforms were found at the foot of both pyramids that probably dated to various occupations of the site. On the south side is a Late Classic Puuc-style pyramid with a frontal platform, faced stone staircase, and vaulted buildings at the summit and on its flanks.

The west causeway, dated to the Preclassic, emanates from the Xcoch cave and travels a short distance to the east edge of the Aguada La Góndola. The southeast causeway travels almost one kilometer before arriving at a natural hill supporting a Preclassic group with two pyramids in the megalithic style placed upon an expansive leveling platform. A third group with a pyramid to the east has three stories with vaulted summit buildings in the Early Classic Proto Puuc style. Two hundred meters south is another Preclassic group with a megalithic pyramid and numerous stone foundations. Less than three hundred meters to the south of this group are two aguadas (one is the South Aguada) within the mechanized parcels of the municipality of Santa Elena. From previous reconnaissance, we know that there are other pyramid groups and substantial settlement one kilometer to the east of the Great Pyramid, other architectural groups in the intermediate zone, and habitation structures to the southeast. Eight hundred meters north of the Great Pyramid are numerous settlement groups including many with pyramids; at least two (the Old Pyramid Group and a pyramid to the east, below) and a small reservoir are dated to the Preclassic period. *Chultuns* (underground water cisterns) are relatively scarce at the site center but more frequent on the site peripheries. They became a ubiquitous feature of residential groups at Puuc sites in the Classic period (Dunning 1992).

Investigation of Water Features

Environmental excavations at Xcoch were largely targeted at topographic depressions that were not obvious reservoirs within the site center and residential zones. Criteria used to distinguish natural depressions from those modified to capture and hold water included: 1) the presence or absence of floors that enhanced water retention; 2) features used to divert water into the depression; and 3) the presence of berms surrounding the depressions that increased water storage capacity. Two of the depressions excavated were located close to the site center, one on the southernmost and lowest terrace of the central acropolis complex, and another on the southeast side of the Old Pyramid Group 200 m north of the Great Pyramid.

Most structures in the Old Pyramid Group lie on a large platform and mapping revealed an archaic pyramid with no clear summit building surrounded by multiple foundation brace buildings on the east and south sides. Test excavation (Op. 43) at the base of the Old Pyramid date this structure to the Preclassic period, though pottery remains in the upper levels of stratigraphy also suggest a reoccupation during the Late Classic as supported by the presence of some of the associated house foundations. Runoff from the platform appears to have been directed into depressions on both the west and southeast sides of

Field Specimen	Lab # NOSAMS	Conventional C-14 Age B.P.	Uncalibrated Calendar Date	Calibrated C-14 Date (2 sigma)	Context
20013	78754	1460+/-25	A.D. 490	A.D. 560-646	Aguada S, Pozo 1(200 cm)
20020	78755	305+/-30	A.D. 1645	A.D. 1488-1603, 1609-1651	Aguada Gondola, Pozo 2 (100 cm)
20045	78756	2520+/-30	570 B.C.	792-716, 695-539 B.C.	Grand Platform, Op. 4, Lev. 6 - Piso V
20046	78757	2550+/-30	600 B.C.	800-743, 689-663, 647-549 B.C.	Grand Platform, Op. 4, Lev. 7 - Piso VI
20059	78758	2560+/-25	610 B.C.	802-749, 687-666, 641-591, 578-567 B.C.	Xcoch Plaza, Op. 5, Lev. 11 - Piso X
20063	78759	145+/-30	A.D. 1805	A.D. 1668-1710, 1717-1781, 1797-1891, 1909-1948	Grand Platform SW, Op. 6 ext. 2, Lev. 1
20072	78760	2570+/-25	620 B.C.	806-751, 686-667, 634-623, 614-594 B.C.	Grand Platform, Niche Bldg, Op. 7, Lev. 3 - Piso II
20076	78761	330+/-25	A.D. 1620	A.D. 1483-1641	Grupo Residencial, Op. 8, Lev. 3 - Piso II
20078	78762	Modern			Grupo Residencial, Op. 8, Lev. 5 - Piso V
20079	78763	245+/-25	A.D. 1705	A.D. 1528-1552, 1633-1673, 1778-1799, 1942-1951	Grupo Residencial, Op. 8, Lev. 6 - Piso V
20082	78764	2490+/-30	540 B.C.	776-508, 458-454, 438-419 B.C.	Grupo Residencial, Op. 8, Lev. 9 - Piso VIII
20088	78765	625+/-25	A.D. 1325	A.D. 1291-1331, 1338-1397	Chultun 2, Op. 15, Lev. 4 (270 cm)
20089	78766	1420+/-30	A.D. 530	A.D. 581-660	Chultun 2, Op. 15, Lev. 5
20124	84303	1750+/-45	A.D. 200	A.D. 139-160, 165-196, 209-398	Aguada Gondola, Pozo 1 (230cm), Lev. 5
20126	84304	2040+/-25	90 B.C.	159-135 B.C., 114 B.C. - A.D. 24	Aguada Gondola, Pozo 1 (310cm)
20131	84305	Modern			East Aguada, Lev. 2
20162	84306	4010+/-30	2060 B.C.	3356-1748 B.C.	Chikin Mul, Op. 26, Lev. 3
20168	84307	1280+/-30	A.D. 670	A.D. 662-779,794-801	Grupo Cuevas, Op. 27, Lev. 7
20185	84308	140+/-30	A.D. 1810	A.D. 1669-1713,1716-1780, 1798-1891, 1908-1944	Mega. F.B., Op. 32, Lev. 3 (150 cm)
20193	84309	2520+/-30	570 B.C.	792-716, 695-539 B.C.	East Pyramid Plaza, Op. 35, Lev. 8, Piso V (below)
20198	84310	2590+/-30	640 B.C.	809.763, 680-673 B.C.	West Sacbé, Op. 36, Lev. 8, Piso III (below)
21001	84311	1250+/-25	A.D. 700	A.D. 678-784, 786-827, 839-864	Gruta Xcoch, Sta. CC3 (A Passage)
21005	84312	175+/-25	A.D. 1775	A. D. 1661-1694, 1727-1813, 1839, 1842, 1853-1859, 1862-1867 AD	Gruta Xcoch, Sta. A4 (A Passage), 1-20 cm
21014	84313	645+/-25	A.D. 1305	A.D. 1283-1324, 1346-1393	Gruta Xcoch, Fire Pit (10 cm), A38
21014A	84314	525+/-30	A.D. 1425	A.D. 1322-1347, 1392-1441	Gruta Xcoch, Fire Pit (25 cm), A38
21019	84315	385+/-30	A.D. 1565	A.D. 1449-1499, 1502-1512, 1601-1616	Gruta Xcoch, Torch, Sta. E13
21020	84316	225 +/-55	A.D. 1725	A.D. 1513-1600, 1617-1706, 1719-1820, 1822-1825, 1832-1884, 1913-1953	Vaca Perdida (30 cm)
20121	84317	1630+/-30	A.D. 320	A.D. 348-369, 378-535	Vaca Perdida, Sala 2
Ya'al Chaac	104687	1530±25	A.D. 420	A.D. 433-494, 505-522, 526-599	Aguada 10 km N of Muna
20251	104688	2250±30	300 B.C .	392-348,317-207 B.C.	S Terrace Pozo 1 85 cm b.s.
20254	104689	1560±25	A.D. 390	A.D. 427-557	S Terrace Pozo 1 135 cm b.s.
21019a	104690	1380±25	A.D. 570	A.D. 614-673	Vaca Perdida Pozo 1 25 cm b.s
21020a	104691	1590±25	A.D. 360	A.D. 418- 538	Vaca Perdida Pozo 2 25-30 cm b.s.

TABLE 1. RADIOCARBON DATES FROM XCOCH, YUCATÁN. ALL DATES WERE CALCULATED USING THE ACCELERATOR MASS SPECTROMETER (AMS) TECHNIQUE FROM THE NATIONAL OCEAN ACCELERATOR MASS SPECTROMETRY FACILITY (NOSAMS) AND THE CALIB RADIOCARBON CALIBRATION PROGRAM.

the platform. A 2 x 2 m pit was excavated near the center of the southern depression.

The strata revealed in the excavation indicate that the depression originated as a small karst doline that was likely expanded for quarrying. Sometime during the Middle Preclassic, the depression began to be used as a garbage dump as reflected in material below 150 cm. At 138-150 cm, the midden material was capped by a poorly preserved floor of clay, sascab, and gravel, thus converting the depression into a small reservoir. Another poorly preserved floor is found at 100-108 cm, this one consisting of plaster and gravel, indicating the renewal of the reservoir. At 50-70 cm there is a discontinuous and variably thick deposit of fine silt most likely an eolian (wind-blown) deposit that probably is indicative of a period of regional aridity and/or cycle of drought perhaps during the Late Classic period as suggested by the diagnostic ceramics found at this level.

Acropolis South Terrace Excavation

A small depression of the southern-most and lowest terrace in the Xcoch acropolis was investigated with a test pit (see Figure 1). The strata revealed in the pit is illustrated in Figure 2. Two probable floors were identified at 80-90 cm (300 B.C.) and 130–140 cm (A.D. 390) but it is not clear why the dates are inverted (Table 1). Both floors were composed of compacted clay and sascab. These floors suggest that the depression served as a water collection tank situated to collect runoff from the paved surface of the terrace. The lower floor was associated only with Preclassic ceramics whereas the upper floor appears to be associated with diagnostic Late/Terminal Classic Cehpech wares.

Excavations in these two smaller depressions at Xcoch revealed that both had been utilized to collect and store rainwater. This finding indicates that the ancient Maya residents of Xcoch were collecting rainwater at multiple scales including large reservoirs such as the huge Aguada La Góndola, modest sized 'tanks' which are appear as depressions at many large platform groups, and household chultuns.

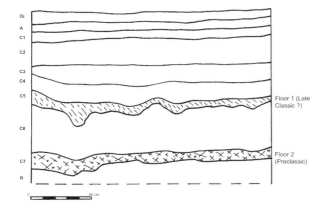

FIGURE 2. PROFILE OF THE WESTERN POZO WALL OF THE SOUTHERN TERRACE OF THE XCOCH ACROPOLIS.

Aguadas and Water Control Systems

Testing at Xcoch has confirmed that three large depression features (*aguadas*) are reservoirs; several others are suspected but not verified (Dunning, Weaver et al. 2014). These aguadas were mapped and sampled by sediment coring and trenching operations to obtain pollen and stratigraphic information that were dated by radiocarbon methods where possible (Figures 3a-b). The sediment cores, unfortunately, produced no usable pollen remains in part because these aguada features have not held water for long periods, which is necessary for pollen preservation. The aguada zone, approximately 1.5 km south of central Xcoch, was the first area to be investigated because it showed evidence for possible irrigation canals associated with ponding features in a rich agricultural zone of modern farm fields of Santa Elena (Smyth and Ortegón 2008).

South Aguada

The South Aguada (Aguada 1) is an irregular depression. In recent years, its surface has been significantly altered by forest clearing and mechanized plowing associated with modern irrigation agriculture. Local informants report that the aguada no longer holds significant quantities of water, but did so within recent memory. Pozo 1 was excavated in the floor of the South Aguada, toward its eastern side (Figures 1 and 3a). A largely decomposed plaster floor was revealed at a depth of about 170 cm. The C3 and C4 horizons overlying the floor show elevated levels of OM (organic matter content) and P and likely represent sediment that accumulated while the aguada was in active use. The charcoal-rich C2 horizon may represent a drying episode in the aguada's history, with wetter conditions likely returning when the sediments comprising the overlying C1 horizon were deposited, providing a suitable habitat for Pomaceae snails.

Pozo 3 was excavated near the apex of the northern berm of the South Aguada (Figure 4). Two probable linings were encountered at 52-67 cm and 75-89 cm and present light-colored sandy clay layers with abundant pebbles, chich cobbles, and charcoal; likely the highly weathered remains of former low quality plaster surfaces and underlying preparation matrixes. An apparent buried, weakly developed surface soil (Ab horizon) appears at 47-52 cm, possibly having formed atop the upper of the two exposed linings and probably reflecting a period of abandonment in the use history of the aguada. The burial of the Ab horizon likely indicates a later reuse of the aguada, including dredging of sediment and deposition on the northern berm. The current surface soil (Ap horizon) shows a loss of organic matter and silt due to modern cultivation. Small numbers of weathered sherds were found at all levels.

The South Aguada is associated with possible irrigation canals passing through the north and south berms. Large boulders near the north berm suggest that these stones may have served as some form of sluice gate, allowing water to be contained and released from the aguada. Canals appear

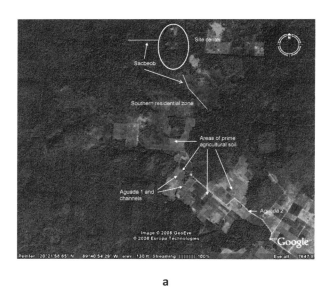

a

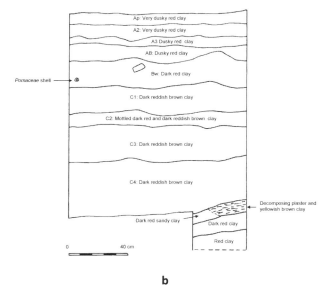

b

FIGURE 3 A-B. (A) AERIAL PHOTO OF THE SOUTH AGUADA ZONE SHOWING AGUADAS 1 AND 2, CANALS, AND THE PRIME AGRICULTURAL SOIL OF SANTA ELENA'S MODERN FARM FIELDS (GOOGLE EARTH 2008); (B) A PROFILE DRAWING OF THE NORTH WALL OF POZO 1 OF AGUADA 1 (SOUTH).

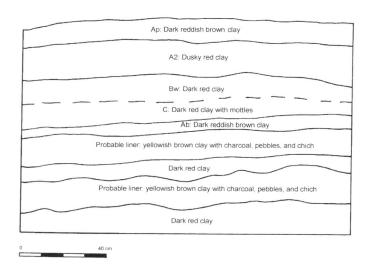

FIGURE 4. PROFILE DRAWING OF THE EAST WALL OF POZO 3 AT THE SOUTH AGUADA.

to run for several hundred meters in both directions but have been badly damaged by modern plowing activity over the years, particularly since the advent of deep plowing with tractors. It is possible that these canals, however, may have been used to transport water from the aguada to surrounding agricultural fields during periods of local *caniculas*, mini dry spells during the rainy season occurring around mid-July. This time is critical in the growth cycle of maize and if sufficient water is not available, maize plants will produce only a few, small ears or no ears at all, even if abundant rainfall returns later. Today, such climatic conditions are countered with irrigation water provided by deep wells and electric pumps, though farmers must pay for the electricity usage.

Aguada La Góndola

Aguada La Góndola lies approximately 100 m west of the Xcoch cave entrance and site center. It is a roughly rectangular depression about 110 m on its east-west axis and 80 m on its north-south axis, though there is an embayment along the south side of the aguada making it somewhat pentagonal in shape (Figure 5). The aguada is currently about six meters deep. There are sluiceways leading into the aguada at its northeast and northwest corners. Low berms are visible around much of the outer rim of the aguada. Alignments of large stone blocks can be seen at varying elevations on each of the interior walls of the depression. Six *pozos* (trenches) were excavated across one such alignment situated about midway up the north wall, into the berm along the northern rim, and in the floor and center of the aguada.

In 2010, the central excavation of Aguada La Góndola, Pozo 1 (Figure 6), revealed a possible badly decomposed floor/lining at a depth of 155 cm. Well preserved floors made of compact clay and sascab were exposed at depths of 250 cm and 310 cm. The sediment immediately above each of these lower floors contained abundant sherds and charcoal. The lowest floor was associated with only Preclassic ceramics suggesting that the reservoir was in place early in the site's history. Late/Terminal Classic ceramics (Cehpech) found in the middle and upper strata suggest that the reservoir continued to be used and refurbished.

On the northern rim, Pozo 2 revealed floors/reservoir linings at depths of 25 cm, 50 cm, and 70 cm; the upper floor was significantly decomposed whereas the lower two floors were still solid (Figure 7). These floors appear to have been associated with low boulder retaining walls, though in this place those walls have partially collapsed. The walls and floors were also exposed in Pozo 3, where these features were better preserved.

Pozo 3, excavated in 2010, was a 1 m x 2.5 m trench in the aguada at a point about 12 m east of Pozo 2. The west profile of Pozo 3 is shown in Figure 8. Into the berm on the northern rim floors/reservoir linings were revealed at depths of 35 cm, 70 cm, and 115 cm; the upper floor was significantly decomposed whereas the lower two floors were still solid. These floors are clearly associated with low boulder retaining walls which appear to have been embedded in the floors and likely served to help keep soil from washing into the reservoir. The lowest floor contained only Preclassic ceramics and likely articulates with the lowest floor exposed in the reservoir floor. Late/ Terminal Classic ceramics were recovered in mid to upper strata, indicating that the reservoir had a long use history.

A 2009 trench excavated across an alignment of large stones situated about midway up the north wall revealed a former linear 'bench' supported by a double retaining wall of large stones seated in a thick plaster reservoir liner, although much of the walls are now fallen (Figure 9). A possible interpretation of the placement of the stones along the walls of the aguada is that these features were benches or steps created within the ancient reservoir so that people could more easily gain access to water even as the water level within the reservoir dropped during the course of the dry season. Weathered ceramics were recovered throughout.

The lowermost floor (310 cm) of the reservoir produced a charcoal-based AMS date of 2040 +/-25 B.P. (1 sigma calibrated range of 89 B.C.–A.D. 1; Table 1). This date is in the Late Preclassic, a finding consistent with weathered Sierra Red ceramics lying within and above the floor (Figure 10). The Middle Preclassic dates associated with the *sacbé* connecting the reservoir with the Xcoch Grotto

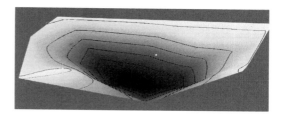

FIGURE 5. 3D DIGITAL ELEVATION MODEL OF AGUADA LA GÓNDOLA CREATED BY ERIC WEAVER. NORTH IS AT THE TOP OF THE IMAGE.

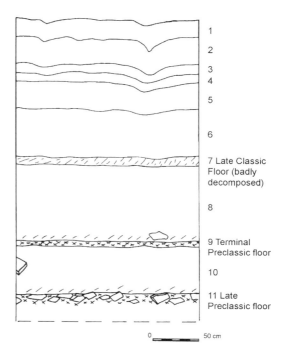

FIGURE 6. AGUADA LA GÓNDOLA 2010 POZO 1: NORTH PROFILE.

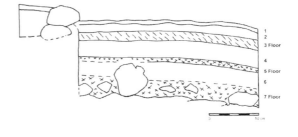

FIGURE 7. AGUADA LA GÓNDOLA 2010 POZO 2: EAST PROFILE.

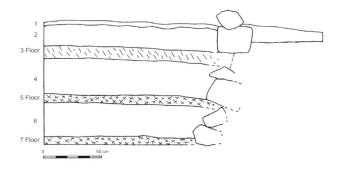

FIGURE 8. AGUADA LA GÓNDOLA 2010 POZO 3: EAST PROFILE.

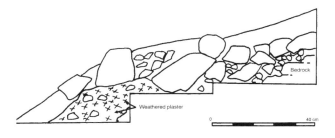

FIGURE 9. AGUADA LA GÓNDOLA 2009 POZO 1: WEST PROFILE.

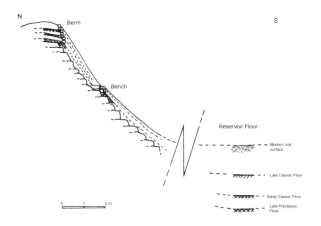

FIGURE 10. CROSS SECTION OF THE NORTH SIDE OF AGUADA LA GÓNDOLA.

suggests that this location may have had ritual significance even before the first known floor was laid, perhaps as a natural sinkhole or pond. However, an undiscovered Middle Preclassic floor cannot be ruled out (Pozo 1 was discontinued in 2010 because of time constraints and safety concerns). The floor at a depth of 230 cm produced a charcoal-based AMS date of 1750 +/- 45 B.P. (1 sigma calibrated range of A.D. 235–377), the Early Classic period. The accumulation of 70-80 cm of sediment in the reservoir between these two floors show signs of a period of abandonment for which there are also indications elsewhere in the site, perhaps occurring towards the end of the Late Preclassic. The second century A.D. was a

notable time of environmental stress, including drought episodes across the Maya lowlands and witnessed site abandonments in many regions (Dunning, Wahl, et al., 2014).

Based upon the findings of stucco floor surfaces sloping to the southwest in Op. 4 (Figures 11a-b) and the absence of stone masonry on the southwest corner of the Grand Platform, a trenching unit (Op. 6) was placed near the SW platform corner (Figures 12a-b). The remains of a stucco feature, an apparent drainage canal, were exposed showing three concave steps that were clearly designed to channel rainwater from the Grand Platform's stucco catchment surface and slow the flow of water downhill towards the Aguada La Góndola some 250 m to the southwest. Additional probes to the south along the Xcoch Plaza revealed stucco and stone canals and a megalithic boulder check damn set in front of the Cave Pyramid that was presumably engineered to turn the flow of water to the south and west before cascading down the terrace edge of the acropolis. At the base of the acropolis, trenching operations exposed a canal of natural bedrock running adjacent to a building platform as well as a junction point (sluiceway) at the northeast corner of Aguada La Góndola where the canals discharged water into the aguada (Figure 12c). In addition, an enormous cobblestone (ch'ich) platform roughly rectangular in shape covering about .75 ha was located along the north side of the aguada, suggesting a massive catchment surface constructed to collect rainwater and direct it into the aguada (Figure 12c).

East Aguada

The East Aguada is a roughly circular depression with a diameter of about 65 m situated a short distance east of the monumental structures on the elevated Xcoch Plaza and Acropolis (Figure 13). The aguada is currently a very shallow depression just over one meter deeper in its center than the surrounding terrain. Vegetation within the depression indicates that it occasionally retains surface water. The aguada is bounded by clear artificial berms on its north and south sides. The west side the aguada abuts limestone outcropping that gives the appearance of having been quarried in ancient times. The east side the aguada is flanked by elevated plazas surmounted by monumental architecture. Several of these plazas appear to be interconnected and canted so that they would funnel rainwater into a clear sluiceway and then into the aguada.

Based on our excavation within the aguada and on the apparent quarry scars on the bedrock exposed along the western flank of the aguada, the Xcoch East Aguada can be best interpreted as having originated as a stone or stone and sascab (lime marl) quarry, although it is possible that a natural depression existed in this spot and was deepened or widened by quarrying. Shortly thereafter, the floor of the quarry was sealed with a layer of compacted, possibly tamped, clay. Ceramics found just above the floor suggest that the reservoir was in place by sometime in the

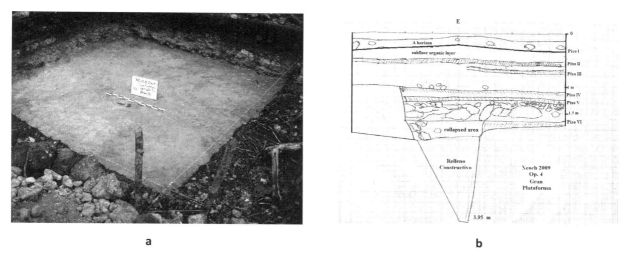

a

b

Figure 11 a-b. (a) Photo of Operation 4, stucco floor III on the Grand Platform looking southwest; (b) Profile drawing of the east wall of this same excavation unit showing all floor levels and construction fill.

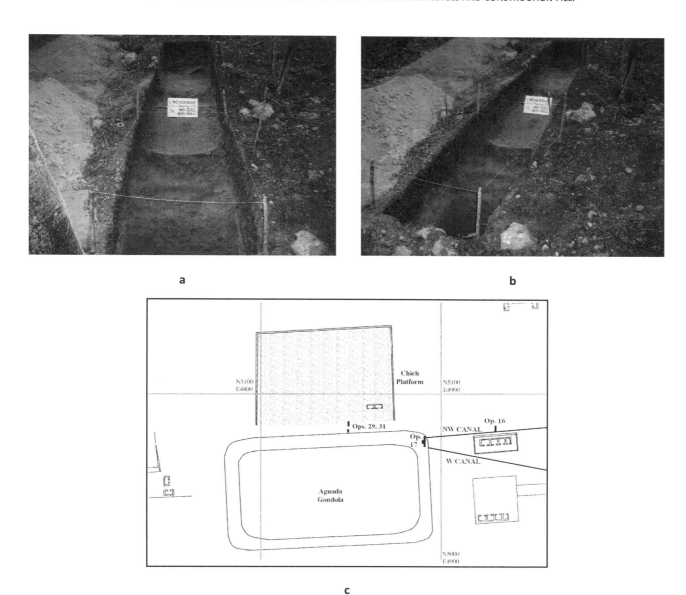

a

b

c

Figure 12 a-c. Photos looking north (a) and northwest (b) of Operation 6 showing the stucco drainage feature with concave steps located near the southwest corner of the Grand Platform; (c) Planimetric map of the Aguada La Góndola, the Chich Platform, and the locations of the northwest (Op. 16) and west canals and junction (Op. 17) at southwest Xcoch.

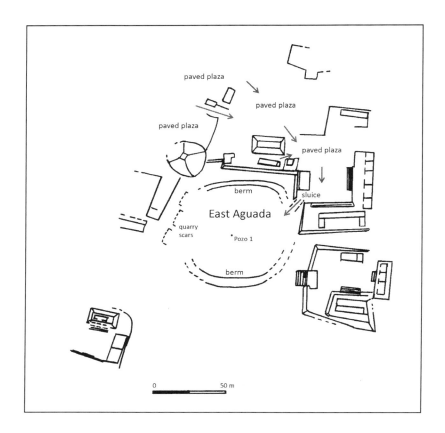

FIGURE 13. SKETCH MAP OF XCOCH EAST AGUADA SHOWING THE SURROUNDING STRUCTURES AND DIRECTION OF RAINWATER MOVEMENT INTO THE AGUADA.

Preclassic period. Clayey sediment began to accumulate after the floor was in place. It is not clear whether or not dredging occurred or whether sediment accumulation was uninterrupted.

Aktun Xcoch

Work at Aktun Xcoch, the Xcoch cave, began in 2009 and included the logistics of opening and preparing the cave for exploration and systematic mapping by a team of experienced cavers as well as pottery collections, soil sampling, and geological and biological survey (Figure 14a-b). These data provide a more comprehensive understanding of the natural and cultural factors that formed this important cave system, the early occupation of the Puuc region, well as the potential for collecting climate based data from this subterranean context.

The Xcoch cave contains a permanent water pool near its bottom with almost inexhaustible surface concentrations of pottery sherds and a number of nearly complete vessels dated from Preclassic to Colonial times, including vessels of the enigmatic Yotolin Patterned Burnished, characterized by long, narrow necks, globular bodies, and long monopod supports (Brainerd 1958; Folan 1968). Yotolin pottery appears to date to the early Middle Preclassic period or contemporaneous with the Early Nabanche phase pottery defined at Komchen (Andrews V 1988, 1990; Ringle and

Andrews 1988). These finds began to provide the context for chronological placement of Yotolin and address the important question of early Middle Preclassic occupation in the Puuc region.

The total surveyed length of the cave is 1,286 km long with a surface length of 103 m. The average diameter of the cave passage is 3.9 m. The cave remains relatively level and then begins to rapidly decline, reaching a depth of 34.9 m over the course of 0.24 km. The average inclination of the cave is 9.8 degrees, indicating a relatively steep slope to the cave passage. The cave appears to have been hypogenic in origin, with several of the large side passages showing evidence of epigenic (hypergenic) development (Klimchouk 2007, 2009). These two processes are so distinctly different within the cave that one may go from one passage or chamber to the next and get the impression of being in two separate caves.

The cave is oriented from the southwest to northeast and is composed of four main chambers. Many of the side passages are mazes of break-aways from and reconnections to the main passage. Numerous pillars in the cave create an even more complex framework within these chambers. The overall layout of the cave appears to be sponge work with some passages exhibiting an anastomotic pattern (Figure 15a). There is no evidence of current water activity in the cave or even water seepage from the walls. The

a

b

FIGURE 14 A-B. (A) A PHOTO OF AN EXCAVATION TRENCH LOOKING EAST EXPOSING A MEGALITHIC-STONE STAIRCASE DESCENDING TO THE MOUTH AND ENTRANCE OF THE CAVE; (B) DETAILED MAP OF THE XCOCH CAVE SHOWING BOTH THE HORIZONTAL AND VERTICAL PROFILES AND DIVERSE CONTEXTUAL INFORMATION.

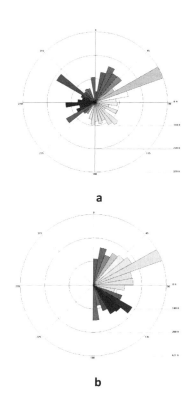

a

b

FIGURE 15 A-B. AZIMUTH DEGREES SHOWING PASSAGE DIRECTION (A) AND WATER FLOW (B).

years. In some areas the soot, when touched, produces an oily residue. The floor of the cave is covered by a loose layer of a rich black soil while the upper passage shows a well-defined trail carved or worn into the floor surface (15-20 cm in depth) suggesting the foot traffic of thousands of visitors over the centuries. The depth of the soil layer throughout the cave has not been determined, but soil samples taken near the cave entrance have recovered remnant pollen (Table 2). The floor of Chamber IV located near the water pool is covered by a hill of broken ceramics and compacted soil and is the only place where the floor is not level; a portion seems to have been built up as a platform.

Pollen Analysis

From the Xcoch cave, five sediment samples from a stratigraphic sequence were analyzed and reported on by John G. Jones (2010). Interestingly, many of the pollen types present in the Xcoch cave samples represent normally rare, insect-pollinated arboreal types, including Passiflora, Solanaceae, Anona, Bauhinia, Ceiba (two species), Pachira, Sapindaceae, and Tiliaceae (Table 2). These taxons are uncommon to rare in most archaeological assemblages. It is suspected that these pollen grains were introduced into the sediments through bat feces; bats consume insects, many of which are pollination vectors. Along with the ingestion of the insects, the bats would have consumed adhering pollen grains, which would pass through the bat gut and ultimately enter the sediment record. A notable quantity of insect chitin was also noted in the samples. The most abundant pollen type (Sapindaceae) in the cave samples is unidentified but is suspected to be something favored by a moth that was consumed by a bat.

Human activity may also be indicated in the Xcoch pollen samples. Cultigens represented by pollen from Gossypium (cotton), Manihot (manioc; probably both wild and domesticated forms) and Zea mays (maize) were noted in

passages have been abandoned and dried out with vague remnants of stalactites, flowstone, and travertine dams. A rose diagram using the passage inclinations shows that the water flowed in northeast, southeast, and easterly directions (Figure 15b).

Throughout the cave, the ceiling is coated black from the soot of the torches used by the Maya over the past 3000

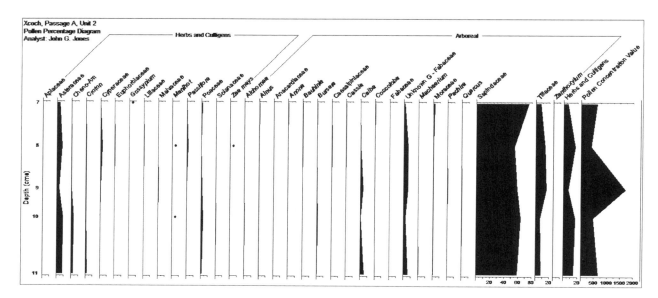

TABLE 2. POLLEN PERCENTAGE DIAGRAM OF THE SOIL SAMPLES FROM THE XCOCH CAVE (JONES 2010).

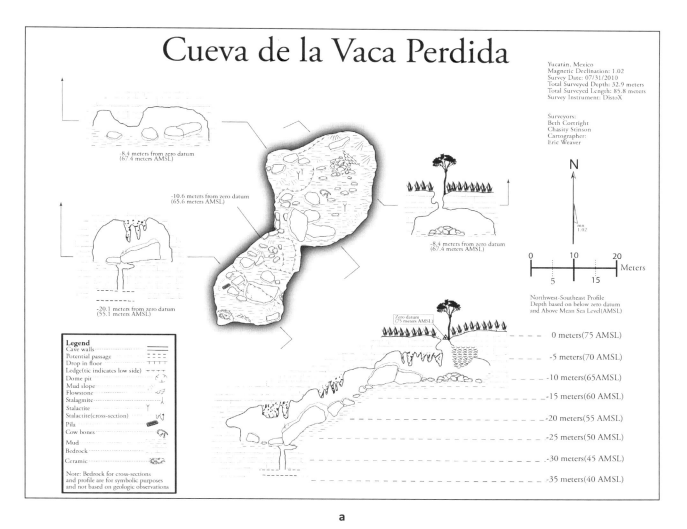

a

b

FIGURE 16 A-B. (A) DETAILED MAP OF LA CUEVA DE LA VACA PERDIDA; (B) PHOTO OF THE ENTRANCE AND VERTICAL SHAFT.

the samples, although they were all present in very low percentages. These grains are all large and heavy and rarely travel far from their source, and their presence in the cave sediments suggests that humans may have deliberately brought these plants and pollen into the cave. Tremendous quantities of particulate carbon were also present in all of the samples, which likely represents past fires in the cave as the sooty particulates would accumulate inside with human activity.

Work at the Vaca Perdida Cave

In 2010, mapping began at Vaca Perdida, a cave located approximately 11.04 km east of Xcoch cave, and several speleothems were collected for paleoclimate analysis (Figures 16a-b). In 2011, equipment was brought in to collect water samples at the sites where the speleothems were collected. The final survey of Vaca Perdida reached a depth of 61 m over a 103.3 m horizontal span. The AMSL (above mean sea level) of the cave's entrance was 71 m based on commercial grade GPS calibrated at sea level in Cancun. The cave covers a brief surface area of 32.2 m. At an average inclination of 31.7 degrees, it is evident that Vaca Perdida acts as a major drain for the hillside. The large amounts of surficial debris washed into the deeper levels of the cave also support this observation. While no active pools of water were present in Vaca Perdida, the lowest levels of the cave are heavily saturated—even containing large muddy puddles of water—very different from the dry passages of Xcoch.

Speleothem Analysis

Speleothem paleoclimate reconstruction attempted to provide a more detailed understanding of the variability of precipitation for Xcoch and the Puuc Region of the Yucatán, Mexico. The Terminal Classic period, A.D. 800-950 or 1200-1050 year BP (before present), is the specific time span of interest. In 2009, speleothems were initially collected from Xcoch cave below the archaeological site. Upon closer examination, these formations were found to be portions of stalactites and other secondary calcite deposits which could not be used for the paleoclimate reconstruction. In 2010, new, usable speleothems were collected from Vaca Perdida. Three stalagmites were of varying lengths, and the two most complete speleothems were selected for the paleoclimate study. The samples were then analyzed for their periods of deposition and stable isotope composition. In 2011, the annual laminae rings of the speleothem samples were counted, dated, and related to the chronology established from other speloethem records for the region. It was hoped that this analysis could shed light of how potential abrupt precipitation changes, such as prolonged droughts, for this particular site may have been partially responsible for adding pressure to the Maya people of this region.

Figure 17 shows the location of the Xcoch study area and other locations that are either other archaeological sites or places where paleoclimate studies have been

Speleothem	Distance from Top (mm)	Age (yr BP)
VP-10-1	3	589± 224
	30	278± 273
	57	-2± 364
	91	2791± 1746
	121	-6363± 5293
	140	1703± 221
	173	2346± 327
	182	975± 232
	217	801± 262
	257	816± 218
	339	551±476
	425	449±346
	435	811±144
	450	2026± 387
VP-10-2	27	580± 88
	43	-19607± 9306
	58	1616± 1242
	89	-14644± 9715
	106	319± 156
	127	298± 99
	153	1677± 215

TABLE 3. ICPMS AGES FOR VP-10-1 AND VP-10-2.

conducted. Of particular interest are the Tecoh cave and Lake Chichancanab sites, whose records have helped create a chronology for our own speleothem record and its interpretation.

Methods

Sample Selection

The two stalagmites, VP-10-1 and VP-10-2, were collected from the Vaca Perdida cave. In the laboratory, each speleothem was cut along its c-axis and then polished. Fourteen and seven 300 mg samples of calcite were removed along each growth axis of VP-10-1 and VP-10-2 respectively, using a computer-controlled micro-drill equipped with a dental burr. These samples were then analyzed for their ages using U-series dating (see below section). The same micro-drill was then used to remove 200 µg samples at 5 mm intervals along the growth axis for each speleothem needed for stable isotope analysis.

Dating Techniques

Uranium series dating techniques, specifically ^{234}U-^{230}Th, were used in order to determine accurate dates for each speleothem, completed at the Radiogenic Isotope Laboratory at the University of New Mexico. Fifty to 150 mg of carbonate powder for the samples were dissolved in nitric acid and spiked with a solution of ^{233}U and ^{229}Th of known concentration, then dried and redissolved in nitric acid and perchloric acid. The samples were again dried, dissolved in nitric acid, and added to anion resin columns to separate the thorium and uranium. Once separated, the thorium and uranium from each sample was run through the ICP-MS. Due to the low counts of ^{234}U and ^{230}Th, the

16

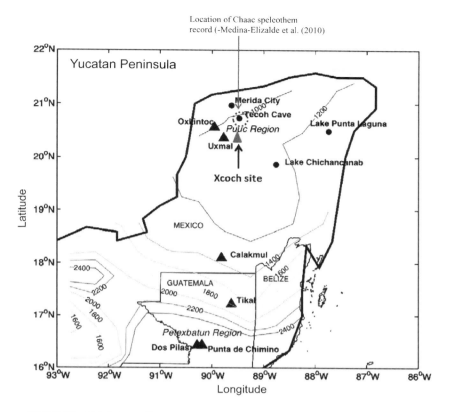

FIGURE 17. LOCATION OF XCOCH AND OTHER SITES USED IN PALEOCLIMATE COMPARISON.

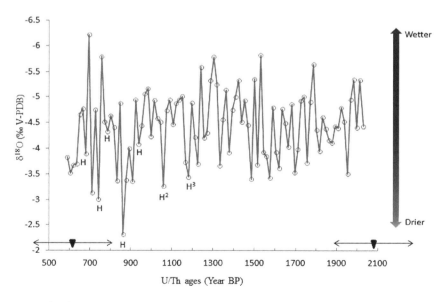

NB: H² & H³ denote number of hiatuses in short succession
←▼→ U/TH date with dating error

FIGURE 18. SPELEOTHEM VP-10-1 Δ¹⁸O (‰) RECORD.

more sensitive SEM was used to measure the amounts of these isotopes.

Stable Isotope Measurements

Once the calcite samples were collected from the speleothems, they were weighed to ~200 μg for stable oxygen isotopic analyses. The calcite was then placed in individual reaction vessels, subjected to anhydrous phosphoric acid in the Keil III carbonate-extraction system coupled to a ThermoFinnigan DeltaPlus XL mass spectrometer. The standard used with conjunction with the cave calcite was the NBS-19 standard, which allowed a precision of <0.1%.

Results

U-series Dates

The ICP-MS ages for each speleothem are given in Table 3; accurate ages for the speleothems could not be obtained. However, the top and base dates appear to be usable due to the low detrital Th and the fact that they were in chronological order. The top date for VP-10-1 also agreed with the top date of VP-10-2, hence this was used for the date that the speleothems cessation of deposition. The construction of the age model for VP-10-1 was simply based on the linear interpolation between the top and base dates. This age model was then used to create a time series for the VP-10-1 stable isotopes values (see Figure 18). With the poor chronological control, a comparison to another, well dated, nearby speleothem record (Tecoh Cave, Medina-Elizalde et al. 2010) was used to help constrain our age model.

Oxygen Isotope Record for VP-10-1

Figure 18 shows the time series for the oxygen isotopes for VP-10-1. The $\delta^{18}O$ values for speleothems in the tropics and this region have been found to record changes in precipitation. The cause of this variability in the $\delta^{18}O$ is due to the amount effect (Lachniet et al. 2004). Consequently, more (less) depleted values in the speleothem are indicative of wetter (drier) conditions. As found in the speleothem c-axis profile, there were numerous hiatuses in the top third of the speleothem. The more prominent of these are marked on Figure 18. H2 and H3 are two very pronounced events where two and three hiatuses occurred in rapid succession. Cessation in deposition is normally induced by drought conditions.

Comparison with other Yucatán Paleoclimate Records

To check the accuracy of the VP-10-1 chronology and our reconstruction of precipitation variability, two different proxies were used. The first is a speleothem record from Tecoh Cave (Chaac $\delta^{18}O$ record, Figure 19a) which is north of our field site. Once again, the Chaac $\delta^{18}O$ isotopic values are interpreted as wetter conditions. Both speleothems, VP-10-1 and Chaac, are plotted on the same y-axis and possess not only very similar $\delta^{18}O$ values but also similar amplitudes. Consequently, our linear interpolation for VP-10-1 appears to be quite accurate when compared to the well dated Chaac chronology. Any differences in the timing of abrupt changes in the $\delta^{18}O$ values can be attributed to the frequent hiatuses in our speleothem, differing growth rates and data resolutions between each record. The Lake Chichanacanab $\delta^{18}O$ record (Hodell et al. 2001) further solidifies both the accuracy of our chronology and our precipitation reconstruction (Figure 20b).

Terminal Classic Period

The Terminal Classic period is of great interest to paleoclimatologists, since it was suggested that major droughts may have contributed to the Maya collapse during this period. Medina-Elizalde et al. (2010), while not being the first study to investigate this question, has provided the most detailed and quantitative analysis of this period to date. The authors demonstrate the possible impact of decreasing precipitation on Maya society in the Yucatán and suggest that precipitation may have been 300 mm below the long term average for their region (Figure 18). More recently, they have suggested that only moderate disruptions in rainfall patterns could have been detrimental to the Maya (Medina-Elizalde and Rohling 2012).

A subsection of the Chaac speleothem record is highlighted in Figure 20, showing precipitation changes for the Tecoh Cave region during the Terminal Classic period. Medina-Elizalde et al. (2010) detailed depiction of the Terminal Classic period demonstrates both rapid changes in precipitation and pronounced droughts, which coincide with pivotal demographic changes for the Maya. One overlying objective of this study is to determine whether these abrupt shifts in precipitation, shown above, were local or more widespread. Precipitation amounts in the Yucatán can vary greatly, even across relatively short distances. In addition, even if the same climate shift occurred across the Yucatán, would its magnitude be uniform or vary locally? For example, could a locale in the same geographic area, such as the Yucatán, experience a different magnitude of change in rainfall compared to another?

In a preliminary attempt to address these questions, Figure 20b displays the Chaac reconstruction of precipitation compared to that of VP-10-1. It is readily apparent that there is a great difference in the resolution of data between the two records. However, there are still several pertinent observations that can be made from this comparison. First, the major changes in precipitation measured at Tecoh Cave (Chaac), especially the prominent droughts, are also found at Vaca Perdida (VP-10-1). Second, the magnitude of change in rainfall at Vaca Perdida appears to be somewhat subdued when matched with the Chaac record. However, it should be noted that this observation may simply be an artifact of the lower resolution of the Vaca Perdida speleothem record.

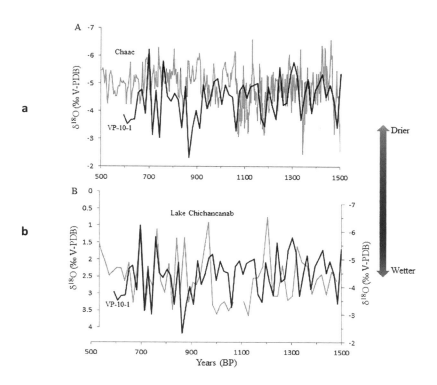

FIGURE 19 A-B. MEDINA-ELIZALDE ET AL. (2010) DEPICTION OF Δ^{18}O ISOTOPIC VALUES FROM LAKE CHICHANCANAB AND THE CHAAC SPECIMEN DURING THE LATE CLASSIC, TERMINAL CLASSIC, AND POSTCLASSIC PERIODS WITH VP-10-01 OVERLAIN TO SHOW SIMILARITIES IN FINDINGS.

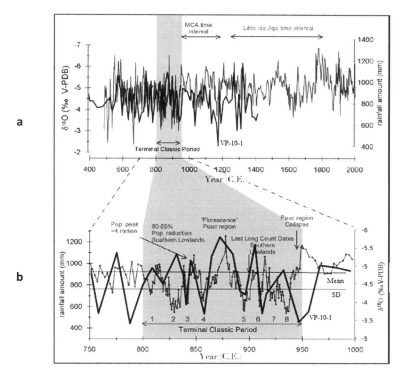

FIGURE 20 A-B. MEDINA-ELIZALDE ET AL. (2010) DEPICTION OF PRECIPITATION DURING THE TERMINAL CLASSIC PERIOD WITH VP-10-01 OVERLAIN TO SHOW SIMILARITIES IN FINDINGS.

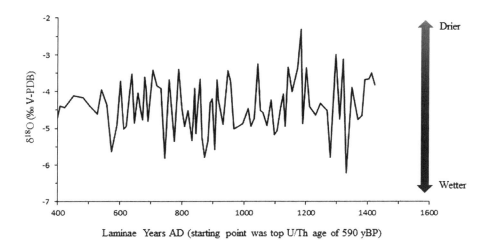

FIGURE 21. PRECIPITATION RECORD WITH VALUES DATED USING ANNUAL LAMINAE YEARS.

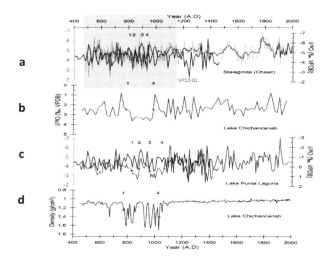

FIGURE 22 A-D. COMPARISON BETWEEN VP-10-01 AND CHAAC STALAGMITE PRECIPITATION RECONSTRUCTION FROM THE NORTHERN YUCATÁN, MEXICO (MEDINA-ELIZALDE ET AL. 2012).

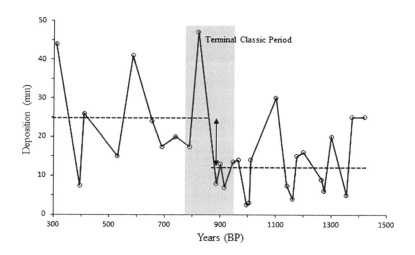

FIGURE 23. VARIABLE DEPOSITION RATE FOR VP-10-01 AROUND A.D. 900.

Based upon the counting of annual laminae rings in the speleothems (similar in principal to counting annual growth rings in trees) of the VP-10-1 stalagmite, a more precise chronology of precipitation reconstruction is now possible. Figure 21 is the precipitation record using the annual laminae starting at A.D. 1422. This new chronology improved the match between our record and the Medina-Elizade (2012) record from Tecoh cave (Figure 22a-d).

One can also see that the change in growth rates occurred around the time of the depopulation of the region (Figure 23). Above rates measured for sections of the stalagmite that had a similar deposition rate. For example, between A.D. 797-892 laminae widths become much thicker than for the period A.D. 972-1014. The obvious conclusion is that deposition rates were generally greater from A.D. 300-870 compared to the period after that. The difference between these two periods is 14 mm.

Summary

The preliminary nature of this pilot study must preclude any definitive conclusions about the magnitude and timing of precipitation changes in the Vaca Perdida region (and Xcoch) over the last 2000 years. The low resolution of the oxygen isotopic record and the issues with the chronology are two major reasons for this tentative approach. However, if the observations outlined in this report have some validity, then an expanded study is warranted. This could entail a higher resolution stable isotope record, possible 14C dating constrained by the two reliable U-series dates. However, the investigation of annual laminae rings in the speleothem has been particularly fruitful. This last mode of study has helped create greater precision for the chronology, a technique long undertaken in dendrochronology and has shown even closer correspondence between VP-10-01 and the Chaac speleothem from Tecoh cave.

Discussion

The beginnings of sedentary farming communities, complex societies, and early community organization in the Puuc region are being addressed by interdisciplinary work at Xcoch and its vicinity. Multiple data sources have identified patterns of chronology and culture process by documenting contextual and behavioral information on architecture and reconstructing the settlement and artifact landscapes. Xcoch was clearly a large Preclassic center in the Puuc hills with special significance because it contained one of the most important water-bearing caves in the region. Indeed, water is such a vital resource in the Puuc region that hydraulic features for water capture and storage may have fundamentally shaped the development of Maya culture as well as its demise (e.g. Dunning 2003a; Ford 1996; Harrison 1993; Scarborough 1993, 1998; Wahl et al. 2007). Xcoch, a site that experienced a long occupation with massive monumental architecture, an agricultural economy, and complex social organization beginning in the Middle Preclassic and lasting through the Late Classic period, also provides significant new environmental data on climate

change, especially patterns of rainfall. Evidence of climate change during the site's long span of occupation includes multiple depopulations, one in the Late Preclassic and another in the Late Classic. The hiatus periods were perhaps brought on, in part, by recurring cycles of intense drought. Investigation at the site also has revealed a sophisticated hydraulic system of water retention that was built and rebuilt over the centuries, including large depression features (aguadas) and potentially dozens of smaller water tanks (household or residential reservoirs), canal systems, and numerous chultuns. These features were constructed to store vast amounts of rain water in response to reoccurring drought cycles for domestic consumption, irrigation, and perhaps even trade.

The material remains within the Xcoch cave indicate that the rulers of the overlying ancient settlement, or ritual specialists acting on their behalf, participated in and manipulated a belief system that highlighted their special relationship with the rain gods. Through ritual, this power would have been publicly expressed as *zuhuy ha* (sacred water) and was likely brought forth annually from the home of the rain gods and poured into the great western reservoir, Aguada La Góndola, helping to initiate the onset of life-giving rains. The physical manipulation of surface flow off of the plastered buildings and plazas of the site center would have provided further control over water in a more pragmatic sense. In the seasonally arid, river-less, and cenote-less Puuc region, reservoirs would, of course, have had tremendous practical importance as community water catchment and storage facilities providing water for domestic uses and facilitating some localized irrigation farming. The creation of large bodies of water within the site center carries potent symbolic meaning as well. Maya cosmology symbolizes water as a transformative boundary, simultaneously connecting and separating cosmic planes. The boundary of the underworld is manifest as a watery surface, reflective of events past, present, and future (Dunning et al. 1999; Isendahl 2011; Scarborough 1998). In this way, the creation or enhancement of such surfaces within an ancient Maya community wielded tremendous symbolic power replicating cosmic structure at the hands of rulers.

The central reservoirs also gave the rulers tremendous practical leverage over the urban population. As noted above, the reservoirs may have supplied a critical backup supply of water useable to supplement or refill chultuns or to enhance urban gardening and farming to tide over prolonged canicular periods as suggested by the South Aguada at Xcoch. The discovery of multiple water tanks integrated into large platforms further extends water management. Puuc Maya rulers may also have attempted to control population distribution by restricting the constructions of chultuns–the water catching/storing cisterns vital to the domestic life of the region's residents. Notably, many 'rural' (intersite) hamlets and farmsteads lack chultuns suggesting that these places were only seasonally occupied and that the rulers of Maya communities may have attempted to control population dispersion by dictating that chultuns could only be constructed in controlled community space (Dunning 2003b, 2004). The later expansion of reservoirs into the outlying portions of Xcoch would have allowed the extension of water-based social control more effectively into the site's hinterland, perhaps analogous to the system of 'water hole group' political control apparent in the Copán Valley.

Climate change in the form of cyclical droughts at Xcoch and its vicinity suggest that significant meteorological events may have played a major role in the dynamics of culture change. Why centers like Xcoch declined and nearby neighbors like Uxmal, continued on for up to another century may be related to the latter's ability to weather severe drought. Uxmal's multitude of aguadas and heavy investment in chultun technology, including those chultun-like structures placed in the bottom of aguadas, may have been a critical adaptation for storing water, especially in times of seasonal shortage. Better water security in hard times coupled with more productive subsistence and storage also would have provided Uxmal a strategic advantage, perhaps allowing military intervention to become a factor in the rapid decline of Xcoch in the 9th century. Though still preliminary, climate change data in concert with excavation, survey, and other environmental data are necessary to provide salient insights into human dynamics and environmental adaptation. The interdisciplinary work at Xcoch and the Puuc region will certainly enhance and advance understanding of the Prehispanic Maya in northern Yucatán and human ecodynamics of climate change and past cultural response.

Acknowledgments. This research was funded by grants from the National Science Foundation (#0940183, #113206), the National Geographic Society (#7989-06), and Waitt Institute for Discovery (W62-09). We are greatly indebted to Anna M. Kerttula, Director of the Arctic Social Sciences Program. This project worked with the permission of Mexico's Instituto Nacional de Antropologia e Historia. We are gratefulness to Dra. Nelly Margarita Robles García (Presidente), Roberto García Moll (Former Presidente) of the Consejo de Arqueología of the Instituto de Antropología e Historia, Eduardo López Calzada Dávila (Director), Federica Solí Miranda (Former Director) and José Huchim Herrera (Coordinator) of the Centro INAH Yucatán. The municipalities and ejidos of Santa Elena and Ticul were supportive, especially Professor Marco Antonio Peez Medina (Municipal President of Ticul); José Gonzalo Peralta Magaña (Communications Director of Ticul), C. Luís Alberto Sansores Mían (Municipal President of Santa Elena), and Ciriaco Chuil Puc and José Grifilio Chulim Sansores (Ejido Commissioners of Santa Elena). We thank Ezra Zubrow, Dustin Keeler, Daniel Griswald, Jeffrey Schieder, and Karen Crissy of the State University of New York at Buffalo (UB) for their services administering the NSF grants and to Dustin Keeler, Gregory J. Korosec, Rebecca Miller, Laurel Triscari, and Caitlin Curtis of the Department of Anthropology at UB who provided fieldwork assistance in November 2011. Radiocarbon dating was conducted by The National Ocean Sciences Accelerator Mass Spectrometry Facility (NOSAMS) at the Woods Hole Oceanographic Institution (NSF Cooperative Agreement number, OCE-0753487). Uranium series dating was performed at the Radiogenic Isotope Lab of the University of New Mexico; Anna Pollock of the University of South Florida prepared the samples. We also want to express our deep gratitude to Daniel Griffin, Pilar Suárez Smyth, Sean-Michael Suárez Smyth, Sebastián Suárez Smyth, Jacob Shedd, Harry and Dorothy Goepel, Beth Cortright, Tammy Otten, Chasity Stinton, Melisa Bishop, Nikki Woodward, Humberto Bonilla Mian, Manuel Bonilla Camal, Marisol Dzul Tuyub, Karina Dzul Tuyub and the local Maya workers of Santa Elena for their dedicated service. And finally, the people of Santa Elena and Muna who kindly shared their friendship, patience, and good humor that have left fond memories and bonds that will be lasting.

References Cited

Andrews, E. Wyllys, V

1988 Ceramic Units from Komchen, Yucatán, Mexico. *Ceramica de Cultura Maya* 15:51-64.

1990 The Early Ceramic History of the Lowland Maya. In *Vision and Revision in Maya Studies*, edited by Flora S. Clancy and Peter D. Harrison, pp. 1-19. University of New Mexico Press, Albuquerque.

Bey, George J., III

2006 Changing Archaeological Perspectives on the Northern Maya Lowlands. In *Lifeways in the Northern Maya Lowlands: New Approaches to Archaeology in the Yucatán Peninsula*, edited by Jennifer P. Mathews and Bethany A. Morrison, pp. 13-37. University of Arizona Press, Tucson.

Brainerd, George W.

1958 *The Archaeological Ceramics of Yucatán.* Anthropological Records, Volume 19. University of California, Berkeley.

Dunning, Nicholas P.

1992 *Lords of the Hills: Ancient Maya Settlement in the Puuc Region, Yucatán, Mexico.* Monographs in World Prehistory No. 15. Prehistory Press, Madison.

2003a Birth and Death of Waters: Environmental Change, Adaptation, and Symbolism in the Southern Maya Lowlands. In *Espacios mayas: representaciones, usos, creencias*, edited by Alain Breton, Aurore Monod Becquelin, and Mario Humberto Ruz, pp. 49-75. Universidad Nacional Autónoma de México, Mexico, D.F.

2003b Along the Serpent's Maw: Environment and Settlement in Xkipché, Yucatán. In *El asentamineto de Xkipché*, edited by Hanns J. Prem, pp. 263-316. Instituto Nacional de Antropología e Historia, México, D.F.

2004 Down on the Farm: Classic Maya Houselots as Farmsteads. In *Ancient Maya Commoners*, edited by Jon Lohse and Fred Valdez, pp. 96-116. University of Texas Press, Austin.

Dunning, Nicholas, Vernon Scarborough, Fred Valdez Jr., Sheryl Luzzadder Beach, Timothy Beach, and John G. Jones

1999 Temple Mountains, Sacred Lakes, and Fertile Fields: Ancient Maya Landscapes in Northwestern Belize. *Antiquity* 73:650-660.

Dunning, Nicholas P., John G. Jones, Timothy Beach, and Sheryl Luzzadder-Beach

2003 Physiography, Habitats, and Landscapes of the Three Rivers Region. In *Heterarchy, Political Economy, and the Ancient Maya: The Three Rivers Region of the East-Central Yucatán Peninsula*, edited by Vernon L. Scarborough, Fred Valdez, Jr., and Nicholas P. Dunning, pp. 14-24. University of Arizona Press, Tucson.

Dunning, Nicholas P., Timothy Beach, Liwy Grasiozo Sierra, John G. Jones, David L. Lentz, Sheryl Luzzadder-Beach, Vernon L. Scarborough, and Michael P. Smyth

2013 A Tale of Two Collapses: Environmental Variability and Cultural Disruption in the Maya Lowlands. *Diálogo Andino* 41:171-183.

Dunning Nicholas P., Eric Weaver, Michael P. Smyth, and David Ortegon Zapata

2014 Xcoch: Home of Ancient Maya Rain Gods and Water Managers. In *The Archaeology of Yucatán: New Directions and Data*, edited by Travis Stanton. BAR International Series, Oxford.

Dunning, Nicholas P., David Wahl, Timothy Beach, John G. Jones, Sheryl Luzzadder-Beach, and Carmen McCormick

2014 Environmental Instability and Human Response in the Late Preclassic East-Central Yucatán Peninsula. In *The Great Maya Droughts in Cultural Context*, edited by Gyles Ianonne, pp. 107-126. University Press of Colorado, Boulder.

Folan, William J.

1968 Un botellón monipodio del centro de Yucatán, México. *Estudios de Cultura Maya* 8:68-75.

Ford, Anabel

1996 Critical Resource Control and the Rise of the Classic Period Maya. In *The Managed Mosaic: Ancient Maya Agriculture and Resource Use*, edited by Scott L. Fedick, pp. 297-303. University of Utah Press, Provo.

Gallareta Negrón, Tomas, and William Ringle

2004 The Earliest Occupation of the Puuc Region, Yucatán, Mexico: New Perspectives from Xocnaceh and Paso de Macho. Paper presented at the 103rd Annual Meeting of the American Anthropological Association, Atlanta.

Harrison, Peter D.

1993 Aspects of Water Management in the Southern Maya Lowlands. In *Aspects of Water Management in the Prehispanic New World*, edited by Vernon L. Scarborough and Barry L. Isaac, pp. 71-119. Research in Economic Anthropology Supplement 7. JAI Press, Greenwich.

Haug, Gerald H., Detlef Gunther, Larry C. Peterson, Daniel M. Sigman, Konrad A. Hughen, and Beat Aeschlimann

2003 Climate and the Collapse of Maya Civilization. *Science* 299:1731-1735.

Hodell, David A., Jason H. Curtis, Mark Brenner, and Thomas P. Guilderson

2001 Solar Forcing of Drought Frequency in the Maya Lowlands. *Science* 292:1367-1370.

Hodell, David A., Mark Brenner, and Jason H. Curtis

2005a Terminal Classic Drought in the Northern Maya Lowlands Inferred from Multiple Sediment Cores in Lake Chichancanab (Mexico). *Quaternary Science Review* 24:1413-1427.

Isendahl, Christian

2011 The Weight of Water: A New Look at Puuc Maya Water Reservoirs. *Ancient Mesoamerica* 22:185-197.

Jones, John G.

2010 Pollen Report of Five Xcoch Cave Soil Samples. The Foundation for Americas Research, Inc., Winter Springs, FL.

Lachniet, Matthew S., Stephen J. Burns, Dolores R. Piperno, Yemane Asmerom, Victor J. Polyak, Christopher M. Moy, and Keith Christenson

2004 A 1500 year El Niño/Southern Oscillation and Rainfall History for the Isthmus of Panama from Speleothem Calcite. *Journal of Geophysical Research 109*: doi:10.1029/2004JD004694.

Medina-Elizalde, Martín Stephen, J. Burns, David W. Lea, Yemane Asmerom, Lucien von Gunten, Victor Polyak, Mathias Vuille, and Ambarish Karmalkar

2010 High Resolution Stalagmite Climate Record from the Yucatán Peninsula Spanning the Maya Terminal Classic Period. *Earth and Planetary Science Letters* 298:255-262.

Medina-Elizade, Martín, and Eelco J. Rohling

2012 Collapse of Classic Maya civilization related to modest reduction in precipitation. S*cience* 335: 956-959.

Ringle, William M., and E. Wyllys Andrews, V.

1988 Formative Residences at Komchen, Yucatán, Mexico. In *Household and Community in the Mesoamerican Past,* edited by Richard R. Wilk and Wendy Ashmore, pp. 171-197. University of New Mexico Press, Albuquerque.

Scarborough, Vernon L.

1993 Introduction. In *Economic Aspects of Water Management in the Prehispanic New World*, edited by Vernon L. Scarborough and Barry L. Isaac, pp. 1-14. Research in Economic Anthropology, Supplement 7. JAI Press, Greenwich.

1998 Ecology and Ritual: Water Management and the Maya. *Latin American Antiquity* 8:135-159.

Smyth, Michael P. and David Ortegón Zapata

2008 A Preclassic Center in the Puuc Region: A Report on Xcoch, Yucatán, Mexico. *Mexicon* 30:63-68.

Smyth, Michael P., Ezra Zubrow, David Ortegón Zapata, Nicholas P. Dunning, Eric M. Weaver, Jane E. Slater, and Philip van Beynen

2011 Paleoclimatic Reconstruction and Archaeological Investigations at Xcoch and the Puuc Region of Yucatán, Mexico: Exploratory Research into Arctic Climate Change and Maya Culture Processes. Report to the National Science Foundation (www.farinco.org).

Smyth, Michael P., David Ortegón Zapata, Nicholas P. Dunning, and Eric M. Weaver

2014 Settlement Dynamics, Climate Change, and Human Response at Xcoch in the Puuc Region of Yucatán, Mexico. In *The Archaeology of Yucatán: New Directions and Data*, edited by T. Stanton. BAR International Series, Oxford.

Stanton, Travis W, and Tómas Gallareta Negrón

2002 Proyecto Xocnaceh: 1ª temporada de campo marzo-julio 2002. Technical report submitted to the Consejo de Arqueología del Instituto Nacional de Antropología e Historia, México, D.F.

Stephens, John Lloyd

1963 *Incidents of Travel in Yucatán*, Volume Two. Dover Publications, Inc. New York

Wahl, David, Thomas Schreiner, Roger Byrne, and Richard Hansen

2007A Paleoecological Record from a Late Classic Maya Reservoir in the Northern Peten. *Latin American Antiquity* 18:212-222.

Webster, James. W., George A. Brook, L. Bruce Railsback, Hai Cheng, R. Lawrence Edwards, Clark Alexander, and Philip P. Reeder

2007 Stalagmite Evidence from Belize Indicating Significant Drought at the Time of Preclassic Abandonment, the Maya Hiatus, and the Classic Maya Collapse. *Palaeogeography, Palaeoclimatology, Palaeoecology* 250:1-17.

In Search of Kilns: The Forms and Functions of Annular Structures in the Bolonchén District

Ken Seligson, Tomás Gallareta Negrón, Rossana May Ciau, and George J. Bey III

Lime powder was one of the most important materials produced and used by the Prehispanic Maya. It was used for construction, sanitary, and dietary purposes and must have played a significant role in the ancient economy. Despite its obvious importance the ephemeral nature of lime production and the lack of structures identifiable as kilns in the archaeological record have limited the investigation of the Prehispanic lime production industry. The recent identification of a series of annular structures hypothesized to be lime pit-kilns in and around the ancient site of Kiuic in the Puuc region of the Northern Maya Lowlands now provides a great opportunity to investigate the lime production industry and its role in the local Puuc economy. This paper presents data from the excavations of seven annular structures during the 2014 summer field season. Preliminary morphological and spatial results suggest that these structures were in fact used as pit-kilns to burn limestone down into lime powder.

Cal era una de los materiales más importantes producidos y utilizados por los Mayas Prehispánicos. Fue utilizado por los fines de la construcción, la higiene, y la dieta, y debe haber jugado un papel importante en la economía antigua. A pesar de su evidente importancia, el estado efímero de la producción de cal arriba del suelo y la falta de estructuras identificables como hornos han limitado la investigación de la industria de producción de cal prehispánico. La reciente identificación de una serie de estructuras anulares que tienen características como hornos en los alrededores del sitio antiguo de Kiuic en la región Puuc de la Yucatán ahora ofrece una gran oportunidad para investigar la industria de la producción de cal y su papel en la economía local antigua. Este capítulo presenta los datos de las excavaciones de siete estructuras anulares durante la temporada de campo 2014 del verano. Resultados morfológicos y espaciales preliminares sugieren que estas estructuras eran de hecho utilizado como hornos más probable para cocinar la piedra caliza para producir polvo de cal.

Powdered lime (calcium oxide, or *cal* in Spanish) was one of the most important materials used by the Prehispanic Maya and the lime production industry and must therefore have played a significant role in the ancient economy. The Prehispanic Maya used lime in order to: produce mortar for the construction of monumental, residential, and utilitarian structures; to create the plaster that covered the facades, walls, and floors of most structures, as well as the plazas between the structures; and also to maintain a healthy diet through the *nixtamalization* process in which corn kernels are soaked in lime-infused water. Despite the obvious importance of lime, archaeologists working in the Maya area have found limited evidence regarding the Prehispanic production of cal. This situation is a result of two main problems: the ephemeral nature of traditional open pyre burning methods in the archaeological record, and the relative lack of structures potentially identifiable as ancient kilns in the Maya area (Barba 2013:27-28; Schreiner 2002). To date archaeologists have only excavated a handful of potential ancient lime kilns in the Maya area (Abrams 1996; Abrams and Freter 1996; Dunning 1991:25; Fauvet-Berthelot 1980:5-7; Freidel and Sabloff 1984; Johnston et al. 1989; Ortíz 2014; Redfield and Villa 1934; Viel 1983). The recent identification of a series of annular structures by the second and third authors hypothesized to be pit-kilns in the Puuc region of the north-central Yucatán peninsula provides a great opportunity to investigate the lime production industry and its role in the local Puuc economy (Gallareta et al. 2014).

The standard annular structure, as it appears in the archaeological record, resembles a rounded mound made of rough limestone blocks arranged in a ring with a depression in the center (Figure 1). Understanding the varying forms and functions of annular structures in the Puuc region is significant for three main reasons: 1) if they were in fact used as kilns for the burning of raw limestone into quicklime, this would contribute to our understanding of indigenous Maya kiln technology; 2) the identification of Prehispanic kilns would have important implications for the amount of fuel necessary to create lime powder and thus affect our understanding of how the ancient Maya managed their environmental resources in a specific sub-region; and 3) the annular structures provide a way to examine an industry that undoubtedly played an important role in the ancient economy. The sheer quantity of annular structures identified by Gallareta Negrón and May during their extensive inter-site survey in the Bolonchén District suggests that they were a significant feature in the local society. The prevalence of these pit-kilns in the Eastern Puuc appears to reflect a sub-regional cultural variation. Thus, in addition providing important information regarding an oft-overlooked Prehispanic Maya industry, investigation of these annular structures contributes to a more detailed understanding of how ancient Maya peoples

Ken Seligson - Department of Anthropology, University of Southern California, Los Angeles (Seligson@usc.edu); **Tomás Gallareta Negrón** - Instituto Nacional de Antropología e Historia (INAH), Mérida, Yucatán (tomasgallareta@gmail.com); **Rossana May Ciau** - Facultad de Ciencias Antropológicas de la U.A.D.Y., Mérida, Yucatán (rossana101@hotmail.com); **George J. Bey III** - Millsaps College, Jackson, Mississippi (beygj@millsaps.edu).

FIGURE 1. ANNULAR STRUCTURE LOCATED IN THE SOUTHEASTERN PERIPHERY OF THE KIUIC URBAN CORE AS IT LOOKED AFTER THE FIRST LEVEL OF EXCAVATION.

living in different sub-regions created distinctive historical trajectories and responded to changing environmental conditions in different ways (Aimers 2007; Bey 2006; Demarest 2009; Dunning et al. 2012).

The current study focuses on the ancient site of Kiuic and its surrounding hinterlands. Since 2000, Tomás Gallareta Negrón, George J. Bey III, and William Ringle have co-directed the Bolonchén Regional Archaeological Project (BRAP), encompassing archaeological surveys and excavations in and around Kiuic (Figure 2). The site center is located in a flat, circular valley surrounded by a ring of low hills in the Bolonchén district of the eastern Puuc region. Excavations in the Dzunun plaza at the Kiuic site center have recovered evidence of occupation dating back to ~800 B.C. and continuing through to a peak era of construction activity between A.D. 700-950 (Gallareta et al 2014:1-7). Kiuic is a medium, rank III size site, containing several monumental structures at the site core, surrounded by a cluster of stone-vaulted residential compounds. It is believed to have been the center of a typical Late and Terminal Classic period Puuc polity (Gallareta et al. 2014).

This study hypothesizes that at least some of the annular structures were used as pit-kilns to produce lime powder from limestone and that the production of lime powder played an important role in the local Puuc economy. The starting point for testing the hypotheses regarding the functions of the annular structures and their role in the lime production industry is the comprehensive inter-site survey completed by the second and third authors and colleagues over the last ten years between the ancient sites of Labná and Kiuic. The survey mapped all archaeological features throughout a nine kilometer long by one kilometer wide transect in the hinterlands between these site centers

(Gallareta et al. 2014) (Figure 3). Among the ancient features recorded were over 140 annular structures that, when added to the half dozen previously identified within the Kiuic site center, provide a wide array from which to sample and examine their spatial contexts. Before getting into the specifics of the current project, it is important to review some of the previous studies regarding the ancient Maya economy, lime production, and annular structures.

Previous Studies

The Ancient Maya Economy

The study of the Prehispanic Maya economy has undergone many changes over the course of the last hundred-plus years in tune with the adoption of evolving economic theories into archaeological studies. Earlier formulations based on cultural ecology and central place theory (Rathje 1971) have been supplemented by more variegated theoretical approaches including a focus on household archaeology (Ford and Fedick 1992; Gillespie 2000; Gonlin 2004; Killion et al. 1989; Robin 2003; Schortman 1989; Wilk and Ashmore 1988; Wilk and Rathje 1982) and agency and practice theory (Clark and Blake 1994; Gillespie 2001; McAnany 2010; Smith and Wobst 2005). It is generally accepted that agricultural production was at the heart of the Prehispanic Maya economy, but it is unclear how the agrarian industry functioned with regard to centralized control and land ownership (Fox et al. 1996; Freidel 1983; McAnany 1989; Robin 2003) and it is quite possible that different systems were used in different sub-regions at different times (Carmean 1990, 1991; McAnany 2010; Montmollin 1989). Another important aspect of the Prehispanic Maya economy was trade, which included networks for the exchange of goods that spanned an

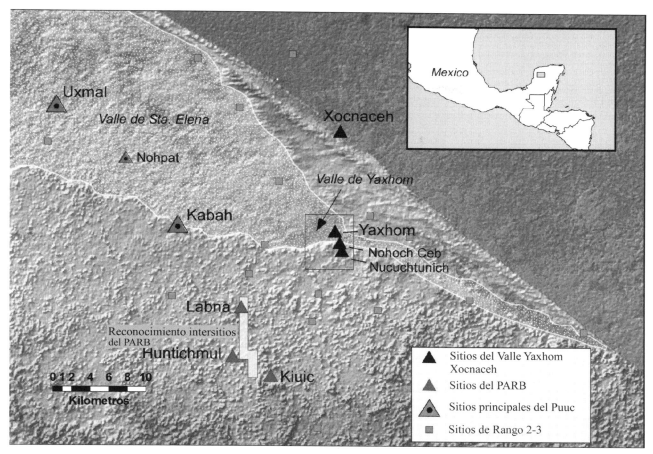

FIGURE 2. MAP OF THE PUUC REGION SHOWING THE LOCATION OF KIUIC IN REFERENCE TO OTHER ANCIENT REGIONAL CENTERS (GALLARETA NEGRÓN ET AL. 2014).

elite-utilitarian spectrum (Andrews et al. 1989; Ashmore 2009; Foias 2002; Freidel et al 2002; Hirth 2003; Potter 1989; Schortman and Urban 1994; Yaeger 2000). Other facets of the Prehispanic Maya economy that have gained specific attention in recent decades are its embedded ritual characteristics (Brady 2005; Gillespie 2001, LeCount 2001; Lucero 2003; McAnany 2014), the ways in which high status groups may have gained and maintained authority through control of necessary resources (Dunning 1992; Lucero 2002; McAnany 1990; Scarborough et al. 1995), and gendered divisions of labor (Neff 2002; Robin 2002).

Most important for the proposed project has been the trend towards examining production on a more localized scale, including at the community and household level (Ashmore et al. 2004; Canuto 2004; Gonlin 2004; Hendon 1991; Robin 2003; Sheets 2002; Yaeger 2000). By studying the production of such durable commodities as ceramics and lithics, archaeologists have found evidence for both attached and independent craftspeople across the ancient Maya social landscape. Archaeologists have suggested that some elite and/or non-elite social groups might have supplemented their wealth through control over the production of these materials (Ball 1989; Hendon 1991; McAnany 1989, 2010; Paris 2008; Potter 1989). Judging from its ubiquitous use throughout the Maya lowlands, lime was likely in high demand and thus lime production may

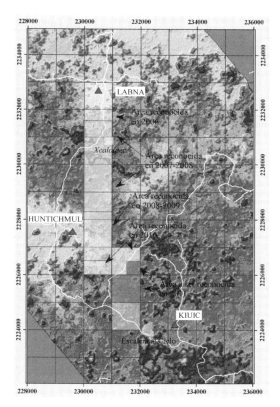

FIGURE 3. A MAP OF THE KIUIC-LABNÁ INTER-SITE SURVEY, DIRECTED BY GALLARETA NEGRÓN AND MAY CIAU (GALLARETA NEGRÓN ET AL. 2011).

27

have been an important source of income for both elite and non-elite members of society. Owing to the difficulty of identifying lime production in the archaeological record, it has not received the same amount of attention with regard to its role in the ancient Maya economy as more durable materials. This study has the potential to shed light on the organization and impact of lime production on the ancient Bolonchén economy at the household level.

The Prehispanic Limestone Industry

There have been many studies about Prehispanic Maya architecture since the 19th century, culminating in the Puuc region with the seminal works of Pollock (1980), Andrews (1990), and Kowalski and Dunning (1999). Studies have focused on all aspects of ancient Maya architecture, including the construction of monumental, residential, and utilitarian structures (Abrams 1994; Abrams and Bolland 1999), the production and identification of different types of lime plaster and mortar (Abrams 1996; Abrams et al. 2012; Alonso 2013; Littmann 1959, 1960, 1966; MacKinnon and May 1990; Russell and Dahlin 2007; Schreiner 2002; Wernecke 2008), and the exploitation of quarries and different types of stone (Carmean et al. 2011; Folan 1978). Considering the ubiquity of lime in the Prehispanic Maya world, there have been relatively few studies about the Prehispanic Maya production of burnt lime specifically (Abrams and Freter 1996; Hansen 2000; Ortíz 2014; Russell and Dahlin 2007; Schreiner 2002).

Working at Chalcatzingo, Morelos in the 1970s, Grove, Guillén, and Martin Arana discovered three pits lined with stone that they contended were used as kilns to produce lime (Grove and Guillen 1987; Martin 1987). Likewise, the Tepeaca Kiln Project, directed by Castanzo and Anderson, discovered more than 80 pit-kilns in the state of Puebla, some of which had evidence of lime production (Castanzo 2004; Castanzo and Anderson 2004). In the Maya area specifically, members of the Sayil Mapping Project of the late 1980s identified at least 24 annular structures in the vicinity of the site core. Nicholas Dunning hypothesized that some may have been used to burn materials to create fertilizer, based on the mixture of limestone, soil, and ash recovered from one such structure (Dunning 1991:25). Abrams and Freter (1996) excavated a feature believed to be a Prehispanic lime kiln on the outskirts of Copán, Honduras that they hypothesized may have been a technological development to increase fuel efficiency in lime production. Other identifications of rudimentary lime pit-kilns have been reported at Cauinal (Fauvet-Berthelot 1980) and Dos Pilas (Johnston et al. 1989) in Guatemala, and at Copán in Honduras (Abrams 1996; Viel 1983). More recently, as part of a federal highway salvage project around the site of Oxkintok directed by Eunice Uc and Raúl Morales, Sol Ortíz Ruíz and colleagues have excavated more than ten annular structures (Ortíz 2014) and Alfredo Barrera Rubio has identified potential kilns in the northeastern Yucatán.

Additionally, there have been experimental studies concerning the production of lime, but the vast majority of these have used the traditional aboveground method of production. The aboveground *calera* technique employs a pyre of green (or wet) wood covered by a small mound of broken down limestone (Barba 2013; Hansen 2000; Morris et al. 1931; Russell and Dahlin 2007; Schreiner 2002). This method of production leaves a trace that is very difficult to identify archaeologically unless you know exactly where to look for it (Russell and Dahlin 2007). These studies demonstrate the possibility of producing great quantities of lime using the calera method, but also raise questions concerning the cost of fuel resources, in this case green wood. Even though some studies have suggested that the necessity of green wood for the production of lime could have led to deforestation and contributed to the disintegration of the Classic Maya civilization (Morris 1931; Schreiner 2002), others have refuted such claims (Abrams and Rue 1988; Dunning et al. 2012; Hansen et al. 2002; Wernecke 2008). It is possible that different methods with different production costs were employed in different sub-regions. It is important to understand the effect that lime production would have had on the environment on a local level.

The Chemistry of Lime Burning

Converting limestone to lime powder involves a process called calcination by which the limestone (calcium carbonate) is heated to at least 800-900° Celsius, releasing all of the carbon dioxide from the limestone and converting it to quicklime (calcium oxide) (Russell and Dahlin 2007; Schreiner 2002). The quicklime, which has caustic properties, can either be slaked immediately or left to absorb moisture from the air over time. The slaking, which renders the material safe to touch, transforms the quicklime into burnt lime (calcium hydroxide), a soft powder that can then be mixed with water and aggregates to produce mortar and stucco, among other materials. When these wet products dry, the excess water evaporates leaving the original material, calcium carbonate, now in a useful shape and form for construction purposes (Schreiner 2002; Wernecke 2008). The full calcination, hydration, and carbonation cycle is represented in elemental formulas as follows:

Calcination: $CaCO_3 + Heat \rightarrow CaO + CO_2$

Hydration: $CaO + H_2O \rightarrow Ca(OH)_2 + Heat$

Carbonation: $Ca(OH)_2 + CO_2 \rightarrow CaCO_3 + H_2O$

Current Study

The current study focuses on the annular structures and the role these important features may have played in the Prehispanic economy of the Bolonchén district of the Puuc. What various functions did the annular structures serve? If they were in fact kilns, how were they involved in the process of converting limestone to powdered lime?

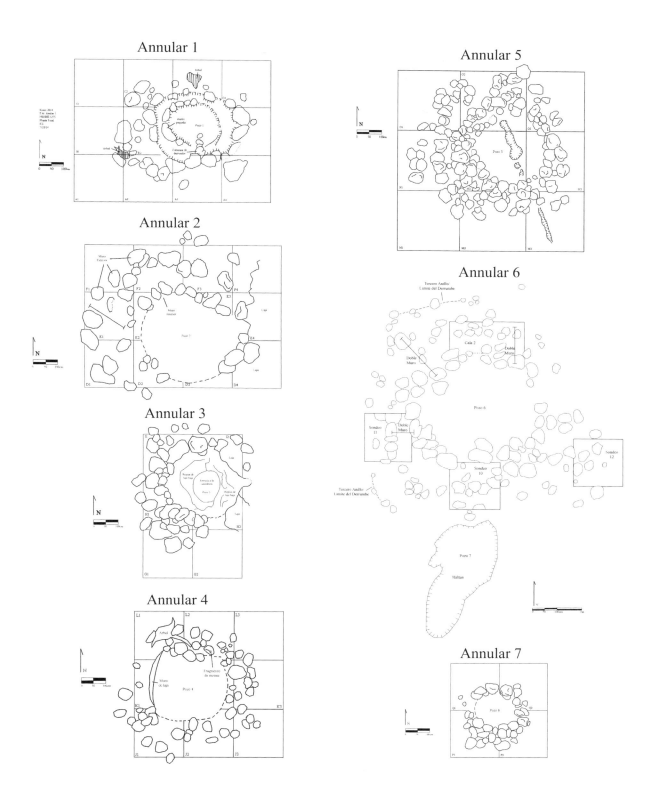

FIGURE 4. DIAGRAM SHOWING A BIRDS-EYE VIEW OF THE SEVEN ANNULAR STRUCTURES EXCAVATED TO DATE TO DEMONSTRATE VARIATIONS IN SIZE AND FORM.

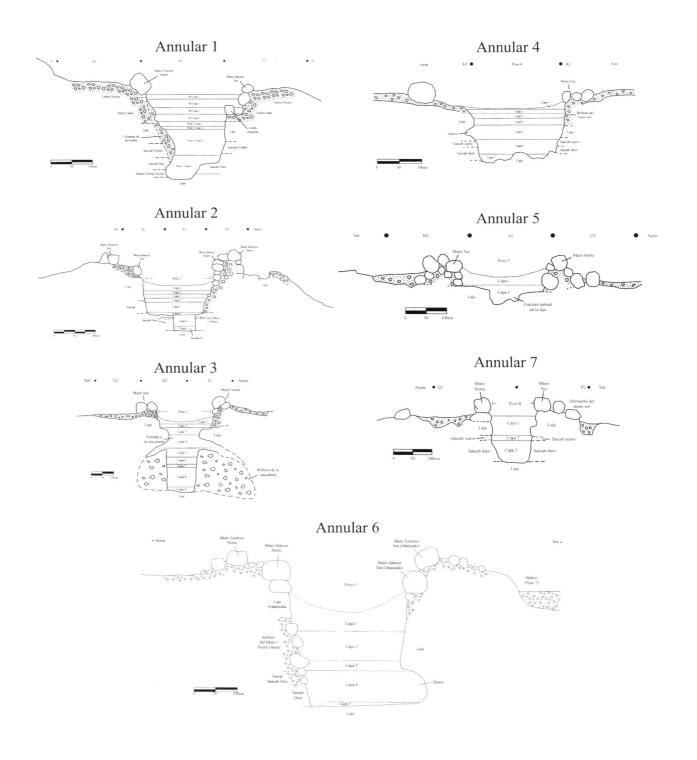

FIGURE 5. DIAGRAM SHOWING A PROFILE CUT VIEW OF THE SEVEN ANNULAR STRUCTURES EXCAVATED TO DATE TO DEMONSTRATE THE VARYING PATTERNS OF CONSTRUCTION.

Were they also used to mix lime plaster? What role did the production of lime play in the local and regional economies? At what social level was the production of lime plaster organized? Did the lime industry change over time? If the annular structures were not used as kilns, what other functions might they have served in Puuc society?

The study tests the hypothesis that the annular structures served as kilns for producing lime from limestone and argues that the lime production industry played a significant role in the local Prehispanic economy. To date 17 annular structures (spanning the urban, suburban, and rural zones in and around Kiuic) have been measured and photographed and seven of these have been excavated and investigated more thoroughly. While the investigations are still ongoing, this paper presents data from preliminary studies conducted during the summer 2013 and 2014 field seasons.

Physical Traits

The annular structures appear in the archaeological record as ring-like formations of small boulders surrounding a central depression. However, investigations over the last two summer field seasons have demonstrated that there is a good deal of variation in their sizes and specific forms (Figure 4). These variations may be linked with such factors as the socioeconomic standing of the people that built and used them, the functions that they served, and/ or the type of lime that they were used to produce among others.

FIGURE 6. PROFILE OF THE SOUTHEASTERN INTERIOR WALL OF THE CENTRAL PIT OF AN ANNULAR STRUCTURE IN THE PIXOY GROUP OF THE KIUIC SITE CENTER (ONE OF THE LARGER ANNULAR STRUCTURES EXCAVATED TO DATE).

The internal walls of the structures generally consist of one to five vertical rows of boulders sitting on top of the bedrock. It is possible that prior to their collapse some of the structures possessed six or seven layers of boulders forming the uppermost levels of the walls (Figure 5). In some cases, the construction process involved excavating through the limestone bedrock and into the layer of softer, whiter limestone known as *sascab*. In these cases, the central depression resembles a well or shaft with nearly vertical walls made of three layers: limestone boulders on top, a layer of limestone bedrock in the middle, and a layer of sascab on the bottom. Some of the annular structures in this category have central depressions that sink more than 3.5 meters below the surface before arriving at a second, final layer of bedrock that often exhibits evidence of repeated exposure to fire (Figure 6). Three of the seven annular structures excavated in 2014 fit into this category, while an additional two followed a similar pattern but did not reach such a great depth. Of the two remaining structures, one consisted of a ring of boulders sitting atop the bedrock, but the central depression did not cross through the surface layer of bedrock. The other consisted of a ring of boulders surrounding the circular entrance to a repurposed *chultún*, or human-made cistern that is a common feature of settlements in the Puuc.

The central depressions of the investigated structures range from 1.2 to 3.3 meters in diameter, the maximum extent of the structures range in diameter from 2.2 to 10.4 meters, and the ring heights above the surrounding terrain range from 0.5 to 1.75 meters. At Sayil, the 24 annular structures identified by the Sayil Mapping Project directed by Jeremy Sabloff and Gair Tourtellot appear to range from approximately 3 to 8 meters in maximum diameter (Sabloff and Tourtellot 1991), and the annular structures studied at Oxkintok range from 4.5 to 10 meters in maximum diameter (Ortíz 2014).

Based on the amount of fill recovered from the central depressions of the structures in the form of limestone rocks ranging in size from fist-size nuggets called *chich* to large boulders, it is possible that some of these annular pit-kilns used a *piib*-like method in which the materials being cooked were covered in insulating layers of rocks and earth. To date only two of the structures yet studied have been found to possess a wall-opening that might have served as a ventilation tunnel. These tunnels presumably allowed for the passage of oxygen into the center of the structure to maintain a fire. It is likely that the collapse of the walls of the other structures have obscured similar ventilation openings.

Evidence for Lime Production

Physical Evidence

Several lines of evidence recovered from excavations during the 2014 summer field season point to the annular structures being used as ovens or pit-kilns. First, large quantities of burnt chich were found scattered on the

FIGURE 7. THE BURNT WALLS AND BEDROCK FLOOR OF ONE OF THE EXCAVATED ANNULAR STRUCTURES.

surface around and within the majority of the annular structures that were investigated. The majority of these small stones are equivalent to the size that would be used to create lime. Limestone is only converted into quicklime when all of the carbon dioxide is removed. It is possible that these burnt pieces of chich represent rocks that did not undergo complete calcination during the firing process and were subsequently discarded outside the structure. Those stones that exhibit evidence of being burnt but are too large for efficient calcination might represent either fill from the walls of the structures or part of layer of stones that could have been used to cover a piib.

The internal walls and floors of the structures also exhibit evidence that supports the use of the structures as ovens or pit-kilns. All of the structures excavated so far possess bedrock walls and/or floors that appear to have been burnt, and those with central depressions that pass through the sascab layer also possess evidence of burnt sascab. The bedrock and sascab encountered in the walls of the deeper structures is extremely friable and the bedrock is often tinted grey or black, indicating burning episodes (Figure 7). In the two structures excavated to date that do not pass through to the sascab layer, the surface layer of the bedrock exhibits similar evidence of having been burnt. In those structures that do pass through the sascab layer, a layer of sascab powder was uncovered that either crumbled from the friable sascab walls or floor. Below the softer sascab layer was a harder layer of sascab resembling a floor. Three of the structures possessed more than one of

these hard sascab floors, in some cases separated by softer sascab tinted reddish-black and in other cases separated by a thin layer of burnt rocks and earth. The lowest layer of all of these structures, sitting immediately above the bedrock floor, consisted of a very hard layer of sascab. The toughness of this final layer resulted either from exposure to multiple firing episodes, the solidification (or carbonation) of previously calcined lime, or represents the natural layer of hard sascab that had not yet been excavated during the Prehispanic period.

Excavators also recovered carbon and ash samples from the lower levels of several of the annular structures that provided evidence for repeated burning episodes inside the structures during their periods of use. Some of the carbon samples will be dated to determine the period when these structures were built and used. Discovering when this form of pit-kiln technology was developed has implications for understanding resource management practices leading up to and through the sociopolitical transformation of the Late and Terminal Classic periods.

In addition to the evidence gathered during the excavations at Kiuic, the hypothesis that the annular structures were used as pit-kilns is supported by the excavation of an annular structure at Sayil and ongoing excavations at Oxkintok. In both cases, archaeologists have encountered evidence of burned materials within the structures (Dunning 1991:25; Ortíz 2014). While these pit-kilns could have been used to cook other materials including food, fertilizer, trash, or even ceramics, the preliminary evidence from Kiuic, Oxkintok (Ortíz 2014), and Sayil (Dunning 1991:25) suggests that at least some were used as lime kilns.

The fact that at least two of the structures in the study area were built on top of *sascaberas*, or sascab quarries, suggests that the features may have served multiple functions. In addition to providing a more efficient lime burning location, the excavation of the central pits would have provided access to sascab that could be used for other purposes. Sascab could be crushed and used as an aggregate in lime plaster or mortar recipes, but could not be used to make lime or to nixtamalize maize (Abrams 1996). Additional functions of the annular structures may include maize storage features during the dry season or as temporary water storage units during the rainy season.

Spatial Evidence

Another line of evidence that suggests the importance of annular structures for the lime production industry is their proximity to limestone quarries. Seven of the nine annular structures identified within the Kiuic site center are located within 20 meters of limestone quarries, limestone outcrops, or sascaberas. A few of the annular structures abut these quarries and sascaberas, and others appear to have been built partially covering a sascabera. A similar construction phenomenon was identified at Sayil, where at least one of the annular structures appeared to have been constructed over the mouth of a sascabera (Dunning 1991). In the southwestern sector of Kiuic, two annular structures were built immediately adjacent to one another and together they are surrounded on three sides by limestone extraction features. These circumstances, combined with the fact that the annular structures are within close proximity to the masonry architecture of the site center, suggest that this may have been a specialized lime production complex dedicated to meeting the lime consumption needs of the site's inhabitants.

More annular structures were identified in close proximity to quarries, sascaberas, limestone outcrops, and chich mounds a little further to the northwest and southwest of the site center, at the base of the hills that ring the Kiuic valley. Of the 26 annular structures identified in this inner 'suburban zone,' 19 (74%) are located within 50 meters of a quarry, sascabera, or chich mound. This high correlation rate suggests that the majority of annular structures were located to facilitate the gathering and transportation of the raw materials to be processed in the kilns. At Sayil, seven of the 24 (29%) identified annular structures are located within 30 meters of a quarry or sascabera, 11 (46%) are within 20 meters of a limestone outcrop, and seven (29%) are within 20 meters of a chich mound. Likewise, at Oxkintok, at least one of the annular structures was built in close proximity to a sascabera, and researchers have identified materials indicative of lime production within most of the excavated structures (Ortíz 2014).

Other features that might have been important to the lime production industry include water gathering and/or retention features such as chultúns and natural depressions in the bedrock called *haltúns*. Two of the larger annular structures excavated at Kiuic during the summer 2014 field season are located in close proximity to haltúns. For one of these structures (Annular Structure 6) the presence of the water catchment feature nearby appears to be the main factor influencing the location of its construction. Annular Structure 6 is the largest annular structure with reference to maximum diameter yet excavated and it is located approximately two and a half kilometers west of Kiuic. The nearest other archaeological feature is more than 50 meters away (Figure 8). The only evident reasons for the construction of such a large kiln so far from a permanent settlement appear to be the presence of several small limestone outcrops (which can be found throughout the Kiuic hinterlands) and more importantly the large haltún that would undoubtedly have collected rainwater. Water is important for slaking the quicklime in order to produce the slaked lime that would have been used for a variety of quotidian activities. This close association of annular structures with other features of the limestone exploitation industry in the Puuc indicates that the annular structures played an important role in the lime production industry.

Discussion and Preliminary Conclusions

Preliminary physical and spatial analyses provide a variety of implications regarding the role of the annular structures and the lime production industry within the local economy of the Prehispanic Bolonchén district. The majority of the annular structures identified in and around the Kiuic site center are located in close proximity not only to limestone industry features but to Prehispanic residential compounds as well. Some of the largest and most well constructed annular structures are located within residential compounds believed to have been inhabited by members of the socioeconomic elite. This claim is based on the presence of stone vaulted architecture in these compounds that required the mustering of large amounts of material and human labor for their construction. The grander scale of these annular structures suggests that the people who commissioned and/or used them to produce lime powder had access to a larger labor force and greater amounts of raw materials, technology, and information in order to produce them. The proximity suggests that these annular pit-kilns were controlled (that is, owned, operated, or overseen) to some degree by the families or social groups that lived within these compounds.

A large quantity of lime powder could have been produced over multiple firing episodes using these larger kilns and this might explain why not every residential compound has its own annular structure. With the exception of a mid-range sized annular structure peculiarly located on a platform within the central civic-ceremonial complex of Kiuic, the annular structures situated in the urban core are all located in residential compounds along the periphery. This abnormal annular structure was excavated by Stephanie Simms in 2008 and did not return any evidence of having been used to fire any materials, let alone limestone (Gallareta et al. 2009:4.37-4.40). The residents of compounds that did possess annular structures could theoretically have produced enough lime powder for their own consumption as well as to distribute to other small-scale corporate groups, and for the construction of monumental buildings in the civic-ceremonial center. The quantity and location of annular structures in the Kiuic site center thus suggest a pattern of small-scale corporate ownership and use of annular structures, which implies that lime-producing social groups could have processed and sold lime manufactured within their compounds.

A similar situation of ownership and use of annular structures likely existed within elite residential compounds further out in the Kiuic periphery, such as the hilltop complex of Escalera al Cielo (EAC). Only one annular structure has been identified atop the hill, which also supported a number of vaulted residential and civic-ceremonial structures (Gallareta et al. 2014). If the entire hilltop compound supported one corporate group or household, it is likely that the annular structure was used to produce lime to meet the group's lime consumption needs. The structure is located at the northernmost tip of the hill's

apex, away from the residential and civic-ceremonial compounds. Steep slopes on other side of this northern promontory make it inaccessible to those not living on the hill. Small-scale corporate ownership and use of at least some annular structures is supported by the location of this pit-kiln atop EAC, as well as the identification of a few other elite hilltop complexes with their own annular pit-kilns.

A slightly different situation is suggested for the production of lime powder on the neighboring hill, just to the east of EAC located slightly closer to the Kiuic site center. More than 20 structures are located on this hill spread over two main clusters, but only one structure possessed a stone vault. This suggests that the inhabitants of these residential clusters were not at the same socioeconomic level as the inhabitants of EAC or the elite compounds on other hills ringing the Kiuic site center. The orientation and contextual relationships of the different residential structures in this EAC-adjacent hill suggests the presence of multiple households or small corporate groups. The two annular structures located on this hill (one in each of the settlement clusters) are of a lower quality than those found on EAC and in the Kiuic site center with regard to both size and shape. Both fall within the smaller range of structure sizes

FIGURE 8. ONE OF THE LARGER ANNULAR STRUCTURES LOCATED IN THE HINTERLANDS TO THE WEST OF THE KIUIC SITE CENTER. THE ANNULAR STRUCTURE IS LOCATED IN THE BACKGROUND AND A LARGE HALTÚN, OR NATURAL DEPRESSION IN THE BEDROCK THAT FILLS WITH WATER, IN THE FOREGROUND.

and are somewhat irregular in form. Neither is located within an easily circumscribed residential compound and it is possible that they were both constructed and used on a more communal basis.

A third situation appears to prevail to the west of the suburban hill zone in the rural hinterlands of Kiuic. The majority of the annular structures identified in this zone are not located in close proximity to any other permanent archaeological features, let alone residential compounds. The lack of permanent structures suggests that these lime pit-kilns were used on a seasonal basis. Perhaps they were used immediately after the rainy season ended, when the risk of potentially disruptive precipitation episodes was diminished but the water reservoirs would have been full. It is difficult to say what types of social organization may have been in place for the operation of these isolated annular structures, but their distance from permanent residential compounds suggests that their use could not have been as strictly controlled.

All of the annular structures excavated thus far exhibit evidence that they were used to cook materials, most likely limestone. All of them possess ring-shaped walls of rough boulders surrounding a central pit that usually crosses through the uppermost bedrock layer to reach the underlying layer of sascab. The walls and floors of the structures, including the layers of boulders, bedrock, and sascab, all have textures and colors that indicate that they were burned. Rock, sascab, and other materials were recovered throughout the excavations and will be subjected to further chemical analyses in order to clarify the type and degree of burning. Although all of the structures share a similar general shape and exhibit evidence for being used as pit-kilns, they also exhibit a range of size and specific construction forms. Of those excavated, the two located within residential compounds immediately outside the Kiuic site center are the most similar in size and shape. They are both cut into the slope of a limestone outcrop, which serves as one side of the inner pit, and they both reach depths of approximately 3.5 meters. The scale and forms of these two structures most likely reflect the greater socioeconomic standing of the corporate groups that commissioned their construction. A third annular structure possesses a comparable shape and size, but is relatively isolated to the west of EAC. Therefore, while its construction and firing process might have been quite similar to the two located within the Kiuic urban core, the social and temporal context for its construction and use may have been quite different.

Future Directions

The next stages of this project will involve a series of laboratory analyses on the material samples recovered from the 2014 summer excavations. These will include chemical and multi-elemental analyses aimed at identifying such variables as: the temperatures to which these kilns were fired; the duration of firing episodes; the materials used as fuel within the kilns; the materials that were being fired in the kilns; and the general time periods when they were constructed and utilized. In addition to the laboratory analyses, the plan is to conduct ethnographic fieldwork to determine the extent of knowledge concerning the traditional production of lime among modern inhabitants of the Bolonchén district. Interviews with local limestone specialists will be used to create a local folk typology for different grades of limestone and their varying importance for lime production. These data can then be compared with material and spatial data recovered from the investigation of the annular structures. Finally, a third line of investigation will involve conducting experiments in the construction and firing of an annular structure. An experimental pit-kiln will be constructed modeled on the Prehispanic annular structures. Limestone will be cooked in order to produce lime powder and produce experimental data for comparison with data recovered from the excavation of the Prehispanic annular structures. The experimental pit-kiln data will also be compared with data recovered from past experimental firings of aboveground *caleras*. Combining these several lines of investigation will provide a better understanding of the forms and functions of the Prehispanic annular structures and their roles within the ancient socio-economy of the Bolonchén district.

Acknowledgements. We would like to thank William Ringle, Sarah Clayton, Stephanie Simms, Betsy Kohut, Evan Parker, Maggie Morgan-Smith, Tomás Gallareta Cervera, Melissa Galván Bernal, and Soledad Ortíz Ruíz for their helpful comments and support. The Bolonchén Regional Archaeological Project takes place under permits by the Consejo de Arqueología del Instituto Nacional de Antropología e Historia (INAH), México. We gratefully acknowledge Eduardo López Calzada, the director of the Centro INAH Yucatán. We thank all project collaborators. Fieldwork was funded by the National Science Foundation (BCS-1445437), INAH, the University of Wisconsin-Madison, and Millsaps College.

References Cited

Abrams, Elliot M, and David J. Rue
  1988 The Causes and Consequences of Deforestation among the Prehistoric Maya. *Human Ecology* 16:4:377-395.
Abrams, Elliot M.
  1994 *How the Maya Built Their World: Energetics and Ancient Architecture*. University of Texas Press, Austin.
  1996 The Evolution of Plaster Production and the Growth of the Copan Maya State. In *Arqueología Mesoamericana: Homenaje a William T. Sanders*, pp. 193-208. Vol 2, Instituto Nacional de Antropología e Historia, Mexico City, D.F.
Abrams, Elliot M. and A. Freter
  1996 A Late Classic Maya Lime-Plaster Kiln from the Maya Centre of Copan, Honduras. *Antiquity* 70:422-428.
Abrams, Elliot M., and Thomas W. Bolland
  1999 Architectural Energetics, Ancient Monuments, and Operations Management. *Journal of Archaeological Method and Theory* 6(4)263-291.
Abrams, Elliot, John Parhamovich, Jared A. Butcher, and Bruce McCord

2012 Chemical Composition of Architectural Plaster at the Classic Maya Kingdom of Piedras Negras, Guatemala. *Journal of Archaeological Science* 39:1648-1654.

Aimers, James A.

2007 What Maya Collapse? Terminal Classic Variation in the Maya Lowlands. *Journal of Archaeological Research* 15:329-377.

Alonso Olvera, Alejandra

2013 Agregados de morteros y conglomerados de cal. In *La Cal: Historia, propiedades y usos*, edited by Luis Barba Pingarrón and Isabel Villaseñor Alonso, pp. 73-94. Universidad Nacional Autónoma de México Instituto de Investigaciones Antropológicas, Distrito Federal, México.

Andrews, Anthony P., E. Wyllys Andrews, and Fernando Robles Castellanos

2003 The Northern Maya Collapse and its Aftermath. *Ancient Mesoamerica* 14:151-156.

Andrews, George

1990 *Architectural Survey Puuc Archaeological Region 1984 Field Season (Jan. 15 April 14, 1984), Preliminary Report.* Arquitectura y Arqueología: Metodologías en la Cronología de Yucatán série II-8. University of Oregon, Eugene.

Ashmore, Wendy

2009 Mesoamerican Landscape Archaeologies. *Ancient Mesoamerica* 20:183-187.

Ashmore, Wendy, Jason Yaeger, and Cynthia Robin

2004 Commoner Sense: Late and Terminal Classic Social Strategies in the Xunantunich Area. In *The Terminal Classic in the Maya Lowlands: Collapse, Transition, and Transformation*, edited by Arthur Demarest, Prudence Rice, and Don Rice, pp. 302-323. University Press of Colorado, Boulder.

Ball, Joseph W.

1989 Pottery, Potters, Palaces, and Polities: Some Socioeconomic and Political Implications of Late Classic Maya Ceramic Industries. In *Lowland Maya Civilization in the Eighth Century A.D.*, edited by Jeremy Sabloff and John Henderson. pp. 243-270. Dumbarton Oaks Research Library and Collection, Washington, D.C.

Barba Pingarrón, Luis

2013 El uso de la cal en el mundo prehispánico mesoamericano. In *La Cal: Historia, propiedades y usos*, edited by Luis Barba Pingarrón and Isabel Villaseñor Alonso, pp. 19-46. Universidad Nacional Autónoma de México Instituto de Investigaciones Antropológicas, Distrito Federal, México.

Bey, George J., III

2006 Changing Archaeological Perspectives on the Northern Maya Lowlands. In *Lifeways in the Northern Maya Lowlands: New Approaches to Archaeology in the Yucatan Peninsula*, edited by Jennifer P. Mathews and Bethany A. Morrison, pp. 13-37. University of Arizona Press, Tucson.

Brady, James E.

2005 The Impact of Ritual on Ancient Maya Economy. In *Stone Houses and Earth Lords: Maya Religion in the Cave Context*, edited by Keith M. Prufer, and James E. Brady, pp. 115-133. University Press of Colorado, Boulder.

Canuto, Marcello A.

2004 The Rural Settlement of Copan: Changes through the Early Classic. In *Understanding Early Classic Copan*, edited by Ellen Bell, Marcello Canuto, and Robert Sharer, pp. 29-49. University of Pennsylvania Museum of Archaeology and Anthropology, Philadelphia.

Carmean, Kelli

1990 The Ancient Households of Sayil: A Study of Wealth in Terminal Classic Maya Society, Ph.D. dissertation, Department of Anthropology, University of Pittsburgh, Pittsburgh.

1991 Architectural Labor Investment and Social Stratification at Sayil, Yucatan, Mexico. *Latin American Antiquity* 2(2):151-165.

Carmean, Kelli, Patricia A. McAnany, and Jeremy A. Sabloff

2011 People Who Lived in Stone Houses: Local Knowledge and Social Difference in the Classic Maya Puuc Region of Yucatan, Mexico. *Latin American Antiquity* 22(2):143-158.

Castanzo, Ronald A.

2004 Tepeaca Kiln Project. Electronic document, http://www.famsi.org/reports/02021/02021Castanzo01.pdf, accessed September 8, 2011.

Castanzo, Ronald A., and J. Heath Anderson

2004 Formative Period Lime Kilns in Puebla, Mexico. *Mexicon* 26(4):86-90.

Clark, John E., and Michael Blake

1994 The Power of Prestige: Competitive Generosity and the Emergence of Rank Societies in Lowland Mesoamerica. In *Factional Competition and Political Development in the New World*, edited by Elizabeth M. Brumfiel and John W. Fox, pp. 17-30. Cambridge University Press, Cambridge.

Demarest, Arthur A.

2009 Maya Archaeology for the Twenty-First Century: The Progress, the Perils, and the Promise. *Ancient Mesoamerica* 20:253-263.

Dunning, Nicholas P.

1991 Appendix A. In *The Ancient Maya City of Sayil: The Mapping of a Puuc Region Center*, Publication 60, edited by Jeremy Sabloff and Gair Tourtellot. Middle American Research Institute, Tulane University, New Orleans.

Dunning, Nicholas P., Timothy P. Beach and Sheryl Luzzadder-Beach

2012 Kax and kol: Collapse and resilience in lowland Maya civilization. *Proceedings of the National Academy of Sciences* 109:10:3652-3657.

Fauvet-Berthelot, Marie-France

1980 Taille de l'Obsidienne et Fabrication de la Chaux: Deux Exemples d'Activite Specialisee a Cauinal. In *Cahiers de la R.C.P. 500 2. Rabinal et la Vallée Moyenne du Rio Chixoy, Baja Verapaz – Guatemala.* pp. 5-37. Centre National de la Recherche Scientifique. Institut d'Ethnologie, Paris.

Foias, Antonia E.

2002 At the Crossroads: The Economic Basis of Political Power in the Petexbatun Region. In *Ancient Maya Political Economies*, edited by Marilyn A. Masson and David A. Freidel, pp. 223-244. Altamira Press, Walnut Creek, CA.

Folan, William J.

1978 Coba, Quintana Roo, Mexico: An Analysis of a Prehispanic and Contemporary Source of Sascab. *American Antiquity* 43(1)79-85.

Ford, Anabel, and Scott Fedick

1992 Prehistoric Maya Settlement Patterns in the Upper Belize River Area: Initial Results of the Belize River Archaeological Settlement Survey. *Journal of Field Archaeology* 19:35-49.

Fox, John W., Garret W. Cook, Arlen F. Chase, and Diane Z. Chase

1996 Questions of Political and Economic Integration: Segmentary Versus Centralized States among the Ancient Maya. *Current Anthropology* 37(5):795-801.

Freidel, David

1983 Lowland Maya Political Economy: Historical and Archaeological Perspectives in Light of Intensive Agriculture. In *Spaniards and Indians in Southeastern Mesoamerica: Essays on the History of Ethnic Relations*, edited by Murdo J. Macleod and Robert Wasserstrom, pp. 40-59. University of Nebraska Press, Lincoln.

Freidel, David A., and Jeremy A. Sabloff

1984 *Cozumel: Late Classic Settlement Patterns*. Academic Press, Orlando.

Freidel, David, Kathryn Reese-Taylor, and David Mora-Marín

2002 The Origins of Maya Civilization: The Old Shell Game, Commodity, Treasure, and Kingship. In *Ancient Maya Political Economies*, edited by Marilyn Masson and David Freidel, pp. 41-84. Altamira Press, Walnut Creek, CA.

Gallareta, Tomas, George J. Bey III, William Ringle, and Rossana May Ciau

2009 *Investigaciones Arqueológicas en las Ruinas de Kiuic y la zona Labná-Kiuic, Distrito de Bolonchén, Yucatán, México*. Informe técnico al Consejo de Arqueología de INAH, Temporada 2008.

2011 *Investigaciones Arqueológicas en las Ruinas de Kiuic y la zona Labná-Kiuic, Distrito de Bolonchén, Yucatán, México*. Informe técnico al Consejo de Arqueología de INAH, Temporada 2010.

2013 *Investigaciones Arqueológicas en las Ruinas de Kiuic y la zona Labná-Kiuic, Distrito de Bolonchén, Yucatán, México*. Informe técnico al Consejo de Arqueología de INAH, Temporada 2012.

2014 *Proyecto Arqueológico Regional de Bolonchén, Yucatán, México*. Propuesta al Consejo de Arqueología del Instituto Nacional de Antropología e Historia, Abril 2014.

Gillespie, Susan D.

2000 Ancient Maya Social Organization: Replacing 'Lineage' with 'House,' *American Anthropologist* 102(3):467-484.

2001 Agency, Personhood, and Mortuary Ritual: A Case Study for the Ancient Maya. *Journal of Anthropological Archaeology* 20:73-112.

Gonlin, Nancy

2004 Methods for Understanding Classic Maya Commoners: Structure, Function, Energetics, and More. In *Ancient Maya Commoners*, edited by Jon C. Lohse and Fred Valdez, Jr., pp. 225-254. University of Texas Press, Austin.

Grove, David C., and Ann Cyphers Guillén

1987 The Excavations. In *Ancient Chalcatzingo*, edited by David C. Grove, pp. 21-55. University of Texas Press, Austin.

Hansen, Eric Floyd

2000 Ancient Maya Burnt-Lime Technology: Cultural Implications of Technological Styles. Unpublished Ph.D. dissertation, Department of Anthropology, University of California, Los Angeles.

Hansen, Richard, Steven Bozarth, John Jacob, David Wahl, and Thomas Schreiner

2002 Climatic and Environmental Variability in the Rise of Maya Civilization: A Preliminary Perspective from the Northern Peten. *Mesoamerica* 13(2):273-295.

Hendon, Julia

1991 Status and Power in Classic Maya Society: An Archaeological Study. *American Anthropologist* 93:894-918.

Hirth, Kenneth

2003 Interregional Exchange as Elite Behavior: An Evolutionary Perspective. In *Mesoamerican Elites: An Archaeological Assessment*, edited by Diane Chase and Arlen Chase, pp. 18-29. University of Oklahoma Press, Norman.

Johnston, Kevin, Takeshi Inomata, and Joel Palka

1989 Excavaciones de Operación 1. In *El Proyecto Archaeological Regional Petexbatun:Informe No. 1*, edited by Arthur Demarest and Stephen D. Houston, pp. 29-52.

Killion, Thomas, Jeremy A. Sabloff, Gair Tourtellot, and Nicholas P. Dunning

1989 Intensive Surface Collection of Residential Clusters at Terminal Classic Sayil, Yucatan, Mexico. *Journal of Field Archaeology* 16:273-294.

Kowalski, Jeff K., and Nicholas P. Dunning

1999 The Architecture of Uxmal: The Symbolics of Statemaking at a Puuc Maya Regional Capital. In *Mesoamerican Architecture as a Cultural Symbol*, edited by Jeff K. Kowalski, pp. 274-297. Oxford University Press, New York.

LeCount, Lisa J.

2001 Like Water for Chocolate: Feasting and Political Ritual among the Late Classic Maya at Xunantunich, Belize. *American Anthropologist* 103:4:935-953.

Littmann Edwin R.

1959 Ancient Mesoamerican Mortars, Plasters and Stuccos: Chiapas.' *American Antiquity* 25(2):264-266.

1960 Ancient Mesoamerican Mortars, Plasters and Stuccos: The Use of Bark Extracts in Lime Plasters, *American Antiquity* 25(4):593-597.

1966 The Classification and Analysis of Ancient Calcareous Materials. *American Antiquity* 31(6):875-878.

Lucero, Lisa J.

2002 The Collapse of the Classic Maya: A Case for the Role of Water Control. *American Anthropologist* 104(3):814-826.

2003 The Politics of Ritual: The Emergence of Classic Maya Rulers. *Current Anthropology* 44(4):523-558.

MacKinnon, J. Jefferson, and Emily M. May

1990 Small-scale Maya Lime Making in Belize: Ancient and Modern.' *Ancient Mesoamerica* 1(2)197-203.

Martin Arana, Raul

1987 Classic and Postclassic Chalcatzingo. In *Ancient Chalcatzingo*, edited by D.C. Grove, pp. 387-399. University of Texas Press, Austin.

McAnany, Patricia A.

1990 Water Storage in the Puuc Region of the Northern Maya Lowlands: A Key to Population Estimates and Architectural Variability. In *Precolumbian Population History in the Maya Lowlands*, edited by T. Patrick Culbert and Don S. Rice, pp. 263-283. University of New Mexico Press, Albuquerque.

2010 *Ancestral Maya Economies in Archaeological Perspective*. Cambridge University Press, Cambridge.

2014 *Living with the Ancestors*: *Kinship and Kingship in Ancient Maya Society* Cambridge University Press, Cambridge.

Méndez-Montealvo, Guadalupe, Francisco J. García-Suárez, Octavio Paredes-López, and Luis A. Bello-Pérez

2008 Effect of Nixtamalization on Morphological and Rheological Characteristics of Maize Starch. *Journal of Cereal Science* 48:420-425.

Morris, Earl H.

1931 *The Temple of the Warriors*. Charles Scribner's Sons, New York.

Neff, Hector

2002 Quantitative Techniques for Analyzing Ceramic Compositional Data. In *Ceramic Production and Circulation in the Greater Southwest: Source Determination by INAA and Complementary Mineralogical Investigations*, edited by Donna M. Glowacki and Hector Neff, pp. 15-36. The Cotsen Institute of Archaeology Press, Los Angeles.

Ortíz Ruíz, Soledad

2014 *Caracterización de las Estructuras Anulares de la Región del Occidente de las Tierras Bajas Mayas*. Unpublished M.A.Thesis, Centro de Estudios Arqueológicos, El Colegio de Michoacan A.C.

Paris, Elizabeth H.

2008 Metallurgy, Mayapan, and the Postclassic Mesoamerican World System. *Ancient Mesoamerica* 19:43-66.

Pollock, Harry E.D.

1980 *The Puuc: An Architectural Survey of the Hill Country of Yucatan and Northern Campeche, Mexico*. Peabody Museum of Archaeology and Ethnology, Cambridge, MA.

Potter, Daniel R.

1989 Analytical Approaches to Late Classic Maya Lithic Industries. In *Lowland Maya Civilization in the Eighth Century*, edited by Jeremy Sabloff and John Henderson. Dumbarton Oaks Research Library and Collection, Washington, D.C.

Rathje, William J.

1971 The Origins and Development of Lowland Maya Civilization. *American Antiquity* 36(30):275-285.

Redfield, Robert, and Alfonso Villa Rojas

1934 *Chan Kom: A Maya Village*. Carnegie Institution of Washington. Publication no. 448. Carnegie Institution of Washington, Washington, D.C.

Robin, Cynthia

2003 New Directions in Maya Household Archaeology. *Journal of Archaeological Research* 11(4):307-356.

2006 Gender, Farming, and Long-Term Change Maya Historical and Archaeological Perspectives. *Current Anthropology* 47(3):409-433.

Russell, Bradley, and Bruce Dahlin

2007 Traditional Burnt-Lime Production at Mayapán, Mexico. *Journal of Field Archaeology* 32(4)407-423.

Sabloff, Jeremy A., and Gair Tourtellot

1991 *The Ancient Maya City of Sayil: The Mapping of a Puuc Region Center*. Publication 60. Middle American Research Institute, Tulane University, New Orleans.

Schortman, Edward

1989 Interregional Interaction in Prehistory: The Need for a New Perspective. *American Antiquity* 54:52-65.

Schortman, Edward, and Patricia Urban

1994 Living on the Edge: Core/Periphery Relations in Ancient Southeastern Mesoamerica. *Current Anthropology* 35(4):401-430.

Schreiner, Thomas Paul

2002 *Traditional Maya Lime Production: Environmental and Cultural Implications of a Native American Technology*. Ph.D. dissertation, Department of Anthropology, University of California, Berkeley.

Sheets, Payson

2002 Soil Chemical Analysis of Ancient Activities in Ceren, El Salvador. *Latin American Antiquity* 13(3):331-342.

Smith, Claire, and H. Martin Wobst

2005 *Indigenous Archaeologies: Decolonizing Theory and Practice*. Routledge, New York.

Viel, René

1983 Evolución de la Ceramica en Copán: Resultados Preliminarios. In *Introducción a la Arqueología de Copán, Honduras*, edited by C. Bandery. pp. 471-550. Vol. 1, Secretaria De Estado en Despacho de Turismo y Cultura, Tegucigalpa.

Wernecke, David C.

2008 A Burning Question: Maya Lime Technology and the Maya Forest. *Journal of Ethnobiology* 28(2):200-210.

Wilk, Richard R., and William J. Rathje

1982 Household Archaeology. *The American Behavioral Scientist* 25(6):617-639.

Wilk, Richard, and Wendy Ashmore

1988 *Household and Community in the American Past*. University of New Mexico Press, Albuquerque.

Yaeger, Jason

2000 The Social Construction of Communities in the Classic Maya Countryside: Strategies of Affiliation in Western Belize. In *The Archaeology of Communities: A New World Perspective,* edited by Marcello A. Canuto, and Jason Yaeger, pp. 123-142. Routledge Press, London.

From Temple to Trash: Analysis and Interpretation of a Dismantled Stucco Façade and its Deposit from Kiuic, Yucatán

Melissa Galván Bernal, George J. Bey III, and Rossana May Ciau

The imagery on building façades in the Maya area has been the object of multiple studies over the years. For the most part such studies have focused on architectonic, iconographic, or epigraphic interpretations. The case presented in this paper focuses on the symbolism of a Maya building façade, but it also gives equal attention to the context and conditions in which the façade was found. In the archaeological site of Kiuic, Yucatán, Mexico, a modeled and painted stucco façade was found dismantled, the remains buried nearby a temple in one of the plazas of the site. In this paper we present the results of the stucco morphological analysis, as well as the associated materials found in the deposit. The objective of this study is to obtain a better understanding of the process of both the construction and dismantling of the stucco façade, which was discovered in a deposit inside the main ceremonial center of Kiuic. Likewise, this study looks for a possible explanation regarding the sociopolitical implications associated with the event and attempts to contextualize it within the greater history of Kiuic.

Las imágenes representadas en las fachadas de los edificios en la zona maya han sido objeto de múltiples estudios a lo largo de los años. Esta información en su mayoría se ha enfocado en arquitectura, iconografía, o epigrafía. El caso que aquí se presenta trata el estudio del simbolismo de la fachada de un edificio maya, pero igualmente de su contexto y las condiciones en las que se encontró la misma. En el sitio arqueológico de Kiuic en la zona Puuc del estado de Yucatán, México, se descubrió una fachada de estuco modelado y pintado la cual fue desmantelada y posteriormente enterrada al lado de un templo en una de las plazas del sitio. En este trabajo se presenta el resultado del análisis morfológico de los fragmentos de estuco así como de los materiales asociados recuperados en el depósito. El objetivo de este estudio fue entender cual fue el proceso tanto de construcción como de destrucción de la fachada. Así mismo, el estudio, busca una posible explicación con respecto a las implicaciones sociopolíticas aunadas al evento, y de esta manera trata de contextualizarlo dentro de la historia de Kiuic.

In the Maya area, change in architectural styles is one of the main topics of archaeological research. In the Puuc region, especially, it represents one of the most important markers of transition from one period to the next. One of the primary question in Puuc archaeology has been: What is the reason for these changes?

The objective behind the research presented in this paper is to describe and interpret a midden located in a plaza at the Maya site of Kiuic in the Puuc region in Yucatán, Mexico (Figure 1). The midden is unusual because it contains a deposit of modeled and painted stucco fragments, which were part of a decorative façade from one of Kiuic's buildings. The uniqueness of the deposit lies in its location and the nature of its burial. According to the stratigraphy, the fragments, discovered four meters to the south of a temple in Plaza Ulum, were most likely deposited in a single event (Bey et.al 2009).

The interest in carrying out this study emerged after careful observation and partial identification of some of the characteristics of the deposit. The latter guided us to realize that no other similar element had been reported in the Maya area. The deposit found at Kiuic is distinct from the *in situ* stucco façades that were recorded at sites such as Acanceh (Miller 1991), Dzibilchaltún (Coggins 1983), Ek' Balam (Vargas de la Peña and Castillo 1999), Palenque (Green 1991; Ruz 1973; Schele 1998:479-517), and Copán (Baudez 1994; Fash 1993).

In this paper, we employ various theoretical models in order to propose an explanation of why the façade ended up buried where it did. Defining the façade's deposition process allows us to distinguish between different types of waste deposits in the archaeological record. Frequently, the characteristics of this kind of element are confusing; there are cases in which a rubbish deposit is not just the result of the disposal of common and daily waste, instead it is the consequence of specific activities, which might include ritual behavior.

Information on local and regional architectural style changes was utilized to better understand how this process was tied, directly and indirectly, to the structures themselves. In the case of the façade deposit, the data recovered from the stucco fragments was analyzed along with the information about Kiuic's architectural style and its changes through time. The latter was aimed to chronologically situate the destruction, removal, and deposition of the façade in order to get a better perspective on the process. The information obtained suggests that this event had a strong symbolic meaning and was not just result of maintenance.

This paper presents the analysis of the façade's deposit, including stratigraphy, the material evidence, and the attempt to interpret both by comparing different theoretical models. The research focuses on the morphological analysis

Melissa Galván Bernal - Tulane University, New Orleans, Louisiana (mgalvan@tulane.edu); **George J. Bey III** - Millsaps College, Jackson, Mississippi (beygj@millsaps.edu); **Rossana May Ciau** - Facultad de Ciencias Antropológicas de la U.A.D.Y., Mérida, Yucatán (rossana101@hotmail.com).

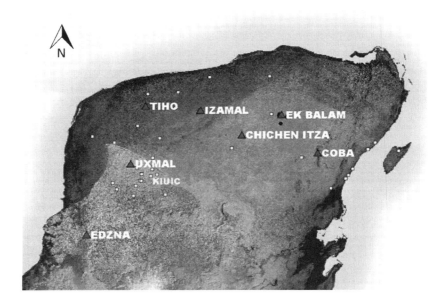

FIGURE 1. MAP OF THE YUCATÁN PENINSULA SHOWING THE LOCATION OF PUUC REGION (BEY ET AL. 2006: FIGURE 1.1).

of the stucco fragments. A typology was developed in order to enable the identification of the façade´s decorative and symbolic elements. This typology is complemented with the data obtained from the associated material assemblage and by placing the façade deposition event within the developmental history of Kiuic.

Background: Kiuic and the Deposit Discovery

Kiuic is located in the southwestern portion of the state of Yucatán, Mexico. The site is classified as Rank III in the *Atlas Arqueológico del Estado de Yucatán* (Garza and Kurjack 1980:104). According to the information assembled over more than a decade, it was founded during the Middle Preclassic period (Bey et al. 2010:7-14). The site´s core contains 17 architectural groups: Pixoy, Yaxché, Kuché, On, Balché, Chulul, Nicté, Zipché, Kiik Che, Sulché, Catzim, Pomol Che, Tuk, Chacáh, Ixim Che, and Habin (Figure 2). Kiuic´s buildings tend to be oriented about 14° east of magnetic north, and many of its platforms face toward the Yaxché group.

The Yaxché group (Figure 3) is located on the east side of the site and includes three plazas: Dzunun, Icim, and Ulum. Excavations at the site showed that this group is the location of the earliest occupation at Kiuic. A Middle Preclassic platform was detected underneath the central plaza at Yaxché. The original platform, known as Plaza Dzunun, was extended, and at least three structures were built on top of it; one on the west side, one on the east side, and another large substructure on the south side of the plaza (sub N1015E1015) (Bey et al. 2009:8-6; 2011:7-4). The excavations at Plaza Icim, adjacent to Plaza Dzunun, showed that at least one platform is located on the west

side of the original platform of the Yaxché group. There is also evidence of another Middle Preclassic settlement located near the Balché and Chulul groups (Figure 2) (Bey et al. 2010:7-14). The evidence suggests that Kiuic had been occupied since this time, as the construction of the Ulum and Dzunun plazas date to the late phase of the Early Classic period, although occupation during the Middle Classic period is still unclear (Bey et al. 2011:5-2).

Ceramics and architectural chronology suggest that the site had two main periods of development, both during the Late Terminal Classic; the first one around A.D. 750 and the second one around A.D. 850 (Bey et al. 2009:8-6). At some point between A.D. 550 and A.D. 650 Yaxché´s original platform was expanded and elevated with new monumental structures on opposite sides (Bey et al. 2008, 2009, 2010). The excavations showed that Floor 3 was also constructed in Plaza Dzunun and the platform was extended towards the north. Substructure N1015E1015 was dismantled and replaced with Structure N1015E1015, a long building with one vaulted room identified as a *popol nah* (council house) (Bey et al. 2009:8-6). During this period, a megalithic substructure, sub-N1065E1025, was also constructed on top of Floor 3 on the north side of Plaza Dzunun (Bey et al. 2010).

During the first of Kiuic´s significant development periods (c. A.D. 750) there was significant construction activity at the site, including dramatic transformation of the Yaxché group. Plaza Dzunun was completely enclosed due to the construction of two other plazas: Plaza Icim on the west and Plaza Ulum on the east. During this period, the first phase of a temple (Structure N1050E1065) was constructed on the east side of Plaza Ulum. Excavations at

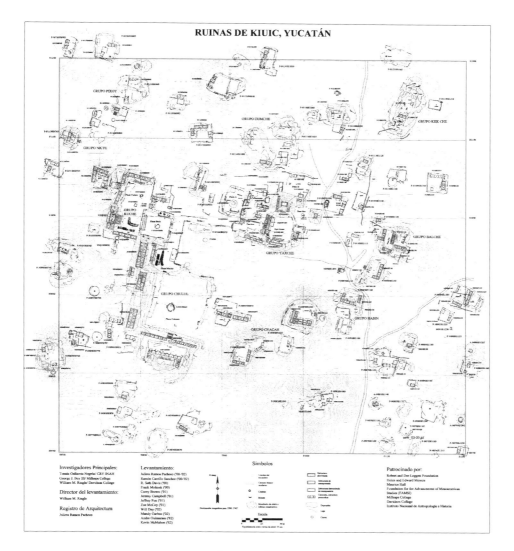

FIGURE 2. MAP OF KIUIC, YUCATÁN. YAXCHÉ GROUP CIRCLED (BEY ET AL. 2003:2.1).

FIGURE 3. TOPOGRAPHIC MAP OF THE YAXCHÉ GROUP AT KIUIC, YUCATÁN (BEY ET AL. 2006:1.5).

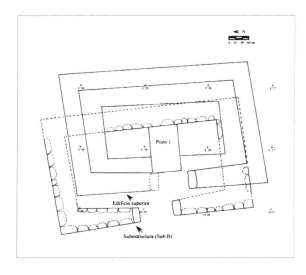

FIGURE 4. STR. N1050E1065. PLAN VIEW SHOWING DIFFERENT CONSTRUCTION STAGES (BEY ET AL. 2008:4-45).

this structure showed that its base (sub-B) consisted of two platforms with stairs and the superior building (sub-Temple A) consisted of one single Early Puuc style vaulted room (Figure 4). Several *espigas* (protruding stones that are the remains of the assembly system that was used to embed stucco decoration on the walls) and numerous modeled stucco fragments were also found among the building collapse, suggesting that it had extensive modeled stucco decoration (Bey et al. 2009:8-7). Inside Plaza Dzunun, Floor 2 was built along with two structures on the west side of the platform and another on the east side. On the west side there was a vaulted building with one room and an Early Puuc style building with columns. On the east side of the plaza another columned building, and possibly a tower, were constructed. The basic form of Structure N1015E1015 in Plaza Dzunun remained unaltered during this period (c. A.D. 750), although the original stairway was dismantled and a new one was constructed with an orientation slightly more toward the east than the original (Bey et al. 2011:7-6).

During Kiuic´s second significant development period (A.D. 800-900), Yaxché underwent a spatial reconfiguration. During this time, the group was an elite residence. Inside Plaza Ulum, a new temple (Temple A) was built on top of Structure N1050E1065. This building has an orientation slightly different from the original. The evidence suggests that the modeled stucco that was decorating sub-Temple A was removed and deposited in the midden on the south side of Temple A; the espigas recovered from the collapse suggest that the second temple, defined as an early Puuc IIa style building, was also decorated with stucco, just as its predecessor. The stairway associated with sub-Temple A was partially dismantled and a new one constructed directly on top (Bey et al. 2008).

Throughout the ninth century, Kiuic experienced a sociopolitical change that was reflected in the site´s unique layout. Yaxché stopped functioning as an elite residence and was integrated into a greater palace complex, which was comprised of the Yaxché and Chulul groups. Despite the social transformation at the site, Yaxché remained in use and evolved as a ceremonial and ritual compound that was connected with the new palace through a *sacbé*, or causeway. During this time, Structure N1065E1025 was transformed from Kiuic´s royal family residence to a 10 meter pyramid with stairs and a vaulted building at the top (Bey et al. 2010).

The Deposit and its Material Assemblage

The stucco deposit was identified during the first field season at Kiuic in 2000 (Bey et al. 2001). Original observations of the area indicated the presence of a midden on the south side of Structure N1050E1065. As a result, three test pits were excavated (Bey et al. 2001:3.17-3.21). The excavation of these pits exposed the stucco deposit. During the 2009 season its contents were defined, resulting in the discovery of a dismantled modeled façade (Figure 5) (Bey et al. 2010:4-32-4-46).

Based on data obtained from excavations, we were able to determine that the deposit covered an area approximately 11 m NS by 6 m EW with a thickness of 40-50 cm, 40 cm from the natural surface (Figures 6 and 7); the deposit begins four meters from the south side of Structure N1050E1065. The façade deposit seemed to be the product of one single event. The deposit had a high concentration of stucco and ceramics, although lithic material was poorly represented. Two bone fragments were also recovered as well as a speleothem and a few burnt shell fragments. Among the modeled stucco fragments, anthropomorphic faces and extremities were identified along with several different decorative elements. The stucco fragments recovered from the main levels of the deposit, those with the highest stucco concentration, were found in good state of preservation, which indicates that the façade was in nearly optimal condition when it was removed from its original place.

FIGURE 5. MAP SHOWING EXCAVATION UNITS IN THE DEPOSIT AREA AND ITS RELATION WITH STR. N1050E1065 (BEY ET AL. 2007:4-10).

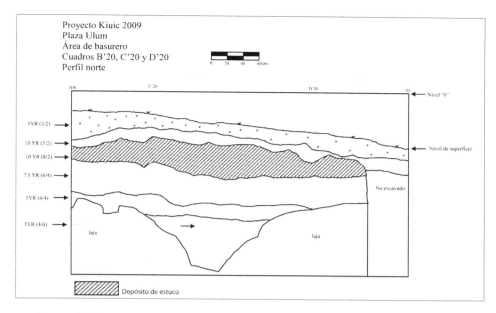

FIGURE 6. 2009 EXCAVATION. NORTH PROFILE SHOWING THE VARIOUS STRATA (GALVÁN 2012).

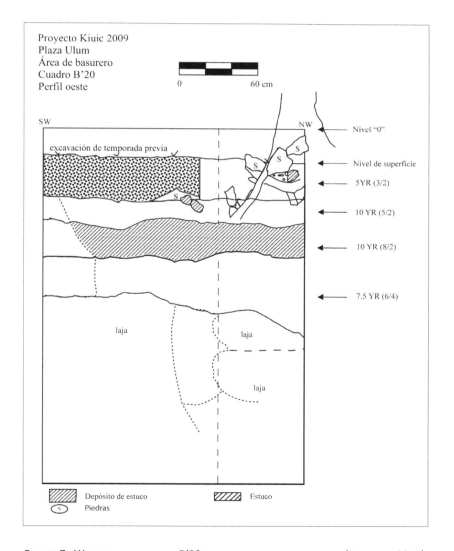

FIGURE 7. WEST PROFILE OF UNIT B´20 SHOWING THE VARIOUS STRATA (BEY ET AL. 2010).

Lines of Inquiry

One of the main aspects discussed in this paper is the formation of the archaeological record (Deal 1985:253; Schiffer 1976, 1996, 2010). The site and the architectural group, where the building to which the stucco façade allegedly belonged is located, remained in use after the façade was destroyed and buried. Ideas about architectural renovation were also considered because the space that was occupied by the original structure was kept in use during the construction of the new building. It is probable that the renovation included termination ritual activities, which would have resulted in the formation of a deposit with complex and difficult to define characteristics (Coe 1959:94-95; Freidel and Schele 1989; Freidel et al. 1998; Pagliaro et al. 2003; Pendergast 1998; Stanton et al. 2008:235; Vogt 1998; Walker 1995). These multiple possibilities directed us to contemplate a range of different scenarios in order to try to explain the deposit's function and meaning.

It has been argued that iconographic analysis is one of the more useful ways to define the function of a civic building (Rivera 1994:51), an aspect we explored in this research. We suggest that the function of the building the façade might have belonged to is directly linked with the treatment that the façade received at the moment of its removal and deposition (Fash et al. 1992:105-115; Freidel et al. 1993:222; Houston 1996:132-151; Kowalski 1987:75).

Another way to interpret the deposit is by combining the concept of ceremonial trash (Walker 1995) with the idea of termination ritual. The concept of ceremonial trash implies that a deposit containing objects utilized in ritual activities, which were discarded after fulfilling their functions tied to those events, might have some symbolic charge (Walker 1995). We propose these ideas based on our observation of the stratigraphy as well as the material recovered from the deposit. Below we explain the classification system and analysis of the stucco fragments and the associated material.

Sources for Comparison

In the Puuc region, modeled stucco sculpture has been recorded, but the examples preserved in situ are minimal. The main reason is that the tradition of modeled stucco façades belongs to an architectural style that predates the Classic Puuc style (Andrews 1986; Gendrop 1998; Pollock 1980), which contains the best preserved examples. The greatest evidence for stucco façades is the presence of espigas in the Early Puuc style buildings (Kowalski 1987; Pollock 1980). Likewise, several modeled stucco fragments have been recovered in excavations in different sites such as Oxkintok (Fernández 1992, 1994), Uxmal (Foncerrada 1965; Kowalski 1987; Pollock 1980), Labná (May 2000; Pollock 1980:34) and Kabah (Pollock 1980). It is more common to find modeled stucco façades in situ in other parts of the Maya area. The reasons may be

innumerable, and a treatment of this issue is not the subject of this paper.

In order to carry out an analysis, the most significant elements were selected from the total sample. Those elements were submitted to a comparative process, using Classic Maya façades as the counterpart. In addition of the recorded representations in the aforementioned Puuc sites, stucco façades present in sites such as Dzibilchaltún (Coggins 1983; Góngora 1997), Acanceh (Miller 1991) and Ek' Balam (Vargas de la Peña and Castillo 2006:60) in Yucatán; Edzná (Benavides 1994:132; 1996:30; 2003:5) and Balamkú (Arnauld et al. 1999; Baudez 1996; García 1994) in Campeche; and Kohunlich (Nalda and Balanzario 2006:43; Velázquez 1995) in Quintana Roo were also taken into account. Likewise, we used examples from several southern lowland sites such as Copán (Argucia 2004), Palenque (Robertson 1983, 1985, 1991; Schele and Mathews 1979), Toniná (Mateos 1996:145; Yadeun 1993), and Yaxchilán (Tate 1992:219) for comparison. These sites were selected because they either contained in situ modeled stucco façades or because evidence of this material was found in association with their buildings.

Stucco Typology

The focus of this investigation is the study of the stucco fragments recovered from the Plaza Ulum deposit, from which a typology was developed. The objectives of such typology and the analysis itself were: 1) to obtain a better understanding about their morphology; 2) to identify shapes present on the façade; 3) to enable the identification of the iconographic elements present on the façade; and 4) to ascertain the approximate size of the figures displayed on the façade. To complement the classification, the features of the fragments, such as quantity and weight, were considered, and we conducted a series of statistical analyses. The stucco typology includes the classification of 8,284 fragments (total amount recovered), which have a combined weight of 464.6 kg (Figure 8).

The fragments were first classified as either modeled fragments or flattened stucco, then separated into five categories (Table 1): 1) Sculptures; 2) Surface Modeling; 3) Decoration/Appliqué; 4) Nuclei; and 5) Flattened. When possible, the fragments were further divided into subcategories (Table 2): 1) Sculptures: a) Extremities, b)

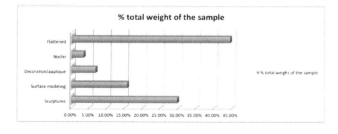

FIGURE 8. WEIGHT PERCENTAGE BY STUCCO FRAGMENTS TYPE.

Type	Quantity	Weight (kg)	% by type from total sample (quantity)	% by type from total modeled sample (quantity)	% by type from total weight
Sculptures	315	137.6	3.80%	18.70%	29.60%
Surface Modeling	438	72.9	5.20%	26.10%	15.60%
Decoration/Appliqué	736	32.2	8.70%	43.60%	6.70%
Nuclei	188	15.6	2.14%	11.40%	3.30%
Flattened	6607	206.3	79.70%		44.30%

TABLE 1. QUANTITIES AND PERCENTAGES OF STUCCO FRAGMENTS TYPES.

Type	Quantity	Weight (kg)	% by type from total sample (quantity)	% by type from total modeled sample (quantity)	% by type from total weight
Sculptures / Extremities	109	86.9	1.30%	6.50%	18.7%
Sculptures / Faces	5	2.8	0.06%	0.3%	0.6%
Sculptures / Unique Forms	4	11.5	0.04%	0.2%	2.5%
Sculptures / Unidentified	197	36.4	2.40%	11.70%	7.8%
Surface Modeling / Moldings	294	57.9	3.50%	17.50%	12.4 %
Surface Modeling / Unidentified	144	15	1.70%	8.6 %	3.20%
Decoration / Unique forms	55	5.1	0.70%	3.40%	1.08%
Decoration / Tables	64	3	0.80%	3.90%	0.60%
Decoration / Half Tables	34	1.6	0.40%	2%	0.30%
Decoration / Feathers	61	4.4	0.70%	3.60%	1 %
Decoration / Half feathers	4	0.1	0.06%	0.20%	0.02%
Decoration / Fangs	11	0.1	0.10%	0.60%	0.02%
Decoration / Leaves	21	0.3	0.20%	1.20%	0.06%
Decoration / Cartouches	12	0.4	0.10%	0.70%	0.08%
Decoration / Knots	9	0.3	0.10%	0.50%	0.06%
Decoration / Beads	32	0.8	0.40%	1.90%	0.20%
Decoration / Discs	21	2.3	0.30%	1.30%	0.50%
Decoration / Bands	49	1.5	0.60%	3%	0.30%
Decoration / Edges	5	0.1	0.06%	0.30%	0.02%
Decoration / Cylindrical Forms	88	1.8	1.00%	5.20%	0.3 %
Decoration / Conical Forms	73	0.5	0.90%	4.30%	0.1%
Decoration / Unidentified	197	9.9	2.3%	11.5%	2.1 %
Nuclei / Simple	184	10.7	2.14%	11.10%	2.3%
Nuclei / Composite	4	4.9	0.04%	0.20%	1%
Flattened > 8 cm	282	131.9	3.40%		28.3%
Flattened < 8 cm	6325	74.4	76.30%		16.00%

TABLE 2. QUANTITIES AND PERCENTAGES OF STUCCO FRAGMENTS SUB-TYPES.

Faces, c) Unique Forms, and d) Unidentified; 2) Surface Modeling: a) Moldings, b) Unidentified; 3) Decoration/Appliqué: a) Unique Forms, b) Tables, c) Half Tables, d) Feathers, e) Half Feathers, f) Fangs, g) Leafs, h) Cartouches, i) Knots, j) Beads, k) Discs, l) Bands, m) Edges, n) Cylindrical Forms, o) Conical Forms, p) Unidentified; 4) Nuclei: a) Tubular [Simple] and b) Composite; and 5) Flattened Stucco.

Sculptures

The sculptures category contains the largest number of three-dimensional fragments. Within this group, we identified both anthropomorphic and abstract shapes. Abstract shapes were classified as unique figures, as these pieces only appear once in the sample and are representations of a specific element. The vast majority of the sculpture type had a tubular stucco nucleus, or the impression of it; this nucleus functioned as the sculpture's frame or support.

The extremities sub-category (Figure 9) contains the appendages of anthropomorphic sculptures. In this group, we identified fragments of arms and legs, including some with painted decoration or appliquéd elements. These fragments have a base of red paint, some with additional painted designs on top. The extremities are a basic cylindrical shapes, modeled with an interior tubular nucleus; the size of this nucleus is proportional to the size of the sculpture. Stucco was built up around the nucleus to form the extremities of these anthropomorphic sculptures. Probably in some cases the nuclei were wrapped with textile or other natural fiber before applying the stucco layers; fragments with impressions of perishable material were recorded (Figure 9c). As explained in more detail below, in some cases there were composite nuclei, which were made to support the heaviest parts of the sculptures.

The crossed bands in white paint present on some extremity type fragments in Kiuic's sample (Figures 9d and 9e) resemble the decoration used on figural representations in murals or on stelae. This kind of decoration is similar to an extended sandal strap, which is crossed like a bandage from the ankle to the knee (Proskouriakoff 1950:figs. 29 c´, d´, i´, j´). While this 'bandage' was not present in every single case, it is common to find it on this form.

The modeling technique used for the Kiuic appendage sculptures seems unusual, as only a few comparable examples were found at Palenque (Schele and Mathews 1979:figs. 47 and 111) and on the façade of Ek' Balam's Acropolis (Vargas de la Peña et al. 2006:56-63). The style of the anthropomorphic representations at Kiuic is similar to some sculptures from the Palace and the Temple of Inscriptions in Palenque (Robertson 1985, 1991; Schele and Mathews 1979:figs. 47 and 111). In some cases, the extremities were decorated with representations of knotted bands, probably a depiction of the ties found under the knee in figural representations (Robertson 1983, 1985, 1991).

In addition to the appendages, five fragments of anthropomorphic faces were recorded: one in profile (Figure 10a), one frontal (Figure 10b), and another fragment of a human nose (Figure 10c). The fourth face was quite different from the first three, both because it has the characteristics of advanced age and is differently colored. This fragment probably represents a god or an ancestor. The fifth face also has anthropomorphic features but is different in style from the previous four pieces. This piece only has the portion of the lips, chin, and right cheekbone. In some cases, the pieces in this sub-category showed evidence that they once had a tubular nucleus as support while others are just solid stucco pieces with a modeled surface (Figures 10a and 10c). All of these pieces have remains of red, black, blue, and orange paint. The modeling style of the first four faces is similar to the modeling style commonly used during the Classic period at Palenque (Schele and Mathews 1979:figs. 138, 248, 291, 845), Toniná (Yadeun 1993:120-124), and Ek' Balam (Vargas de la Peña et al. 2003:56-63).

The three-dimensional modeled forms that are not part of the anthropomorphic sculptures, and not repeated in the sample, were placed in the unique figures sub-category. In these figures polychrome is widely used, with colors such as red, orange, yellow, blue, green, black, and brown. Some of these pieces had a tubular nucleus as a support or frame, although there are cases in which the sculptures only had mortar and small stones as a fill. The surface modeling of these pieces is complex in every case, since they have additional appliquéd elements.

Surface Modeling

Pieces of flattened stucco with an elevated surface, the great majority with angular modeling, were classified as surface modeling. This category was divided between a) moldings and b) unidentified.

In a molded form, modeling creates a relief on the surface. In our examples, the shape is angular and longitudinal, maintaining an identical profile; these pieces are identified as part of the façade wall (Figure 11). We have suggested that these moldings were part of a façade framework, perhaps demarcating specific areas. Multiple colors were identified in these type of fragments, red the most common (44.8%), followed by a combination of red-blue (11.68%), and lastly red-black (4.54%).

Decoration or Appliqué

The fragments classified in the decoration or appliqué category are pieces that were created to be attached to a surface as decorative elements; these surfaces could have been part of a wall or a sculpture. The shapes found within this type are variable, but have a common attachment mark. In general, these pieces were found in a good state of conservation, several pieces were even complete. The reason for this is that these elements were crafted separately and then plastered to a surface. When the façade

46

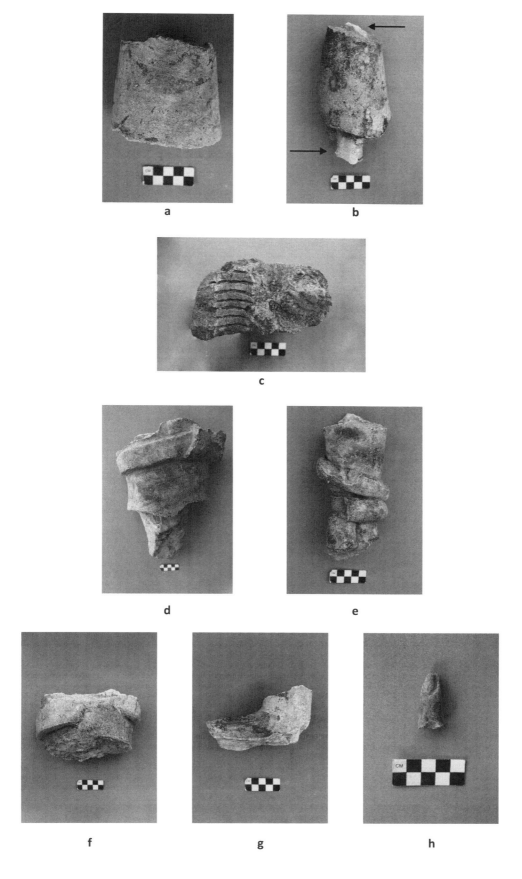

FIGURE 9 A-H. EXTREMITY FRAGMENTS WITH (A) CROSSED BANDS IN PAINT; (B) NUCLEUS; AND (C) DETAIL OF THE TEXTILE IMPRESSIONS ON THE INTERIOR OF THE STUCCO FRAGMENT. (D) PROBABLY A LEG; (E) PROBABLY AN ARM; (F-G) VARIOUS EXTREMITY TYPES; (H) HUMAN FINGER SHAPED FRAGMENT.

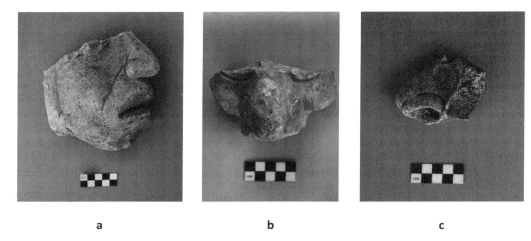

FIGURE 10 A-C. (A) STUCCO FRAGMENT SCULPTURE/FACE NO.2; (B) STUCCO FRAGMENT SCULPTURE/FACE NO. 4; (C) STUCCO FRAGMENT SCULPTURE/FACE NO. 5.

FIGURE 11. STUCCO FRAGMENTS OF SURFACE MODELING/ MOLDINGS.

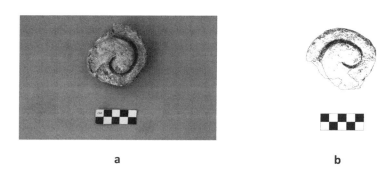

a   b

FIGURE 12 A-B. STUCCO FRAGMENT DECORATION/UNIQUE FORM NO. 12 (IU90005). (A) PHOTOGRAPH; (B) DRAWING.

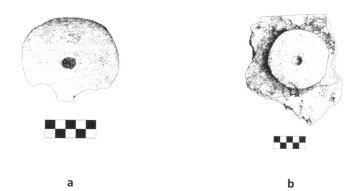

a   b

FIGURE 13 A-B. CHALCHIHUITES. (A) STUCCO FRAGYENT DECORATION/UNIQUE FORM NO. 25 (KIU90011); (B) STUCCO FRAGMENT DECORATION/UNIQUE FORM NO. 8 (KIU900105).

was dismantled, these decorative elements would have detached easily. Decoration/appliqué pieces are small to medium sized, ranging between 1.5-15 cm long and 0.9-13.8 cm wide.

Within this category, 16 sub-categories were created: a) Unique Forms; b) Tables; c) Half Tables; d) Feathers; e) Half Feathers; f) Fangs; g) Leaves; h) Cartouches; i) Knots; j) Beads; k) Discs; l) Bands; m) Edges; n) Cylindrical Forms; o) Conical Forms; p) Unidentified. The modeling technique used to form these pieces is simple; they were crafted in solid stucco without a nucleus or frame. In some cases, the surface was decorated or modeled, using incisions, perforations, or painted designs. These decorative pieces provide uniqueness to the anthropomorphic sculptures and to the façade in general.

The shapes of the pieces classified as unique forms are not repeated in the sample, and the polychrome technique is widely used (Figures 12-15). This type of fragments is, possibly, the most significant of the entire sample; the state of preservation along with the information provided by their unique designs make these decorative pieces extremely important to the study. For practical purposes, only the most representative are described in this paper (for a complete catalog see Galván 2012).

The fragment depicted in Figure 12 is almost complete (90%). It is a modeled disc shape, and its anterior face is carved with a spiral design with remnants of red paint. On the posterior face, the surface was flattened and smoothed. Coggins (1983:26) has argued that these spiral designs resembles marine gastropods, and these images make a reference to aquatic themes. This spiral shape has been utilized frequently within this sort of context as sites such as Altun Ha (Zender 2010:89) and in the mural in the Temple of the Warriors at Chichén Itzá (Cobos 2010:199).

Another example is the solid stucco disc shaped pieces, perforated in the center, with remains of blue-green paint on the surface (Figure 20). Coggins (1983:65) identified this shape on the façade of Str.1-sub at Dzibilchaltún and associated it with the chalchiuite, or precious water, symbol (Figure 13). Since the pieces at Kiuic share a similar form and color, we argue that it is the same symbol (Schele and Mathews 1979:fig. 760).

The pieces in the knot sub-category have an oval concave shape with carved relief designs on the anterior face. The design consists of curved thin lines crossing each other (Figure 14). This design has been associated with the four-sided knot symbol, which has been linked with the Palenque Triad God GI (Schele and Mathews 1979:figs. 765, 766, 829).

The pieces in the feathers sub-category are modeled triangular forms with rounded and curved tips in solid stucco. The feathers have decorative paint on the surface with a rugged attachment mark (Figure 15). The vast

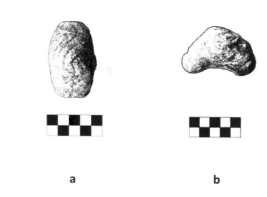

FIGURE 14 A-B. STUCCO FRAGMENT DECORATION/UNIQUE FORM NO. 37 (KIU90038). (A) TOP VIEW; (B) SIDE VIEW.

FIGURE 15 A-B. (A) FEATHER AND HALF FEATHER TYPE STUCCO FRAGMENTS; (B) DETAIL OF A FEATHER TYPE STUCCO FRAGMENT.

majority of these fragments have red, green, and blue paint. Some of them are well-preserved.

The pieces in the half feathers sub-category have a design similar to the feathers explained above; they are triangular shaped with rounded tips. But, unlike the feathers, these pieces are not elongated and have the attachment mark on one of its ends (inferior) instead on the posterior face like the feathers (Figure 15). Half feathers were crafted in solid stucco, painted in red and blue.

We suggest that both feathers and half feathers represent the ends of overlapping feathers. There are several examples on sculptures, reliefs, and stelae that depict headdresses with layers of feathers similar in shape to those in our sample. Several pieces from Kiuic are marked with impressions (most likely fingerprints), creating a 'wave' effect (Figure 16); this was possibly a representation of a serrated feather (Robertson 1991:45, fig. 128).

The fragments classified as leaves are small, conical pieces that are modeled but flattened and curved on the end (Figure 17). We suggest that these pieces could represent leaves because of their size, shape, and color. Aprons and collars were often made, or at least decorated, with these

a   b

FIGURE 16 A-B. STUCCO FRAGMENT DECORATION/UNIQUE FORM NO. 4. (KIU000068). (A) PHOTOGRAPH; (B) DRAWING.

a   b

FIGURE 17 A-B. STUCCO FRAGMENTS DECORATION/LEAF.

FIGURE 18. STUCCO FRAGMENTS DECORATION/CARTOUCHES.   FIGURE 19. STUCCO FRAGMENTS DECORATION/KNOTS.

leaf shapes (Patrois 2008:94; Robertson 1983:figs. 237, 238, 245, 269 and 298).

The cartouches sub-category is composed of rectangular, flat pieces modeled in solid stucco; they have rounded corners and are painted. Cartouches also have incised designs on one face. These designs are composed with a series of dots and lines within a rectangular frame demarcating the entire face of the piece (Figure 18). The entire sample of this sub-category has paint on the anterior face; the combination of red and blue is the most common. Cartouches generally have an attachment mark on the posterior face that was not painted or finished in any other way. Based on its features, we suggest that cartouches were part of glyphic elements (Schele and Mathews 1979:fig. 669).

The knot-type fragments are incomplete forms; just the ends of these pieces were recovered. In the sample, knots refer to pieces with elongated and bulky modeling, with a low relief line along the middle of the piece (Figure 19). Knots are solid stucco pieces, tubular but both curvy and flattened. Their ends are rounded and all of them were decorated with paint. These pieces are only fragments of the original form, which makes their identification in other contexts almost impossible, although some similarities have been observed with regard to their shape. Tripartite flowers contain shapes that resemble those of the knots at their terminus (Schele and Mathews 1979:fig. 97, 767). The ends of representations of knots, often present in glyphs, are also similar to the elements found at Kiuic (Schele and Mathews 1979:figs. 675, 724, 737, 739).

The bead fragments are three-dimensional pieces with a circular ball-like shape. Within this subcategory we identified two types of beads: spherical and flattened.

a

b

c

FIGURE 20 A-C. (A, B) STUCCO FRAGMENTS DECORATION/SPHERICAL BEADS; (C) STUCCO FRAGMENTS DECORATION/FLATTENED BEADS.

The spherical beads, as the name suggest, are small pieces with a spherical shape (3.1 cm average diameter) (Figure 20a and 20b). These beads have one, two, or three attachment marks, which could serve as evidence that they were joined to each other and then attached to the façade surface. The paint on these beads covers the entire piece, except the attachment mark, which was rough.

The flattened beads are circular shaped solid stucco, although they are more flat than spherical (average diameter of 3.0 cm and average thickness of 1.3 cm) (Figure 20c). These pieces have paint and ink designs on one of the faces. In Maya iconography, flattened beads are frequently worn by important individuals. These beads are often used in collars, wristbands, headdresses, or belts. These beads may also reference blood. There are some images depicting human sacrifice where blood is portrayed as rows of flattened beads (Proskouriakoff 1950:figs. d, g, h, k, o, w; Robertson 1985:figs. 73, 80, 81, 83, 91, 96, 97, 99, 120, 121, 169, 226, 228, 244; Robertson 1991:fig. 129; Schele and Mathews 1979:figs. 96, 802, 813, 818, 819).

There were two stucco pieces within the Kiuic sample that resemble parts of zoomorphic figures. The first piece is a three-dimensional modeled fragment with a shape similar to an animal's tail. This piece was attached to another surface, which could not be defined. Both parts are painted with yellow-orange designs and a mottled pattern of dark brown ink asterisks. We suggest that this piece is a feline tail (Figure 21a and 21b). The second example is the representation of an animal leg and paw, presumably that of a dog (Figure 21c and 21d). This piece was modeled

in solid stucco with a basic cylindrical form with the paw shaped design at the end. It was painted red and was attached to the façade wall.

Nuclei

The nuclei are fragments of the frame or support that held up the figures from the inside; these are basically the 'skeleton' of the façade sculptures. We identified two forms: a) Tubular (Simple) Nuclei and b) Composite Nuclei. The simple tubular nucleus was used to support the smallest or lightest sections of the sculptures while the composite nucleus was designed to support the largest and heaviest parts.

The simple pieces have a tubular form composed of a long solid stucco cylinder (Figure 22a). The majority of these fragments are found among the extremities of anthropomorphic sculptures, although they are not exclusive to them. In some cases, we found evidence that these stucco cylinders were wrapped in textile or other perishable fiber material in order to be covered later by stucco layers, creating the fill for the sculptures. We were able to find line impressions on the interior of the sculptural fragments. All the pieces in the sample are fragments of the original, and therefore every one was different from the other. However, they were consistent in diameter, which ranges between 1.9 cm and 4.9 cm. The surfaces of these pieces were smooth, without paint or decoration. In some cases, the nucleus was slightly curved, but in general are straight.

51

a   b

c   d

FIGURE 21 A-D. ZOOMORPHIC STUCCO FRAGMENTS. (A-B) DECORATION/UNIQUE FORM NO. 42 (KIU90041); (C-D) DECORATION/UNIQUE FORM NO. 12 (KIU000105).

a   b

FIGURE 22 A-B. STUCCO NUCLEI. (A) SIMPLE TUBULAR NUCLEI; (B) COMPOSITE NUCLEUS.

The composite nuclei were formed by stones, mortar, and one, two, or three tubular nuclei (Figure 22b). Composite nuclei supported the heaviest and largest sections of the façade sculptures. There is evidence that suggests these pieces existed on the inside of the extremities of anthropomorphic sculptures.

Stucco Analysis

After completing the stucco analysis, we concluded that the fragments were in fact the deposit of a single façade. This argument is based upon the following evidence:

-Style homogeneity, showed by the stucco pieces distinguished by naturalistic, curvy, and fluid design.

-Modeling technique homogeneity. Two techniques were identified based on the stucco fragments: 1) round shape (tridimensional), in which stucco nuclei (tubular or composite) are used as support or frame for the biggest sculptures. 2) Solid stucco modeling with surface finish and decoration (incisions, low relief, paint, or perforations). These pieces were manufactured separate and then assembled to the rest of the façade.

-Material homogeneity. The stucco used to form the façade is of high quality and consists a fine mixture, providing solidity to every sculpture and element of the façade.

Likewise, we are able to define the morphological elements of the façade, which include:

-Sculptures of human figures: represented in the sample by fragments of extremities, legs, arms, and fingers, as well as by anthropomorphic faces.

-Complementary decorative elements: the shapes on these pieces were varied, but at the same time repetitive (catalogued as decoration/appliqué). These decorative components provided a uniqueness and significance to the imagery theme displayed on the façade.

-Moldings: fragments with an angular elevation modeling, which might have functioned as the façade frame.

-Flattened surface: these fragments were most likely part of the façade wall functioning as 'a background' for the sculptures. These pieces were catalogued as flattened fragments.

Based on the comparative analysis, the evidence suggests that the stucco fragments collected from Kiuic´s Plaza Ulum were part of a single façade. The presence of human extremities, arms, and legs, supports the idea that the façade had a historic narrative theme, which 'portrayed' important individuals associated with the site (Schele 1998:506). The façade incorporated at least three historical figures with feathered headdresses and decorative motifs on the extremities in seated or standing positions. The appliqué on the façade suggests aquatic themes and a possible association with the GI god of the Palenque Triad (Robertson 1991:27, 28; Schele and Mathews 1979). One of the most interesting aspects of the data recovered is the similarity with the Classic Maya style. The execution of the modeling on the Kiuic façade shows a greater resemblance to the continuous, fluid lines of the Classic Maya than to the characteristic angular shapes of Classic Puuc style.

Associated Material

Apart from the stucco fragments, a significant amount of ceramics was recovered from the deposit, along with some lithic fragments, a couple of shell pieces, and a small fragment of stone from a cave.

Ceramics

George Bey and Christopher Gun completed the type-variety analysis of the 23,313 sherds recovered from the deposit and the area surrounding it. From the total amount of sherds, only 33% belonged to the stucco stratum. The results of this analysis are shared below (Figure 23).

As the graph demonstrates (Figure 24), the ceramic recovered from the stucco deposit consisted mainly of types pertaining to the Ceh complex of Kiuic (Table 3), which is equivalent to Cehpech complex defined by Smith (1971), specifically Muna Slate and Yokat Striated (A.D. 800-1000). Based on this evidence, it has been suggested that the most intense occupation of this particular area of the site was during the Terminal Classic; the vast majority of the ceramics recovered in Plaza Ulum in general, as well as in the deposit area, belonged to the Cehpech sphere. However, a significant amount of earlier sherds was also collected; this included wares from the Yuc complex, dated to the Late Classic (equivalent to Motul complex and extended with early slate wares, early thin slate wares and early red wares) (Boucher 1992; Varela 1993). The ceramic types associated to the Yuc complex that were collected from the deposit area included early slates and early thin slates, essentially domestic wares that are associated with the Motul complex. However, in the deepest units some ceramic types from the Early Classic, Late Preclassic, and Early Preclassic were present. Likewise, Posclassic ceramic types were found in the more superficial levels.

In the stucco stratum, the vast majority of the ceramic types correspond to the Ceh complex (48.74%), with a significant percentage of Yuc-Ceh types (32.81%) (Figure 25); the overwhelming majority corresponded to Muna Slate (36.11%) and Yokat Striated (36.11%) types. The sherds from other complexes such as Bah-Och from the Preclassic (4.89%), Chiich from the Early Classic (1.97%), and Zodz from the Post-Classic (0.04%) were minimal in contrast with those dating to the Late/Terminal Classic. Based on the evidence presented, we suggest that the façade deposit occurred during the Terminal Classic period, which coincides with the theories proposed by researchers

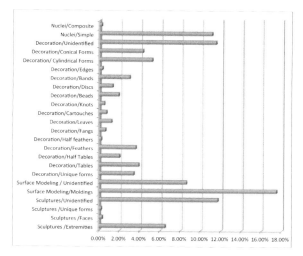

FIGURE 23. CHART SHOWING THE PERCENTAGE OF EACH TYPE OF FRAGMENT, BASED ON THE QUANTITY OF FRAGMENTS OF THE TOTAL SAMPLE.

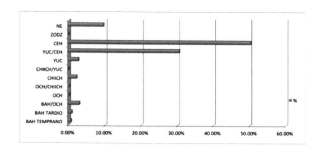

FIGURE 24. PERCENTAGES FOR EACH COMPLEX PRESENT ON THE CERAMIC RECOVERED FROM THE STUCCO DEPOSIT AREA (CHRISTOPHER GUNN, PERSONAL COMMUNICATION 2011; BEY ET AL. 2010).

PERIOD	COMPLEX	CHRONOLOGY
PRECLASSIC	EARLY BAH	800 – 600 B.C.
	LATE BAH	600 – 300 B.C.
	OCH	300 B.C. – A.D. 300
CLASSIC	CHIICH	A.D. 300 – 600
	YUC	A.D. 600 – 800
	CEH	A.D. 800 – 950
POSTCLASSIC	ZODZ	A.D. 950 – 1300 (?)

TABLE 3. CERAMIC COMPLEXES DEVELOPED FOR THE SITE OF KIUIC (BEY ET AL. 2010).

at Kiuic. This further implies that the building to which the façade was once attached was constructed during the Late Classic period. The façade would have been destroyed and deposited at some moment during the Terminal Classic.

Regarding the ceramic forms found in the stucco strata, the majority were Muna Slate (18.25%) and Yokat Striated ollas (26.75%). There also was a significant presence of Muna Slate bowls (6.48%) and cazuelas (5.91%). The amount of ollas and cazuelas, both vessels of considerable size, points to food preparation on a large scale. It is interesting to note the low percentage of bowls; in a regular

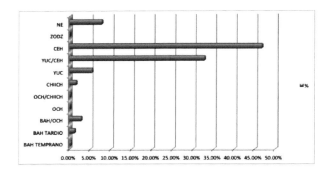

FIGURE 25. PERCENTAGES FOR EACH COMPLEX PRESENT IN THE CERAMIC SAMPLE RECOVERED FROM THE STUCCO STRATA.

midden we would expect to find a high concentration of ceramics used for food consumption.

The predominant ceramic forms present in the stucco deposit suggest we are looking at the remains of an event where a considerable amount of food was prepared in association with the façade deposit. Although we could consider this waste deposit the result of maintenance activities, the ceramic forms suggest otherwise. Furthermore, the evidence does not explicitly indicate ritual events at the moment of the façade's destruction and deposit, since the ritual ceramic forms such as censers (0.2%) and drinking cups (1.8%) were scarcely represented in the stucco strata. Nevertheless, looking at the midden as a whole there is a real possibility that ritual behavior was involved in the event of the façade deposit.

Lithics

The lithic material found in the deposit was not atypical for a common midden. The majority of the recorded pieces are fragments of retouched flakes and a few tools and chert bifacial fragments. However, lithic debitage was minimal. The presence of obsidian pieces was small, merely consisting of few flakes and prismatic blades.

Others

It is interesting to note the presence of materials that are often considered uncommon in a daily rubbish midden, such as shell pieces and the cave stone fragment. We also draw attention to the absence of grinding tools, which are frequently found in middens in the Maya area.

General Considerations

-The stratigraphy showed that the stucco deposit occurred as a single event or within a short period of time.

-The optimal state of preservation of the façade fragments suggests that the façade was in good condition at the time it was removed from the building.

-The analysis of the stucco fragments showed that the deposit was composed of the remains of a single façade and suggests that it had a historic-narrative theme with representations of important figures from Kiuic.

-Similar to Classic Maya representations, the images on the Kiuic façade are naturalistic and highlight the divinity of the characters.

-The architectural style of the structure that the façade decorated coincides with that of the earliest building of Structure N1050E1065—an Early Puuc structure, which one of its main features is the stucco decoration on its friezes.

-The ceramic showed that the deposit of the dismantled façade coincides chronologically with the construction of the second building of Structure N1050E1065.

-The two construction phases of Structure N1050E1065 correspond chronologically to the two main periods of development and political changes at Kiuic and the spatial changes in the Yaxché Group.

The Façade Deposit as Part of the History of Kiuic

After carrying out the analysis of the deposit and the material recovered from it, we attempted to contextualize this event within the history of the Yaxché Group, the site of Kiuic, and the region. The starting point was the information obtained from the excavation of a deposit at the nearby Structure N1050E1065, identified as a temple (Bey et al. 2007). This building had two construction stages; the first one was completed during the Late Classic (A.D. 600-800) while the second one was erected during the Terminal Classic (A.D. 800-1000) (Bey et al. 2007:4-2). Sub-N1050E1065 was dismantled and its stones were reutilized as construction fill for the superstructure, Temple A (Structure N1050E1065). The Temple A excavation indicated that its interior floor was burned. It also showed evidence of a post-abandonment cult; several Chen Mul censers and an offering were placed after the partial collapse of Temple A, suggesting that the later building had a great ritual significance.

The sub-B architectural style was identified as Early Puuc; one of its main characteristics is the modeled and painted friezes. The construction of the second building coincides chronologically with the stucco façade deposition just four meters to the south of the structure. The latter makes the argument that the studied façade belonged to the first building of Structure N1050E1065 very plausible. As for the rest of Yaxché Group, it underwent changes during the Late Classic (A.D. 700-800), at which time there was considerable construction activity.

The stucco façade recovered from Plaza Ulum must have being an important part of the decoration of sub-Temple A (Sub-N1050E1065). The impact that this probably have had within the Yaxché Group landscape would have been of great magnitude. The figures represented in the façade decoration were life-size, displaying important historic characters in a naturalistic style. Structure N1050E1065 was part of a ritual complex used by the Kiuic elite. The latter accentuates the importance of this building and allows us to propose the possibility of a careful and respectful destruction, probably within a ritual ambience.

It is a fact that the use of modeled stucco decoration as well as the representations displayed on Kiuic´s buildings, as in the rest of the region, changed between the Late Classic and the Terminal Classic periods. During the Late Classic, the use of molded stucco was common (Andrews 1986; Gendrop 1998; Pollock 1980), with representations leaning towards the Classic Maya style with naturalistic and historic images. During the Terminal Classic, the use of stucco decreases, and the Classic Puuc carved stone façades tend toward the geometric and abstract. The reason for the changes in the representations displayed on the buildings is not well understood yet. Foncerrada (1965:121) suggested that the difference between the Classic Puuc style and Classic Maya style from the Lowlands lies in religion. She argued that during the period of greatest splendor in the Maya Lowlands religion was concentrated on Maya lords and the power that these governors had to manipulate the gods and nature. In contrast, in the Puuc region the focus was on the gods and nature itself.

The evidence that we have so far suggests that the façade fragments once decorated Sub-Temple B of Structure N1050E1065 of Kiuic. At the time the site reached a moment of strong political change and spatial restructuring, Structure N10501065 became obsolete and was destroyed, probably within a ritual atmosphere. These activities resulted in the dismantling of the façade and its subsequent deposition to the south of Structure N1050E1065. Later, the building was completely destroyed in order to be replaced by the construction of Temple A. The significance of the destroyed façade is reflected by the images that were displayed on it and the particular treatment that it received at the moment it was discarded.

These events coincide with a transitional moment in the Puuc region, evident in the decorative architectural techniques. The façade elements became more geometric and abstract during the Late to Terminal Classic transition, with later monumental constructions executed using mosaic decoration. The sociopolitical implications that were likely associated with all these stylistic changes are not understood yet, but the events experienced by the Yaxché Group during this period may help in the understanding of this transition in the region.

References Cited

Agurcia F, Ricardo
  2004 Rosalila: Temple of the Sun-King. In *Understanding Early Classic Copan,* edited by Ellen E. Bell, Marcello A. Canuto, and Robert J. Sharer, pp. 101-111. University of Pennsylvania Museum of Archaeology and Anthropology, Philadelphia.

Andrews, George F.
  1986 *Los estilos arquitectónicos del Puuc: una nueva apreciación.* Colección Científica 131. Instituto Nacional de Antropología e Historia, México, D.F.

Arnauld, Charlotte, Dominique Michelet, Gregory Pereira, Fabienne de Pierrebourg and Philippe Nondédéo
  1999 Balamkú: tercera temporada de campo, 1998. In *XII simposio de investigaciones arqueológicas en Guatemala, 1998,* edited by Jean Pierre Laporte and Hector Escobedo, pp. 613-627. Museo Nacional de Arqueología y Etnología, Guatemala.

Baudez, Claude F.
  1994 *Maya Sculpture of Copan: The Iconography.* University of Oklahoma Press, Norman.
  1996 La Casa de los Cuatro Reyes de Balamkú. *Arqueología Mexicana* 3(18):36-41.

Benavides, Antonio
  1994 Edzná y el suroeste de la región Puuc. In *Hidden Among the Hills: Maya Archaeology of the Northwest Yucatan Península,* edited by Hanns J. Prem, pp. 121-132. Acta Mesoamericana, Vol. 7. Verlag Von Flemming, Möckmühl.
  1996 Edzná, Campeche. *Arqueología Mexicana* 3(18):26-31.
  2003 Se localizan vestigios de un mascaron en Edzná, Campeche. *Arqueología Mexicana* 10(60):5.

Bey, George, Tomás Gallareta and William Ringle
  2001 Informe Técnico y solicitud de autorización para proseguir investigaciones al Instituto Nacional de Antropología e Historia. Proyecto Investigaciones Arqueológicas en las Ruinas de Kiuic y la zona Labná-Kiuic, Distrito de Bolonchén, Yucatán, México. Temporada 2000.
  2002 Informe Técnico y solicitud de autorización para proseguir investigaciones al Instituto Nacional de Antropología e Historia. Proyecto Investigaciones Arqueológicas en las Ruinas de Kiuic y la zona Labná-Kiuic, Distrito de Bolonchén, Yucatán, México. Temporada 2001.
  2005 Informe Técnico y solicitud de autorización para proseguir investigaciones al Instituto Nacional de Antropología e Historia. Proyecto Investigaciones Arqueológicas en las Ruinas de Kiuic y la zona Labná-Kiuic, Distrito de Bolonchén, Yucatán, México. Temporada 2004.
  2006 Informe Técnico al Consejo de Arqueología del Instituto Nacional de Antropología e Historia. Proyecto Investigaciones Arqueológicas en las Ruinas de Kiuic y la zona de Labná-Kiuic, Distrito de Bolonchén, Yucatán, México. Temporada 2005.
  2007 Informe Técnico al Consejo de Arqueología del Instituto Nacional de Antropología e Historia. Proyecto Investigaciones Arqueológicas en las Ruinas de Kiuic y la zona de Labná- Kiuic, Distrito de Bolonchén, Yucatán, México. Temporada 2006.
  2008 Informe Técnico al Consejo de Arqueología del Instituto Nacional de Antropología e Historia. Proyecto Investigaciones Arqueológicas en las Ruinas de Kiuic y la zona de Labná-Kiuic, Distrito de Bolonchén, Yucatán, México. Temporada 2007.
  2009 Informe Técnico al Consejo de Arqueología del Instituto Nacional de Antropología e Historia. Proyecto Investigaciones Arqueológicas en las Ruinas de Kiuic y la zona de Labná-Kiuic, Distrito de Bolonchén, Yucatán, México. Temporada 2008.
  2010 Informe Técnico al Consejo de Arqueología del Instituto Nacional de Antropología e Historia. Proyecto Investigaciones Arqueológicas en las Ruinas de Kiuic y

la zona de Labná-Kiuic, Distrito de Bolonchén, Yucatán, México. Temporada 2009.

2011 Informe Técnico al Consejo de Arqueología del Instituto Nacional de Antropología e Historia. Proyecto Investigaciones Arqueológicas en las Ruinas de Kiuic y la zona de Labná-Kiuic, Distrito de Bolonchén, Yucatán, México. Temporada 2010.

Cobos, Rafael
2010 The Maya Ports Isla Cerritos and Uaymil. In *Fiery Pool: The Maya and the Mythic Sea,* edited by Daniel Finamore and Stephen D. Houston, pp. 163-165. Peabody Essex Museum, Salem, MA.

Coe, William R.
1959 *Piedras Negras Archaeology: Artifacts, Caches, and Burials.* The University Museum, University of Pennsylvania, Philadelphia.

Coggins, Clemency
1983 *The Stucco Decoration and Architectural Assemblage of Structure 1-sub, Dzibilchaltun, Yucatan, Mexico.* Middle American Research Institute, Publication 49. Tulane University, New Orleans.

Deal, Michael
1985 Household Pottery Disposal in the Maya Highlands: An Ethnoarchaeological Interpretation. *Journal of Anthropological Archaeology* 4:243-291.

Fash, William L., Richard V. Williamson, Carlos Rudy Larios y Joel Palka
1992 The Hieroglyphic Stairway and its Ancestors: Investigations of Copán Structure 10L-26. *Ancient Mesoamerica* (3):105-115.

Fash, William L.
1993 *Scribes, Warriors, and Kings: The City of Copan and the Ancient Maya.* Thames and Hudson, London.

Fernández, María Yolanda
1992 *Excavaciones en el Grupo May, Oxkintok, Yucatán, México.* Thesis from the Departamento de Historia de América II (Antropología de América), Universidad Complutense, Madrid, España.
1994 Historia arquitectónica del Grupo May, Oxkintok, Yucatán. In *VII Simposio de Investigaciones Arqueológicas en Guatemala, 1993*, edited by Jean Pierre Laporte y Hector Escobedo, pp. 543-557. Museo Nacional de Arqueología y Etnología, Guatemala.

Foncerrada de Molina, Marta
1965 *La escultura arquitectónica de Uxmal.* Imprenta Universitaria, México, D.F.

Freidel, David A. and Linda Schele
1989 Dead Kings and Living Temples: Dedication and Termination Rituals among Ancient Maya. In *Word and Image in Maya Culture: Explorations in Language, Writing, and Representation*, edited by William F. Hanks and Don S. Rice, pp. 233-243. University of Utah Press, Salt Lake City.

Freidel, David A., Linda Schele and Joy Parker
1993 *Maya Cosmos: Three Thousand Years on the Shaman's Path.* Harper Collins Publishers, New York.

Freidel, David A., Charles K. Suhler and Rafael Cobos P.
1998 Termination Ritual Deposit at Yaxuna: Detecting the Historical in Archaeological Context. In *The Sowing and the Dawning: Termination, Dedication, and Transformation in the Archaeological an Ethnographic Record of Mesoamerica*, edited by Shirley B. Mock, pp. 135-144. University of New Mexico Press, Albuquerque.

Galván, Melissa
2012 *Análisis, descripción e interpretación de una fachada de estuco desmantelada y su depósito: El caso de la Plaza*

Ulum de Kiuic, Yucatan. Unpublished licenciatura thesis, Universidad de las Américas, Puebla.

Garcia, Florentino
1994 Balamkú: un sitio maya de Campeche. *Arqueología Mexicana* 1(5):59-60.

Garza Tarzona, Silvia and Edward B. Kurjack
1980 *Atlas arqueológico del Estado de Yucatán.* Instituto Nacional de Antropología e Historia, México, D.F.

Gendrop, Paul
1998 *Rio Bec, Chenes and Puuc Styles in Maya Architecture.* Labyrinthos Press, Lancaster, CA.

Góngora, Angel G.
1997 *Los estucos modelados de Dzibilchaltún.* Licenciatura thesis, Universidad Autónoma de Yucatán, Mérida.

Houston, Stephen D.
1996 Symbolic Sweatbaths of the Maya: Architectural Meaning in the Cross Group at Palenque, Mexico. *Latin American Antiquity* 7(2):132-151.

Kowalski, Jeff K.
1987 House of the Governor: A Maya Palace of Uxmal, Yucatan, Mexico. University of Oklahoma Press, Norman.

Mateos, Frida
1996 Toniná, un recorrido por los relieves. In *Octava Mesa Redonda de Palenque, 1993*, edited by Merle Greene Robertson, pp. 143-152. Pre-Columbian Art Research Institute, San Francisco.

May, Rossana
2000 *Análisis de las torres este y oeste de la estructura 8 de Labná, Yucatán.* Unpublished licenciatura thesis. Universidad Autónoma de Yucatán, Mérida.

Miller, Virginia E.
1991 *The Frieze of the Palace of the Stuccoes, Acanceh, Yucatan, Mexico.* Dumbarton Oaks Research Library and Collection, Washington, D.C.

Nalda, Enrique, and Sandra Balanzario
2006 Kohunlich y Dzibanché: los últimos años de investigación. *Arqueología Mexicana* 13(76):42-47.

Patrois, Juilie
2008 *Etude iconographique des sculptures du nord de la péninsule du Yucatán à l'époque classique.* BAR International Series 1779. Paris Monographs in American Archaeology 20. Archeopress, Oxford.

Pagliaro, Jonathan B., James F. Garber, and Travis W. Stanton
2003 Evaluating the Archaeological Signatures of Maya Ritual and Conflict. In *Ancient Mesoamerican Warfare*, edited by M. Kathryn Brown and Travis Stanton, pp.75-89. AltaMira Press, Walnut Creek.

Pendergast, David M.
1998 Intercession with the Gods: Caches and Their Significance at Altun Ha and Lamanai, Belize. In *The Sowing and the Dawning: Termination, Dedication, and Transformation in the Archaeological an Ethnographic Record of Mesoamerica*, edited by Shirley B. Mock, pp. 55-63. University of New Mexico Press, Albuquerque.

Pollock, Harry E. D.
1980 *The Puuc: An Architectural Survey of the Hill Country of Yucatan and Northern Campeche.* Memoirs of the Peabody Museum, Vol. 19. Harvard University, Cambridge.

Proskouriakoff, Tatiana
1950 *A Study of Classic Maya Sculpture.* Carnegie Institution of Washington, Washington, D.C.

Rivera, Miguel
1994 Notas de arqueología de Oxkintok. In *Hidden among the Hills: Maya Archaeology of the Northwest Yucatan*

Peninsula, edited by Hanns J. Prem, pp. 44-58. Acta Mesoamericana, Vol. 7. Verlag Von Flemming, Möckmühl.

Robertson, Merle Green

1983 *The Sculpture of Palenque: The Temple of the Inscriptions.* Vol. I. Princeton University Press, Princeton.

1985 *The Sculpture of Palenque: The Early Buildings of the Palace and the Wall Paintings.* Vol. II. Princeton University Press, Princeton.

1991 *The Sculpture of Palenque: The Cross Group, the North Group, the Olvidado, and Other Pieces.* Vol. IV. Princeton University Press, Princeton.

Ruz, Alberto

1973 *El Templo de las Inscripciones, Palenque.* Instituto Nacional de Antropología e Historia, México, D.F.

Schele, Linda

1998 Iconography of Maya Architectural Facades during the Late Classic Period. In *Function and Meaning in Classic Maya Architecture,* edited by Stephen D. Houston, pp. 479-517. Dumbarton Oaks,Washington, D.C.

Schele, Linda, and Peter Mathews

1979 *The Bodega of Palenque, Chiapas, Mexico.* Dumbarton Oaks, Harvard University, Washington, D.C.

Schiffer, Michael B.

1976 *Behavioral Archeology.* Academic Press, New York

1996 *Formation Processes of the Archaeological Record.* University of New Mexico Press, Albuquerque.

2010 *Behavioral Archaeology: Principle and Practice.* Equinox Publishing Ltd, London.

Smith, Robert E.

1971 *The Pottery of Mayapan.* Papers of the Peabody Museum of Archaeology and Ethnology. Vol. 66. Harvard University, Cambridge.

Stanton, Travis W., M. Kathryn Brown, and Jonathan B. Pagliaro

2008 Garbage of the Gods? Squatters, Refuse Disposal, and Termination Rituals among the Ancient Maya. *Latin American Antiquity* 19(3):227-247.

Tate, Carolyn E.

1992 *Yaxchilan: The Design of a Maya Ceremonial City.* University of Texas Press, Austin.

Varela, Carmen

1998 *El Clásico Medio en el noroccidente de Yucatán: la fase Oxkintok regional en Oxkintok (Yucatán) como paradigma.* British Archaeological Reports, International Series 739. Archaeopress, Oxford.

Vargas de la Peña, Leticia , and Víctor R. Castillo

1999 La acrópolis de Ek´Balam, el lienzo en el que plasmaron lo mejor de su arte los antiguos pobladores. *Boletín Informativo* 10-11(V):26-30.

2006 Hallazgos recientes en Ek Balam. *Arqueología Mexicana* 13(76):56-63.

Velázquez, Adriana

1995 Cosmogonía y vida cotidiana en Kohunlich. *Arqueología Mexicana* 3(14):32-36.

Vogt, Evon Z.

1998 Zinacanteco Dedication and Termination Rituals. In *The Sowing and the Dawning: Termination, Dedication, and Transformation in the Archaeological and Ethnographic Record of Mesoamerica,* edited by Shirley B. Mock, pp. 20-30. University of New Mexico Press, Albuquerque.

Walker, William H.

1995 Ceremonial Trash? In *Expanding Archaeology,* edited by James M. Skibo, William H. Walker, and Axel E. Nielsen, pp. 67- 79. University of Utah Press, Salt Lake City.

Yadeun, Juan

1993 *Toniná.* Ediciones del Equilibrista. México, D.F.

Zender, Marc

2010 The Music of Shells. In *Fiery Pool: The Maya and the Mythic Sea,* edited by Daniel Finamore and Stephen D. Houston, pp. 86-89. Peabody Essex Museum, Salem, MA.

Un Acercamiento al Patrón de Asentamiento de Kabah, Yucatán

Luis Raúl Pantoja Díaz

El área cultural conocida como Puuc (localizada en la parte sur del estado de Yucatán, México) se caracteriza por ser la zona alta del estado, alcanzando en algunos lugares hasta 100 metros sobre el nivel del mar. Por ello, las poblaciones humanas que se asentaron en tiempos prehispánicos fueron capaces de adaptarse a condiciones particulares que forman un patrón de asentamiento en toda la región. De ahí que, el presente estudio es un acercamiento a la comprensión e interpretación de los asentamiento humanos en el sitio arqueológico de Kabah, lugar que posee una especial posición en el contexto cultural, político y social de la región en diversos periodos del desarrollo de la misma.

The Puuc cultural area (located in the southern part of the state of Yucatán, Mexico) has a number of unusual geographical features, among them that it is the highest zone in the state, in some places reaching 100 meters above sea level. Human populations that settled in ancient times adapted to the local conditions, forming a regional settlement pattern. The study presented here is an approach to the understanding and interpretation of human settlement at the archaeological site of Kabah, a place that holds a special position in the cultural, political, and social context of the region in diverse periods of regional development.

Kabah es un sitio arqueológico localizado en la región y área cultural del Puuc. Su importancia es notable puesto que es mencionado en el libro del Chilam Balam de Chumayel, al ser uno de los documentos históricos que narran el paso de los Itzaes en las tierras bajas del norte (Mediz Bolio y de la Garza 1988:57). Los sitios de la región Puuc ocupan una temporalidad muy larga, al menos los orígenes de Kabah se remontan del Preclásico Medio (600-300 a.C) hasta el Clásico Terminal (950-1050 d.C), momento en el que esa ciudad alcanzó su mayor desarrollo; aunque su época de mayor apogeo fue hacia el año 800 d.C., coincidiendo con la de Uxmal (Andrews 1975, 1986; Gendrop 1983).

Kabah es uno de los sitios más amplios del área, tanto así que su extensión hasta ahora es desconocida. Fue el segundo centro religioso más grande de la región Puuc, después de Uxmal, ubicándose en un valle donde se aprovechan los afloramientos rocosos y los lomeríos que cierran dicho valle por el oeste, en el que se edificaron los distintos conjuntos arquitectónicos. Las estructuras principales se encuentran en un área de aproximadamente de 1 km de norte a sur y de 1.2 km de este a oeste. Dunning (1989) reporta que las estructuras que se encuentran en la periferia tienden a situarse sobre los puntos más altos del terreno y reporta la presencia de otros conjuntos abovedados, algunos de ellos tienen una pequeña pirámide y considera que el asentamiento tuvo una extensión cercana a los 5 km (Toscano et al. 2009).

El sector nuclear de Kabah presenta varias estructuras equiparables en tamaño a las que se encuentran en sitios como Uxmal y Chichén Itzá, y constituyen magníficos ejemplos del estilo arquitectónico Puuc. Los principales edificios localizados Kabah se distribuyen en tres grupos alineados en un eje este-oeste. El resto del asentamiento se encuentra disperso, formando pequeños conjuntos en forma de patios y/o plazas. Hasta la fecha se desconoce cuál fue la traza original del sitio; sin embargo, todo parece indicar que hacia el periodo Clásico Terminal, todos los edificios que actualmente se observan se encontraban funcionando (Toscano 2009:14).

Los trabajos de registro y de prospección recientes en la periferia del sitio, forman parte de uno de objetivos de investigación del proyecto Kabah, el cual plantea conocer su extensión, lo que ha permitido visualizar las dimensiones de la ciudad prehispánica y otras características importantes, lo cual es tema del presente trabajo.

Generalidades

Kabah se localiza a 120 km al sur de la Ciudad de Mérida y a 23 km al sureste de Uxmal por la carretera federal 261, a la altura del Km 120. En la actualidad es parte del área natural protegida con carácter de Parque Estatal mediante el decreto publicado en el Diario Oficial del Estado de Yucatán el 9 de junio de 1993, que cuenta con una superficie de 949.76 hectáreas protegidas como área de reserva ecológica (SEDUMA http://www.seduma.yucatan.gob.mx/areas-naturales/kabah.php) (Figura 1). En este parque se localizan numerosos restos arqueológicos de valor incalculable característicos del estilo arquitectónico Puuc. También presenta escenarios naturales poco alterados con recursos suficientes para el aprovechamiento local, como las selvas medianas caducifolias en buen estado de conservación, las cuales resguardan diversas especies de fauna, entre las que destacan especies endémicas de la península de Yucatán.

Por consiguiente, Kabah es un sitio clasificado con rango II, de acuerdo a las categorías propuestas de Garza y Kurjack (1980) en el atlas arqueológico del estado. Cabe mencionar que, esta categoría se caracteriza por la presencia de varios conjuntos arquitectónicos monumentales y un asentamiento que ocupa un área extensa, lo que supone una

Luis Raúl Pantoja Díaz - Instituto Nacional de Antropología e Historia (INAH), Mérida, Yucatán (lupandi10@hotmail.com).

FIGURA 1. VISTA DEL GRUPO ESTE DE KABAH.

comunidad que controló una amplia zona de sustentación (Garza y Kurjak 1980; Toscano 2009:13). Asimismo, la región arqueológica a la que pertenece Kabah incluye a los sitios de Uxmal, Labná, Sayil, y Xlapak, misma que fue declarada Patrimonio de la Humanidad por la UNESCO en 1996 (Figura 2).

Antecedentes

La referencia más antigua de Kabah es la que aparece en el Chilam Balam de Chumayel, cuando es abandonada (Mediz Bolio y de la Garza 1988:57). A fines del siglo XIX, las primeras visitas y los reportes fueron realizados por el explorador Teobert Maler, quien hizo referencia al lugar como: Kabahau-can: (*kab*, mano; *ah ahau*, señor; *can*, serpiente, es decir, 'El señor que sujeta a la serpiente o el que tiene la serpiente real en la mano')

John L. Stephens (1993) realizó el primer plano de Kabah, publicándolo en 1843; mientras que para 1928, Ignacio Marquina (1981) publicó un nuevo mapa, sin embargo, un año antes H.E.D. Pollock (1980) publicó el plano del área central del sitio (Figura 3). Los primeros trabajos de índole arqueológica se llevaron a cabo alrededor de 1952 y 1953, cuando el arqueólogo Ponciano Salazar (1952, 1953) restauró parcialmente la fachada oeste de la Estructura 2C6, conocida como el Codz Pop. En este mismo periodo, el arqueólogo Alberto Ruz realizó algunas excavaciones en tumbas, en el sector norte del Grupo Este (Toscano et al. 2009).

Después de estas primeras exploraciones, el sitio no fue intervenido hasta 1990, año en el que el Instituto Nacional de Antropología e Historia (INAH) inició un proyecto a

mediano plazo dirigido por el arqueólogo Ramón Carrasco Vargas, quien dio inicios a los trabajos de reconocimientos de superficie con el objetivo de estudiar la extensión del sitio (Carrasco et al. 1992).

A partir del año 2002, y hasta la fecha, el proyecto es dirigido por la arqueóloga Lourdes Toscano Hernández, quien ha continuado con las investigaciones en el Codz Pop, y últimamente el grupo Yax Kan, con el objetivo de retomar los estudios sobre el patrón de asentamiento, y conocer tanto las dimensiones como sus características constructivas.

Como parte de los trabajos de investigación de Kabah en la temporada 2010, dirigida por Toscano (2011:62), se propuso la realización del reconocimiento del asentamiento en el sector noroeste con el fin de darle continuidad al trabajo de recorrido realizado anteriormente por Carrasco, para establecer los límites del asentamiento y delimitar un área de protección. Otro de los objetivos del proyecto fue proponer el desvío de la carretera Mérida-Campeche vía la región Chenes, dando continuidad al estudio de patrón de asentamiento que se enfocó principalmente en el sector noroeste del sitio, en el área cercana al sacbé Kabah-Nopat-Uxmal.

Posteriormente, en la temporada de campo en 2010 (Toscano 2011) se registraron 27 grupos arquitectónicos, contemplando una descripción superficial de cada uno de los conjuntos antes reportados en la década de 1990 (Carrasco et al. 1991, 1992). Sin embargo, en el plano general estos grupos aparecieron representados únicamente con el contorno de sus basamentos, por lo que no fue fácil distinguir su eje posicional.

FIGURA 2. UBICACIÓN DE KABAH (GOOGLE MAPS).

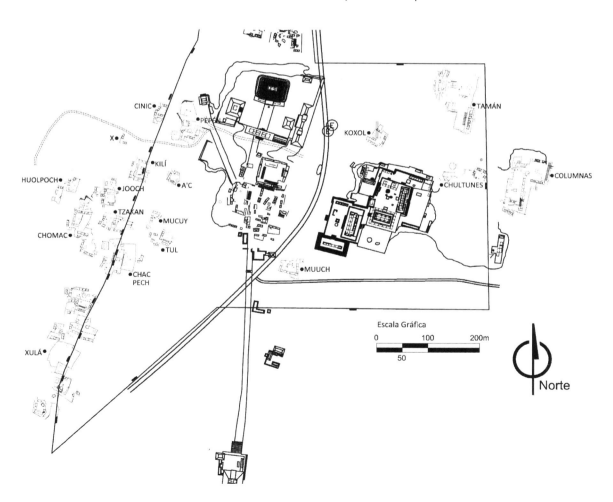

FIGURA 3. PLANO DEL NÚCLEO DE KABAH (MODIFICADO DE POLLOCK 1980).

FIGURA 4. EJEMPLO DE ARQUITECTURA DE KABAH, COMO ESCENARIO DE LA VIDA COTIDIANA.

El espacio y territorio construido

Antes de entrar de lleno al desarrollo del patrón de asentamiento de este espacio histórico hay que considerar que la conjunción de toda la evidencia arqueológica registrada y estudiada comprende lo que se considera un territorio, el cual es concebido como el paisaje en el que transcurrió la historia. Para el caso que nos ocupa, cuando una porción del espacio es habitada por uno o más grupos humanos ocurre una 'apropiación social' del espacio; esto es lo que los geógrafos denominan el 'espacio socialmente construido' o 'territorio.' Es la expresión de la interacción entre la naturaleza y la cultura, es decir, aquellos espacios identificados individual y colectivamente como propios frente a los espacios de 'los otros' (Velásquez 1997:113).

El término 'territorio' (desde la tradición ecológica) puede entenderse como sinónimo de medio natural, con lo que suele hablarse de relaciones entre sociedad y territorio. Sin embargo, desde la práctica social, el territorio se entiende como el sistema socioecológico que reúne la sociedad y el medio que ésta habita que pretende estudiar tanto en sus relaciones verticales (entre sociedad y medio físico), sus características (organización económica, política, demográfica, espacio construido, medio físico en cuanto condiciona a la sociedad) y sus relaciones horizontales (entre los diversos sub-territorios que lo conforman). Es por ello que se identifican diversos espacios físicos que conforman el territorio, pues éste incluye a los elementos del paisaje biótico o 'natural,' modificado mediante las

actividades involucradas en el sistema de producción y los asentamientos donde se localizan las viviendas, de manera que se encuentran espacios diferenciados por la acción organizada de los habitantes de las comunidades.

De hecho se identifica la existencia de un espacio arqueológico, aunque en el pasado no existía conciencia del espacio social. Por lo tanto, hay que considerar la comprensión del territorio como un indicio fundamental en el análisis arqueológico de una sociedad del pasado, dado que es en éste donde se materializan y concretan los elementos significativos para abordar su explicación. El logro de dicha comprensión requiere identificar en el espacio los ámbitos geográficos con peso histórico y reconocer las prácticas sociales que se dan en su seno, con la intención de identificar los procesos de trabajo y las características del sistema productivo a través de los materiales culturales y, en efecto, en un conjunto arqueológico donde se intervienen las áreas de actividad como unidades mínimas con significación social.

El estudio del territorio va de la mano con el estudio del patrón de asentamiento, considerando las condiciones naturales del medio ambiente y los factores de tipo cultural, en conjunto desempeñan un papel integral en la dispersión de los grupos humanos y sus poblaciones en un área particular. Para algunos autores (Kurjack y Garza 1981; Haggett 1965), los factores naturales no son los únicos involucrados en la disposición de los patrones de asentamiento, ya que son múltiples los elementos que

FIGURA 5. LA AQUITECTURA SE ASOCIA A LAS ACTIVIDADES CÍVICO, CEREMONIALES COMO A LO REDISENCIAL.

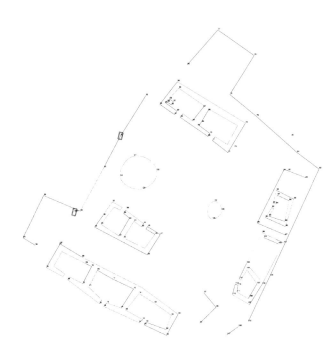

FIGURA 6. UNIDAD HABITACIONAL REPRESENTATIVA DE KABAH.
GRUPO COXOL.

condicionan la distribución de la geografía humana. Las actividades agrícolas pudieron ser determinantes en la distribución de los asentamientos en Yucatán, aunque no se puede derivar de ello que los sitios pequeños y dispersos solamente eran cultivadores dedicados al sistema de roza, ya que el tipo de arquitectura en estos lugares indica que fueron comunidades más complejas.

Por ello es importante que partamos de elementos tangibles como la arquitectura (Figura 4), misma que se ha de entender en esta ocasión como el espacio en el que se desarrolla un múltiple y complejo mundo de acontecimientos y actividades de orden cultural, así como otras funciones de semejante índole (Ashmore 1981:39). Para conocer el patrón de asentamiento de un sitio es preciso comenzar por analizar la localización y la distribución en un determinado espacio geográfico, las diversas características y categorías de estructuras que conforman aquella unidad, así como aspectos naturales relacionados. En especial se hace énfasis en la distribución del espacio y los restos de las estructuras arqueológicas construidas, tanto de tipo cívico-ceremonial como las de habitación (Figura 5).

En este sentido, el aspecto arquitectónico se relaciona con la estratificación social, además de la densidad de población, de su manera de asentarse, así como de convivir, ya sea de manera compacta o dispersa (Robina 1959:607). Además, el clima y el entorno ejercen influencia que sobre la localización de las unidades de habitación, desde un

FIGURE 7. ESTRUCTURA ARQUEOLÓGICA QUE REPRESENTA UN CIMIENTO.

punto de vista general (Willey 1956:1 10-3; Willey et al. 1965).

Con base en lo anterior, en esta investigación se centra la atención en el estudio de las estructuras fuera del área cívico-administrativa de Kabah. En especial en aquellas que representan la casa-habitación materializada, en las plataformas arqueológicas (Ashmore 1981:47; Rice y Puleston 1981:137; Wauchope 1934; Willey et al. 1965:11) y otros tipos de estructuras, entre ellas las áreas de producción y culto, así como de las unidades residenciales relacionadas con su entorno, y que a su vez pertenecen a un conjunto social (Figura 6).

Análisis espacial

El análisis espacial arqueológico parte de las diversas construcciones que se registran en campo. Cabe mencionar que se ha definido el concepto de estructura arqueológica como toda construcción hecha por el hombre, en la que se refleja su forma de vida pasada y sobre la cual quedan sus restos materiales como cerámica, metates, etc. Para este estudio se usaron dos categorías: la primera es la plataforma (entendida como el elemento estructural básico de la arquitectura maya prehispánica en general); mientras que la segunda consiste en las estructuras de menores como los cimientos o desplantes, y con este concepto nos referiremos a las bases de aquellas construcciones habitacionales mayas o las huellas de estas, ya que en su caso la mayoría fue construida de materiales perecederos (Figura 7).

La suma de los elementos arquitectónicos anteriores proporciona el siguiente nivel de estudio; el de sitio arqueológico. El argumento tradicional dice que un sitio es una acumulación de estructuras o artefactos, bien definida en términos de espacio, circunscrita por espacio vacío o por una disminución de densidad de estructuras o artefactos (Blanton et al. 1982; Sanders et al. 1979). Cuando disminuye la densidad del asentamiento, las unidades domésticas son dispersas; asimismo la calidad,

la hechura y las dimensiones decrecen, lo cual resulta en menos contactos de interacción personal y cuando ésta no existe, los habitantes no forman parte de una misma 'comunidad,' creando de alguna forma una frontera (Figura 8).

De ahí que, la investigación ha girado en torno a una perspectiva ecológica cultural sugiriendo que el medio ambiente es uno de los factores que influye preponderantemente, pero no exclusivamente, en el modo de asentamiento de los grupos humanos (González, 1979; Sanders, 1956; Steward, 1973). Retomando a Sanders quien publica en 1956, que: el patrón de asentamiento es ecología humana, ya que se refiere a la distribución de la población sobre el paisaje y con la investigación de las razones del porqué esa distribución. Se privilegian las interpretaciones funcionales, donde el concepto básico es la adaptación dada por el nivel tecnológico, aunque se consideran los factores culturales e históricos (Bohanan y Glazer 1993).

Enfatizando los aspectos de distribución demográfica sobre el ambiente fisiográfico se encuentran Willey (1953), Chang (1968) y Sanders (1979). De acuerdo con Willey (1953:1), el patrón de asentamiento es:

el modo en el cual el hombre se desarrolla en el medio ambiente en que vive, se refiere a las viviendas, su arreglo o distribución y a la naturaleza y disposición de otros edificios en relación a la vida comunal. Estos asentamientos reflejan el medio ambiente natural, el nivel tecnológico de sus habitantes, y varias instituciones de interacción social y control que esa cultura mantenía.'

Por su parte, Steward (1973) se enfoca en el análisis de la tecnología de explotación o producción (en el presente caso representado por las probables estrategias agrícolas o de extracción de materia prima), el medio ambiente (como la topografía y los recursos acuáticos), y el análisis de la influencia de estas estrategias adaptativas tanto en lo social como en lo económico, al igual que el grado en que estos factores afectan otros aspectos de la cultura.

En este trabajo se ha tomado de la ecología cultural la importancia de los factores tecnoeconómicos en la adaptación al medio ambiente, aunque se ha tomado consciencia del peso que la cultura y la organización social juegan en la distribución de los grupos sobre el paisaje fisiográfico. En este sentido se toma como apoyo a Haggett (1965), quien afirma que 'son múltiples los elementos (naturales, sociales, culturales, entre otros) que condicionan los patrones de la geografía humana.' Por lo tanto, la manera en que los grupos humanos se disponen en el espacio va a depender de los distintos niveles de interacción del medio ambiente físico con la tecnología de subsistencia, combinado con la manera en que estos factores se organizan socialmente para ello, 'ecuación que no es única ni estable' (Sanhueza et. al. 2007:104).

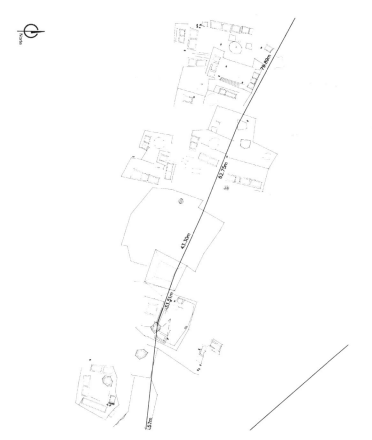

Figure 8. Conjunto de estructuras que conforman el grupo Xula.

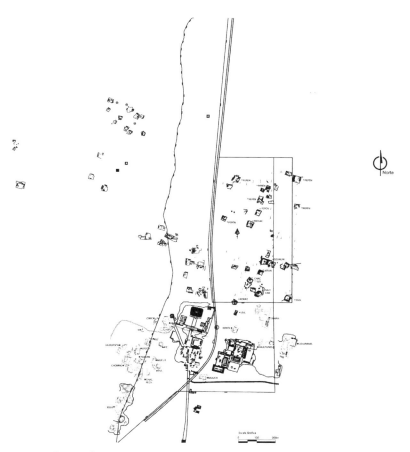

Figure 9. Plano resultante de las temporadas 2012 y 2013.

FIGURE 10. ESTRUCTURA ARQUEOLÓGICA QUE REPRESENTA UNA PLATAFORMA.

FIGURE 11. ACCIDENTE DE LA TOPOGRAFÍA QUE FUE APROVECHADO, POSIBLE CANTERA.

FIGURE 12. SASCABERA. ÁREA DE EXTRACCIÓN DE MATERIAL PÉTREO CALCÁREO, ASOCIADO A LA CASA-HABITACIÓN.

FIGURE 13. EJEMPLO DEL SISTEMA DE CONSTRCUÓN DE UNA PLATAFORMA LA CUAL SOPORTA OTRA CONSTRUCIÓN.

FIGURE 14. ESTRUCTURAS DE MAMPOSTERÍA, REPRESENTA LA INVERSIÓN DE MANO DE OBRA Y UNA ESTRATIFICACIÓN SOCIAL.

FIGURE 15. BASAMENTO PIRAMIDAL, ASOCIADO GRUPOS DE CASA-HABITACIÓN.

FIGURE 16. ESTRUCTURAS DE MAMPOSTERÍA QUE CORRESPONDE A UNA CASA-HABITACIÓN.

Con lo mencionado anteriormente, también se ha intentado comprender las formas de organización familiar, social y política reflejadas en los asentamientos arqueológicos, así como las formas de gobierno y las relaciones comerciales (Millon 1981; Pantoja et al. 2009).

Las estructuras y elementos arqueológicos

En Kabah, los trabajos de registro han permitido tener un panorama de su territorio, pues además del registro del grupo central se ha podido avanzar por sectores hacia el noroeste; por lo que tanto Carrasco (1991) como Toscano (2011) realizaron el registro de plataformas con construcciones de tipo habitacional. En 2012 se realizó el reconocimiento en un sector entre los grupos monumentales; el grupo oeste y el grupo este, registrando nuevamente con mayor detalle algunas de las construcciones reportadas por Pollock (1980), y de algunas que no contaba con registro.

En la temporada de 2013 se recorrió un polígono de aproximadamente 350 metros de este a oeste y de 1500 metros al norte, paralelo a la carretera a Santa Elena que consistió en un rectángulo al noreste del grupo central, detectando un total de 29 plataformas construidas aprovechando las elevaciones del terreno, y compensando alturas con rellenos constructivos que mostraron en alguno de sus lados grandes alturas (Figura 9).

Como en todo el Puuc, Kabah presenta un patrón de construcción similar a los otros sitios del área, no solo por sus característica por el uso piedra de recubrimiento en sus construcciones, sus plataformas desplantadas sobre altillos naturales (Figura 10), y construcciones menores con un sin número de metates y chultunes, posiblemente destinados a la producción de alimentos, sino también por construcciones relacionas a diversas actividades de producción. Como por ejemplo, hay espacios donde la roca madre que aflora cercana a los grupos y presenta tanto fracturas como restos de piedras de menor tamaño, lo que podría indicar la presencia de canteras especiales

(Figura 11), al estar cercanas al área administrativa del sitio, bancos de extracción de materiales pétreos (sascab) (Figura 12) para la construcción; y algunos contextos peculiares que pudieron haber tenido la función de hornos, los cuales están asociados a depósitos de agua.

Los registros realizados muestran la existencia de cuatro grupos definidos hasta ahora en el área de estudio, sin contar los grupos central, este, y oeste, mismos que corresponde a estructuras de élite. Dichos grupos están compuestos por estructuras que muestran una inversión de mano de obra considerable, decorados con elementos característicos como son los tamborcillos en los zócalos y algunos diseños simples en la moldura superior. Entre estos conjuntos de construcciones estuvieron posiblemente las residencias de grupos con un estatus social alto o intermedio al contar con estructuras abovedadas, algunas de cuartos simples, otras de múltiples recintos (doble fila de cuartos), y hasta ahora uno de dos niveles (Figuras 13 y 14).

La presencia de plataformas que soportaron basamentos piramidales (al menos dos reportadas fuera de los grupos centrales) podría indicar una función especial de actividad cívico-ceremonial, al menos de estos conjuntos de construcciones asociadas, los cuales podrían indicar una exclusividad del grupo social que los habitó (Figura 15).

Es importante mencionar que llama la atención una de las estructuras, cercana al grupo central, que a pesar de su simple manufactura al ser una plataforma simple contuvo secciones de mosaicos de piedras que correspondieron a los mascarones que decoraron las principales estructuras Kabah, lo que probablemente indica un espacio de producción o almacenamiento de estos elementos decorativos. Asimismo, se puede inferir que se estos conjuntos de estructuras, separados uno de otro, podrían indicar un control y uso autónomo entre grupos domésticos, pero bajo la hegemonía de una misma élite gobernante.

El patrón de asentamiento de estos conjuntos de estructuras parece estar normado por el aprovechamiento del terreno, ya que la topografía es determinante, pues los altillos fueron aprovechados al máximo y en ellos se perforaron los chultunes, del cual dependían las familias de cada grupo residencial.

Las similitudes que fueron encontradas en el patrón de asentamiento de los grupos fueron las siguientes:

1. Plataformas construidas sobre los afloramientos de roca, sobre todo en las que poseen mayor altura respecto a los espacios bajos, donde se encuentran extensiones de tierra propensa a ser inundable en las épocas de lluvia; por lo que sobre éstas se edificaron una variedad de edificaciones de diversas características constructivas y funciones, pero principalmente para uso residencial.

2. Presencia de al menos un chultún por plataforma, aunque se pudo observar que en algunas plataformas

con desniveles y anexos se pueden encontrar chultunes asociados.

3. Presencia de al menos una construcción de mampostería de uno o dos recintos, como elemento principal en los patios compuestos de otra construcciones de menor calidad. Se puede inferir que no todas estas construcciones de mampostería tuvieron cubiertas de piedra, lo que indica que éstas fueron techadas con materiales vegetales.

Consideraciones finales

La principal clase de estructura de mayor dimensión encontrada en los polígonos estudiados fue la de plataforma, en todas sus variantes, partiendo de nivelaciones simples del terreno a basamentos bien elaborados, aunque prevaleció la presencia de plataformas simples. Mientras que en el caso de las estructuras menores, se observó a los montículos *chii'ch*, seguido de los cimientos o desplantes que indicaron la presencia de diversas estructuras construidas de material perecedero, y finalmente los recintos de mampostería de uno o más cuartos, algunos de un solo acceso y otros con presencia de accesos de tres vanos y columnas (Figura 16). Asimismo de estructuras complementarias.

Por su parte, las relaciones entre medio ambiente y el hombre son notorias en esta área, ya que se apreció una interacción por parte de los grupos humanos con el medio natural que los rodeó. Los datos recabados en campo permiten inferir que el asentamiento original fue planeado y construido tomando en cuenta la localización de las condiciones de la topografía y las extensiones de tierra fértil para el cultivo, sin dejar de lado el aprovechamiento de la fauna del lugar, por medio de la caza, los intercambios comerciales entre caseríos, sitios cercanos y la costa; sin embargo, estas ideas serán corroboradas en un futuro a través de las excavaciones.

Se sugiere entonces, desde una perspectiva ecológica cultural, que el medio ambiente influyó principal pero no exclusivamente en el modo de asentamiento de los grupos arquitectónicos construidos por los habitantes de Kabah (Chang 1968; González 1979; Sanders 1956; Steward 1973; Willey 1953). Un mayor entendimiento de la distribución de los caseríos sobre el paisaje y de las razones del porqué esa distribución podrá verse reflejado en los resultados de las futuras excavaciones de dicha área de estudio. Arquitectónicamente las estructuras registradas podrían no ser tan simples como se observaron en la prospección.

Como en la generalidad de los sitios Puuc, Kabah presenta un tipo de asentamiento disperso, distribución que permitió un manejo del medio más acorde con las características ecológicas y topográficas propias del pequeño valle donde se encuentra. La ubicación generalizada de las estructuras en las cotas más altas del terreno permitía un aprovechamiento de los suelos fértiles para desempeñar

actividades productivas y el aprovechamiento de éstas como canteras. La importancia de la ecología y de la misma geografía en la conformación de la sociedad (Borhegyi 1956:101) fue de relevante importancia debido a que en esta parte de la península las tierras ricas y la dependencia de las fuentes de agua fue determinante para la subsistencia de los sitios. Nicholas Dunning (1989), quien recorrió los alrededores del sitio, reportó la existencia de una aguada de tamaño mediano hacia el noroeste del área central (Toscano et al. 2009:14). En el asentamiento existen numerosos chultunes cerca de los edificios grandes o pequeños (Andrews 1990; Dunning 1989; Pollock 1980; Toscano et al. 2009:14).

A pesar de ello, se encaminará a establecer siempre la cantidad, distribución y función de las estructuras, así como determinar los patrones de asentamiento, analizando tanto su aspecto social como ecológico (Borhegyi 1956; Voght 1956); pues varios investigadores han coincidido que la calidad y cantidad arquitectónica es considerada como un elemento característico y definidor del patrón de asentamiento maya (Ashmore 1981:56; Ashmore y Willey 1981:14; Hammond 1981:50; Haviland 1981:100-1; Sanders y Price 1968:165; Trigger 1968:55; Turner 1981:75).

En la mayoría de las poblaciones mayas se admite la presencia de un núcleo central compacto de construcciones público-monumentales y privadas, por lo general de alta densidad demográfica a pesar de que el resto de la población se disgregó en grupos periféricos a manera de 'barrios,' alrededor del núcleo central (Andrews 1981:329; Haviland 1970; Kintz 1983:179).

Varios estudio han presentado estas características e inferimos que los patrones de asentamiento en el área maya del norte de Yucatán, y en particular en el Puuc, presentan similitudes. Pues la distribución de las estructuras en el espacio que ocupa cada asentamiento permite inferir que se repite de manera más sencilla, sin embargo en Kabah, aún nos falta continuar realizando trabajos de reconocimiento, para conocer más sobre su patrón de asentamiento, y las diferencias y similitudes con otros sitios del Puuc.

Por otra parte, como bien se mencionó al principio, aún es desconocida la traza original de asentamientos; sin embargo, este trabajo preliminar permitirá un acercamiento al conocimiento de la extensión real de Kabah y cómo se fue moviendo en el tiempo. Hasta ahora los resultados parciales de los análisis parecen indicar que hacia el período Clásico Terminal todos los edificios que actualmente se pueden observar se encontraban funcionando (Toscano 2011:14).

Tal parece que en Kabah los arquitectos mayas prefirieron agrupar sus construcciones en conjuntos delimitados por enormes plataformas, sobre las que organizaron los espacios abiertos y los edificios. Un aspecto que hay que recalcar aquí es que los tres grupos principales del asentamiento se construyeron aprovechando las partes más elevadas del terreno, permitiendo que las escaleras jueguen un factor muy importante en la organización del medio ambiente construido, ya que a través de ellas los mayas lograron darle un carácter público o restringido a los espacios.

La interacción o la complejidad de un sitio no solo se ve a través del espacio socialmente construido, sino que existen contacto o relaciones sociales con regiones más cercanas o lejanas que pueden ser estudiados principalmente por la cultura material y que no es únicamente el espacio edificado. No obstante y en efecto, para conocer un sitio es necesario registrar de forma sistemática todos aquellos rasgos arquitectónicos y naturales que se ven a simple vista, los cuales permitan identificar un posible patrón que haya tenido tal asentamiento para explicar su forma de organización.

Aún queda mucho por hacer, se espera continuar caminando en la majestuosa selva de Kabah para responder aquellas interrogantes en torno a la dimensión de la ciudad y su interacción con el medio ambiente.

Referencias Citadas

Andrews, George F.

1975 *Maya Cities: Placemaking and Urbanization*, Volumen 131 de Civilization of the American Indian series. University of Oklahoma Press, Norman.

1986 *Los estilos arquitectónicos del Puuc: Una nueva apreciación*. Colección Científica No. 131. Serie Arqueología. Instituto Nacional de Antropología e Historia, México, D.F.

1990 *Architectural Survey at Kabah*. Archivo de la sección de arqueología del Centro INAH Yucatán, Mérida, Yucatán.

Andrews, E. Wyllys, V

1981 Dzibilchaltun. In *Supplement to the Handbook of Middle American Indians*, Vol. l, Archaeology, editado por Victoria R. Bricker and Jeremy A. Sabloff, pp. 313–341. University of Texas Press, Austin.

Ashmore, Wendy (editor)

1981 *Lowland Maya Settlement Patterns*. University of New Mexico Press, Albuquerque.

Ashmore, Wendy, y Gordon Willey

1981 A Historical Introduction to the Study of Lowland Maya Settlement Patterns. En *Lowland Maya Settlement Patterns*, editado por Wendy Ashmore, pp. 3-18. University of New Mexico Press, Albuquerque.

Blanton, Richard E., Stephen Kowalewski, Gary Feinman, y Jill Appel

1982 Monte Albán's Hinterland, Part I: The Prehispanic Settlement Patterns of the Central and Southern Parts of the Valley of Oaxaca, Mexico. University of Michigan, Ann Arbor.

Bohannan Paul y Glazer Mark

1993 Antropología. Lecturas. McGraw Hill Interamericana, España.

Borhegyi, Stephan F. de

1956 Settlement Patterns in Meso-America and the Sequence in the Guatemala Highlands Past and Present. En Prehistoric Settlement Patterns in the New World, editado por Gordon R. Willey, pp. 101-106. Viking Fund Publications in Anthropology, No. 23. Wenner-Gren Foundation for Anthropological Research, New York.

Carrasco Vargas, Ramón, Josep Ligorred Perramón, y Eduardo Pérez de Heredia

1991 Proyecto Kabah, Centro Regional Yucatán, Informe de los trabajos realizados en la temporada 1990. Archivo del Consejo de Arqueología, Instituto Nacional de Antropología e Historia, México, D.F.

Carrasco Vargas, Ramón, Josep Ligorred Perramón, Luis Millet, Fabienne de Pierrrebourg, Antonio Centeno, Eduardo Perez de Heredia, y Sylviane Boucher

1992 Proyecto Kabah, Centro Regional Yucatán, INAH Informe de los trabajos realizados en la temporada 1991. Archivo del Consejo de Arqueología, Instituto Nacional de Antropología e Historia. México, D.F.

Chang, Kwang-Chin

1968 *Settlement Archaeology*. National Press Books, Palo Alto, CA.

Dunning, Nicholas

1989 *Archaelogical Investigations at Sayil, Yucatan, Mexico: Intersite Reconnaissance and Soil Studies during the 1987 Field Season*. Publications in Anthropology, No. 2. University of Pittsburgh, Pittsburgh.

Garza Tarazona, Silvia y Edward Kurjack

1980 *Atlas arqueológico del estado de Yucatán*. Instituto Nacional de Antropología e Historia, Secretaria de Educación Pública. México, D.F.

Gendrop, Paul

1983 *Los estilos Río Bec, Chenes y Puuc*. Facultad de Arquitectura. Universidad Nacional Autónoma de México, México, D.F.

González Crespo, Norberto

1979 *Patrón de asentamiento prehispánico en la parte central del bajo balsa: un ensayo metodológico*. Instituto Nacional de Antropología e Historia, Secretaria de Educación Pública, Departamento de Prehistoria, México, D.F.

Haggett, Peter

1965 *Locational Analysis in Human Geography*. Edward Arnold, Ltd, London.

Hammond, Norman

1981 Settlement Patterns in Belize. En *Lowland Maya Settlement Patterns*, editado por Wendy Ashmore, pp. 157-186. University of New Mexico Press, Albuquerque.

Haviland, William A.

1970 Maya Settlement Patterns: A Critical Review. En *Archaeological Studies in Middle America*, pp. 23-47. Middle American Research Institute, Tulane University, New Orleans, LA.

1981 Dover House and Minor Centers at Tikal, Guatemala: An Investigation into the Identification of Valid Units in Settlement Hierarchies. En *Lowland Maya Settlement Patterns*, editado por Wendy Ashmore, pp. 89-117. University of New Mexico Press, Albuquerque.

Kintz, Ellen R.

1983 Class Structure in a Classic Maya City. En *Coba: A Classic Maya Metropolis*, editado por William Folan,

Ellen R. Kintz, y Laraine A. Fletcher, pp. 161-179. Academic Press, New York.

Kurjack, Edward B., y Silvia Garza Tarazona de González

1981 Una vision de la geografiá humana en la regíon serrana de Yucatán. In *Memoria del Congreso Interno 1979*, pp. 39-54. Instituto Nacional de Antropologia e Historia, Centro Regional del Sureste, México, D.F.

Marquina, Ignacio

1981 *Arquitectura prehispánica*. Instituto Nacional de Antropología e Historia, Secretaria de Educación Pública México, D.F.

Mediz Bolio. Antonio, y Mercedes de la Garza

1988 *Libro de Chilam Balam de Chumayel*. Secretaria de Educación Pública-Cien de México. México, D.F.

Millon René

1981 Teotihuacan: City, State, and Civilization. En Supplement to the Handbook of Middle American Indians. Vol. I: Archaeology, editado por Jeremy A Sabloff, pp. 198-243. University of Texas Press, Austin.

Pantoja Díaz, Luis, Cecilia Medina Martín, y María José Gómez Cobá

2014 San Pedro Cholul: un asentamiento arqueológico del Clásico Tardío en la región de Mérida, Yucatán, México. En *The Archaeology of Yucatán,* editado por Travis W. Stanton, pp. 165-180. Pre-Columbian Archaeology 1. Archaeopress, Oxford, England.

Pollock, Harry E. D.

1980 *The Puuc: An Architectural Survey of the Hill Country of Yucatan and Northern Campeche, Mexico*. Harvard University and the Carnegie Institution of Washington, Cambridge, MA.

Rice, Donald, y Dennis Puleston

1981 Ancient Maya Settlement Patterns in the Peten, Guatemala. En *Lowland Maya Settlement Patterns*, editado por Wendy Ashmore, pp. 121-156. University of New Mexico Press, Alburquerque.

Robina, Ricardo

1959 La arquitectura. En *El esplendor del México Antiguo*, Tomo II, pp. 607-650. Centro de investigaciones Antropológicas de México. Editorial del Valle de México, D.F.

Sanders, William T.

1956 The Central Mexican Symbiotic Region: a Study. En *Prehistoric Settlement Patterns in the New World*, editado por Gordon R. Willey, pp. 115-127. Viking Fund Publications in Anthropology, No. 23. Wenner-Gren Foundation for Anthropological Research, New York.

Sanders, William T., y Barbara J. Price

1968. Mesoamerica. The Evolution of a Civilization. Random House, New York.

Sanders. Wiillian T, Jeffrey R. Parson, y Robert S. Santley

1979 *The Basin of Mexico. Ecological Processes in the Evolution of the Civilization.* Academic Press, New York.

Sanhueza, Lorena R., Luis Cornejo B., y Fernanda Falabella G.

2007 Patrones de asentamiento en el período Alfarero Temprano de Chile central. Volumen 39, Nº 1, pp. 103-115. Revista de Antropología Chilena, Chungara.

Steward, Julian

1973 Theory of Culture Change. The Methodology of Multilinear Evolution, 2a. edición. University of Illinois Press, Urbana.

Toscano Hernández, Lourdes

2009 *Proyecto Kabah: Investigación y conservación del Codz Pop*. Archivo técnico del Consejo de arqueología. México, D.F.

Toscano Hernández, Lourdes, Roció Jiménez, Gustavo Novelo, David Ortegón, Aarón Duarte, Karla Castro, Nelda Marengo, Oyuki García, y Julián Cruz

2011 *Informe de la temporada 2010. Proyecto de Investigación y restauración arquitectónica en Kabah*. Archivo técnico del Consejo de arqueología. México, D.F.

Turner, Ellen Sue, Norman Turner, and R.E.M. Adams

1981 Volumetric Assessment, Rank Ordering, and Maya Civic Centers. En *Lowland Maya Settlement Patterns*, editado por Wendy Ashmore, pp. 71-88. University of New Mexico Press, Albuquerque.

Trigger, Bruce G.

1968 The Determinants of Settlement Patterns. En *Settlement Archaeology*, editado por Kwang-Chin Chang, pp. 53-78. National Press Books, Palo Alto, CA.

Velázquez, Emilia

1997 La apropiación del espacio entre nahuas y popolucas de la Sierra de Santa Marta, Veracruz. En *Nueve estudios sobre el espacio. Representación y formas de apropiación*, editado por Odile Hoffmann y Fernando I. Salmerón Castro, pp. 113-131. CIESAS-ORSTOM, México, D.F.

Voght, Evon Z.

1956 An Appraisal of Prehistoric Settlement patterns in the New World. En *Prehistoric Settlement Patterns in the New World*, editado por Gordon R. Willey, pp. 173-182. Viking Fund Publications in Anthropology, No. 23. Wenner-Gren Foundation for Anthropological Research, New York.

Wauchope, Robert and Edith H.B. Ricketson

1934 *House Mounds of Uaxactun, Guatemala*. Contributions to American Archaeology, no. 7. Carnegie Institution of Washington Publication, no. 436, Washington, D.C.

Willey, Gordon R.

1953 *Prehistoric Settlement Patterns in the Virú Valley, Perú*. Smithsonian Institution. Bureau of American Ethnology, Bulletin 155, 82nd Congress, no. 309.

Willey, Gordon R. (editor)

1956 *Prehistoric Settlement Patterns in the New World*. Viking Fund Publications in Anthropology, No. 23. Wenner-Gren Foundation for Anthropological Research, New York.

Willey, Gordon R., William R. Bullard, John B. Glass y James C. Gifford

1965 *Prehistoric Maya Settlements in the Belize Valley*. Papers of the Peabody Museum of Archaeology and Ethnology. Harvard, Cambridge, MA.

Investigación y Restauración Arquitectónicas en el Codz Pop de Kabah, Yucatán

Gustavo Novelo Rincón

Los trabajos de conservación e investigación que se han venido realizando desde 2006 en el Codz Pop de Kabah tienen como objetivo no sólo detener el deterioro y devolverle parte de su apariencia original, sino también entender al edificio a partir del estudio de su arquitectura, la iconografía de sus ricamente ornamentadas fachadas, los materiales asociados, así como de su ubicación dentro del conjunto palaciego del asentamiento, en donde residió la familia gobernante durante el período Clásico Terminal (800-1000 d.C.) y que debió ser un espacio destinado también a la administración y el ejercicio del poder político. La información recuperada a lo largo de estos años junto con el reciente hallazgo de dos jambas esculpidas en el cuarto 1 del edificio, ambas con una fuerte carga iconográfica, nos han permitido ampliar nuestro conocimiento sobre las transformaciones del espacio construido y las posibles funciones que ahí se desarrollaron a través del tiempo, así como acerca de la estructura social y política de los grupos de élite que habitaron en Kabah.

The objective behind the conservation and research carried out at the Codz Pop Kabah since 2006 is to not only stop the deterioration and restore some of its original appearance, but also to understand the building's architecture, the iconography of the richly ornamented facades, its associated materials, and its location within the palace complex of the settlement, where the ruling family resided during the Terminal Classic period (A.D. 800-1000) and must have also been a space for the administration and to exercise political power. The information recovered over the years, including the recent Discovery in Room 1 of two iconographically charged sculpted jambs, have allowed us to expand our knowledge about the transformations of the built space and possible functions that developed over time, as well as about the social and political elite groups that inhabited Kabah.

En 2010 inició el Proyecto investigación y restauración arquitectónica en Kabah, en el que se concibe al Grupo Este del asentamiento como un conjunto palaciego que durante el Clásico Tardío/Terminal (750-900/1000 d.C.) sirvió como residencia de la familia gobernante y espacio para actividades públicas, religiosas, y administrativas asociadas el ejercicio del poder político.

Este proyecto tiene dos objetivos principales: 1) asegurar la conservación de las estructuras, deteniendo el proceso de deterioro y devolviéndoles, en la medida de lo posible, su apariencia original; y 2) obtener información que permita identificar las distintas funciones que ahí se desarrollaron, a partir del estudio de la arquitectura, la iconografía plasmada en las fachadas y/o espacios internos, así como los materiales muebles asociados (Toscano 2009). Para cumplir con ambos objetivos, la principal herramienta utilizada es la restauración, entendiéndola como el conjunto de actividades que permite recuperar datos tanto para la investigación, como asegurar la permanencia de los bienes inmuebles.

Como relatar las labores en todo el conjunto sería muy extenso, este escrito se enfocará en las exploraciones y resultados preliminares de los trabajos en el Codz Pop, sin duda la construcción más importante del Grupo Este. Para ello el texto se ha dividido en tres apartados: en el primero se ubica a la ciudad prehispánica de Kabah y al edificio dentro del asentamiento; seguidamente se describe la metodología de trabajo; y por último se exponen los resultados del análisis de los datos arquitectónicos.

El asentamiento y el Codz Pop

Kabah se localiza en la región del Puuc (Figura 1), palabra que en maya-yucateco significa 'sierra' y que abarca la parte sur de Yucatán y noreste de Campeche (Andrews 1990; Pollock 1980). En la literatura arqueológica, esta zona es considerada la cuna de una tradición arquitectónica reconocida por el uso de la mampostería de recubrimiento o 'encofrado perdido' (Andrews 1986; Prem 1995), una refinada técnica constructiva que se desarrolló en el Clásico Tardío-Terminal y que se caracteriza por el excelente trabajo de cantería y alta calidad de los morteros, que permitió a los arquitectos construir edificios abovedados más amplios y ornamentarlos con mosaicos de piedra (Toscano et al. 2007).

A juzgar por los vestigios de su medio ambiente construido, durante la época prehispánica Kabah debió ser una de las ciudades más grandes e importantes del Puuc. Si bien su ocupación se extiende desde el Preclásico Tardío (800 a.C.-100 d.C.) hasta el Posclásico (1000/1200-1300 d.C.), fue durante el Clásico Tardío-Terminal (750-900/1000 d.C.) cuando el asentamiento alcanzó su máxima ocupación y se construyeron la mayoría de los conjuntos arquitectónicos monumentales del área central, dándole a ésta su conformación final.

El núcleo central del asentamiento abarca una superficie de aproximadamente 1.2 km² y fue organizado a partir de un eje principal norte-sur, formado por el Grupo Central, el *Sacbé* 2 y el Grupo Sur, el cual posiblemente definió la

Gustavo Novelo Rincón - Instituto Nacional de Antropología e Historia (INAH), Mérida, Yucatán (codzito73@gmail.com).

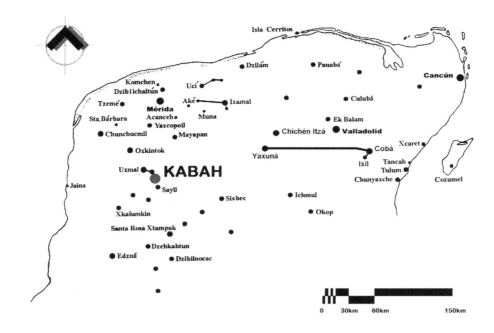

FIGURA 1. MAPA DE YUCATÁN.

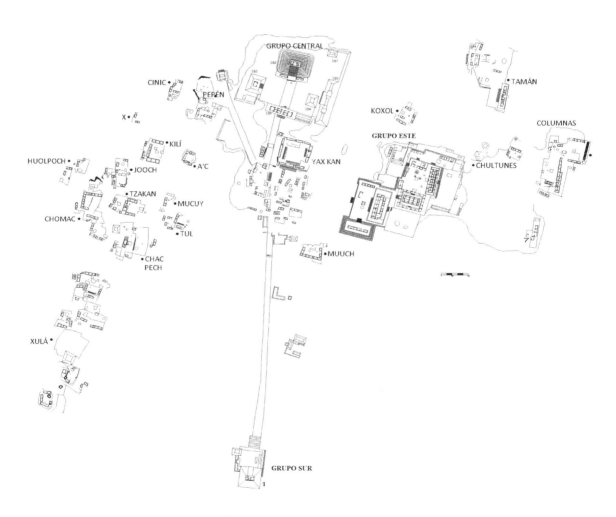

FIGURA 2. EL NÚCLEO CENTRAL DEL ASENTAMIENTO DE KABAH.

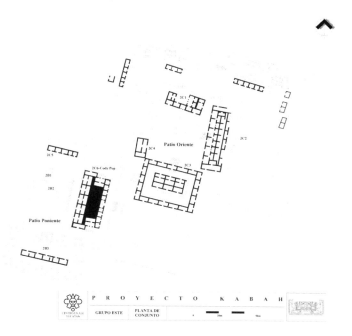

FIGURA 3. PLANTA DE CONJUNTO DEL GRUPO ESTE DE KABAH.

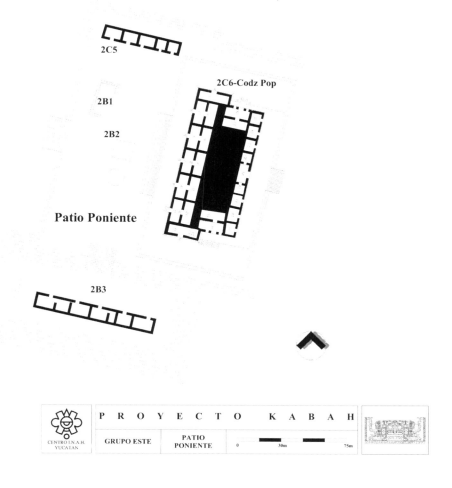

FIGURA 4. PLANTA DE PATIO PONIENTE.

FIGURA 5. ESTRUCTURA 2C6 O CODZ POP.

traza urbana de la ciudad desde el Clásico Temprano (400-600 d.C.) (Toscano et al. 2004) (Figura 2).

Al oriente de esta calzada se localiza el Grupo Este, el más grande e importante de Kabah durante el Clásico Tardío-Terminal (Figura 3). Este enorme conjunto, cuyo eje visual se dirige hacia los Grupos Central y Oeste, está formado por nueve edificios multicámaras y numerosas construcciones elaboradas principalmente de materiales perecederos, organizados alrededor de dos grandes espacios abiertos (Plazas Oriente y Poniente) y siete patios ubicados en distintos niveles e intercomunicados (Toscano y Novelo 2012). Viendo el arreglo espacial del conjunto, es claro que las escaleras jugaron un factor muy importante en la organización del ambiente construido, ya que a través de ellas los mayas lograron darle un carácter público o restringido a los espacios (Toscano 2009; Toscano et al. 2004).

El Codz Pop (estructura 2C6) se localiza en el extremo oriental del Patio Poniente[1], formado además por otras cuatro construcciones (2B1, 2B2, 2B3, y 2C5) (Figura 4). Este monumental edificio (Figura 5), que descansa sobre un gran basamento con una amplia escalinata en su costado oeste, está formado por un macizo de mampostería central rodeado por 26 cuartos: en su lado poniente cuenta con dos crujías paralelas divididas en cinco recintos cada una; nueve habitaciones forman el costado oriente, en el sur se localizan cuatro cuartos, en tanto que en el norte se encuentran tres recintos.

La crestería que coronaba la cima del macizo central junto con la rica y variada ornamentación de sus fachadas, sin duda el rasgo más sobresaliente del Codz Pop, remarcan la importancia y jerarquía del edificio y hacen que sea considerado el rasgo arquitectónico más sobresaliente del Grupo Este e incluso del asentamiento (Pollock 1980), así como uno de los mejores ejemplos de la arquitectura Puuc Mosaico de Yucatán (Andrews 1986).

Exploración y excavación del Codz Pop

Para lograr los objetivos del proyecto, la principal herramienta utilizada en el Grupo Este de Kabah es la restauración integral, concibiéndola como la serie de acciones que nos permiten conocer y explorar de manera sistemática las estructuras, recuperar datos fidedignos para la investigación y lograr su conservación mediante una correcta intervención. En otras palabras, vemos en la restauración un medio ideal para estudiar la arquitectura prehispánica y al mismo tiempo asegurar su permanencia (Toscano 2009).

A lo largo del proceso de restauración, la metodología de trabajo aplicada nos ha permitido planear y ejecutar las distintas acciones de investigación y conservación. El primer paso fue elaborar una detallada historiografía del edificio, que inicia con el análisis de los relatos e imágenes de los viajeros-exploradores del siglo XIX (Stephens y Catherwood en 1842; Charnay en 1857; Maler hacia 1888-1891) así como de los reportes de los inspectores de monumentos prehispánicos del Gobierno Mexicano, que visitaron Kabah en la primera parte del siglo XX. La segunda parte contiene una síntesis de los estudios e

---

[1] Para una descripción de los Patios Oriente y Poniente ver Andrews (1990) y Pollock (1980).

FIGURA 6 A-D. EXCAVACIÓNES EN EL CODZ POP. (A) EXCAVACIÓN CON CALAS ALTERNADAS; (B) CAÍDA ORDENADA DE LA BÓVEDA DEL CUARTO 1; (C) COLAPSO EN BLOQUE DEL TÍMPANO NORTE DEL CUARTO 3; (D) ORDEN DE CAÍDA DE LA CASCADA DE MASCARONES DE LA ESQUINA SURESTE DEL CUARTO 14.

intervenciones arqueológicas efectuadas a partir de 1935, que incluye los trabajos de Pollock (1980), Ruz (1950), Pavón (1951), Salazar (1952 y 1953), Andrews (1990) y del Proyecto Kabah dirigido por Ramón Carrasco Vargas (Carrasco et al. 1991 y 1992). La elaboración de esta historiografía nos permitió tener un registro gráfico y diacrónico del edificio a partir de 1842, año de la visita de Stephens y Catherwood, en el cual se observa su estado en conservación y proceso de deterioro desde esa fecha hasta la segunda mitad del siglo XX.

A continuación hicimos un minucioso reconocimiento del edificio y su derrumbe para conocer su estado de conservación, los rasgos en superficie más sobresalientes, así como las afectaciones o alteraciones ocasionadas por acción natural y/o humana. Con los datos del reconocimiento y la historiografía elaboramos una detallada descripción arquitectónica y un diagnóstico de deterioro, a partir del cual se programaron las exploraciones y los trabajos de excavación, consolidación y reintegración de elementos, que han servido para ir solventando los problemas de conservación del edificio.

Al igual que Molina (1975), quien propuso que una buena técnica de excavación es requisito indispensable para recuperar la información y los elementos necesarios para lograr una correcta restauración, consideramos que la excavación sistemática del derrumbe representa una de las partes más importantes del trabajo arqueológico, ya que de ahí obtenemos los datos necesarios y confiables para la investigación, así como los elementos necesarios realizar una consolidación y reintegración de elementos fidedignas.

Siguiendo el planteamiento de Molina (1975), hemos aplicado una estrategia metódica con la cual exploramos de manera extensiva el edificio, localizando los sectores in situ y retirando de manera sistemática las partes colapsadas. Este meticuloso proceso nos permitió detectar evidencias de actividades rituales anteriores al abandono del edificio (ver Toscano y Huchim 2014) y las causas que ocasionaron su colapso, así como encontrar varios sectores del edificio que se desplomaron en bloque y por ende conservaban un excelente orden de caída, tales como las bóvedas de los cuartos 1, 13, y 15, así como las cascadas de mascarones de las esquinas noreste del recinto 1 y sureste del cuarto

FIGURA 7. DECORACIÓN DE LA FACHADA OESTE DE 2C6/1°A.

14, la primera del zócalo a la moldura media, y la última completa hasta el cornisamento (Figura 6).

Resultados y avances en la investigación

Los trabajos efectuados en el Codz Pop de Kabah han contribuido a su conservación e incrementado nuestro conocimiento de su arquitectura e historia. Conjuntando la información de todos los trabajos realizados en el edificio hemos logrado identificar cómo los mayas modificaron tanto su forma como el discurso plasmado en sus fachadas, lo que sugiere que los dirigentes del asentamiento tuvieron una necesidad constante de transformar el espacio construido, ya sea para ampliar las dimensiones de las áreas de circulación y el número de cuartos, o bien para modificar u ocultar los elaborados diseños que ornamentaban las fachadas (ver Toscano et al. 2007; Toscano et al. 2012).

El análisis de los datos indica que el Codz Pop tiene una compleja secuencia arquitectónica, formada por al menos siete períodos de construcción[2]. Aunque no la podemos considerar como integral, ya que no todas las modificaciones están conectadas espacialmente lo que hace difícil interrelacionarlas, pensamos que es una secuencia bastante completa que ilustra de manera clara cómo se fue transformando el espacio construido.

La construcción más antigua fue designada 2C6/2°A. Corresponde a una estructura anterior al Codz Pop localizada bajo el pórtico del cuarto 15, en el costado sur del edificio; desafortunadamente sólo hallamos parte del muro de contención y la cima de un basamento, elaborado con piedras burdamente talladas en forma de bloques rectangulares, que en algunas partes aún conservaba el recubrimiento de estuco. Posteriormente, esta plataforma fue ampliada hacia el sur (2C6/2°B), modificación que conservó el sistema constructivo del relleno, el tallado de la piedra del muro, así como en la textura y color del estuco.

El segundo período es 2C6/1°A y corresponde a la construcción, sobre el basamento de la etapa anterior, de lo que ahora conocemos como el Ala Oeste del Codz Pop (cuartos 1-14). Este edificio tenía dos crujías longitudinales, cada una dividida en cinco recintos frontales y cinco posteriores (2-12), rematados por dos cuartos al sur (13-14) y uno al norte (1). Por lo menos tres de sus fachadas estaban ornamentadas con mascarones desde el zócalo hasta el friso, pintados en color rojo y en menor medida negro; en la parte inferior la decoración se interrumpe por las entradas, todas flanqueadas por columnas de medios mascarones; en el friso de la fachada oeste la continua ornamentación de mascarones también cambia a la altura de los accesos, ya que sobre éstos se colocó un complejo diseño formado una columna de tres mascarones completos flanqueada por mascarones de perfil con las fauces abiertas, enmarcados por un diseño trenzado. Llama la atención que esta decoración sólo se presenta en el oeste, ya que en las fachadas norte y sur el friso presenta exclusivamente mascarones completos.

---

[2] Esta información fue tomada de Toscano et al. 2007 y Toscano et al. 2012. Existen otras evidencias de modificaciones y alteraciones en el edificio, tales como fragmentos de esquinas, empalmes de muros, niveles de piso y diferencias en el tallado de las piedras. Sin embargo, estas evidencias no han sido exploradas por lo que aún no tenemos una idea clara del elemento del cual formaron parte (ver Toscano et al. 2007 y Toscano et al. 2012).

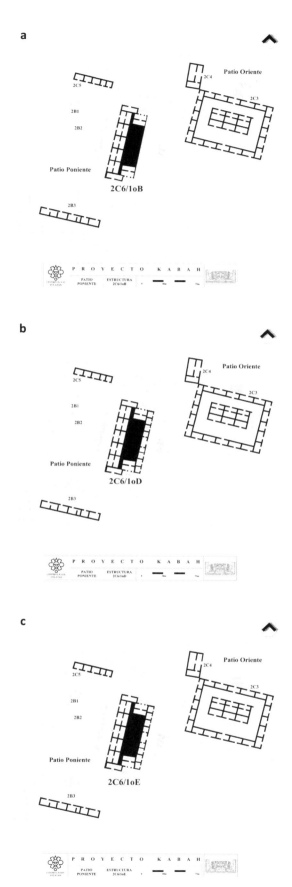

FIGURA 8 A-C. ETAPAS DE CONSTRUCCIÓN DEL CODZ POP. (A)
2C6/1°B; (B) 2C6/1°D; (C) 2C6/1°E.

Desafortunadamente, los mayas desmantelaron la fachada oriente, aunque suponemos que debió tener una ornamentación similar.

Los mascarones del friso descansan sobre la moldura media, que rodea el edificio y representa el cuerpo ondulante de la serpiente emplumada rematado con cabezas de ofidio en cada esquina (ver Pollock 1980), en tanto que en la parte superior estuvieron coronados por una fila de elementos circulares y una de almenas triangulares (Figura 7).

El sistema constructivo de este período difiere radicalmente del anterior, ya que muestra una excelente calidad en la cantería de las piedras, los núcleos y morteros que se reflejó en el uso de una delicada ornamentación de mosaico, el fino enlucido de estuco y el uso de color. Esto sugiere que transcurrió un espacio considerable de tiempo que permitió el desarrollo de una refinada técnica de construcción, así como contar con arquitectos, canteros, escultores, y artesanos más calificados.

La gran inversión de recursos utilizada en la construcción del edificio y su fuerte carga iconográfica, con complejos diseños en los que se plasman los símbolos y el discurso de la clase gobernante, indican que desde su planeación el Codz Pop fue concebido como el rasgo más importante del Grupo Este, una majestuosa construcción que debió ser visible desde todos los conjuntos importantes de la ciudad (Toscano et al. 2007).

El siguiente momento fue designado 2C6/1°B (Figura 8a). Para este período se construyeron cuatro recintos, dos en la esquina noreste (26-27) y dos en la sureste (15-16), así como el macizo y la crestería del edificio, que remarcó la jerarquía del Codz Pop dentro del Grupo Este.

En esta fase el diseño en planta del edificio era similar al primer piso de la Estructura 2C1 del Grupo Noroeste, o Dos Altos de Kabah, ya que ambos tenían un macizo de mampostería central con cuartos en tres de sus costados. Esta distribución no es común en los edificios de la región Puuc cuentan con un macizo al centro, ya que por lo general los recintos se distribuyen a lo largo de los cuatro lados, tal y como se observa en las Estructuras 2C2 y 2C3 de Kabah (ambas en el Patio Oriente del Grupo Este) y en los Palacios Norte y Sur de Sayil (ver Pollock 1980).

En este período aumentó la variedad de diseños ornamentales, lo que se reflejó en la organización y decoración de las fachadas; los cuartos 15 y 26 desplantaban sobre una plataforma adosada al zócalo de 2C6/1°A y decorada con mascarones flanqueados por guilloches, junquillos, y paños de celosías; en ambos frentes, el acceso a los recintos se lograba a través de escalinatas, que al menos en el costado norte estuvo formada por peldaños junquillos rematados por fajas de listeles.

Los cuartos frontales 15 y 26 tienen un zócalo sencillo y presentan un pórtico de tres vanos y cuatro pilares en la fachada, en el primero está enmarcado por columnas de

FIGURA 9. PLATAFORMA BASAL DE 2C6/1°D.

FIGURA 10. FRISO DE LOS CUARTOS 21 Y 22 DEL ALA ORIENTE DE 2C6/1°D.

mascarones de perfil con las fauces abiertas, iguales a los del friso sobre las entradas de la fachada oeste, en tanto que en el extremo opuesto (recinto 15) sólo el extremo oeste presenta un panel liso. En ambos la decoración se concentró en el friso, que estuvo recubierto por paneles de 12 mascarones, organizados en cuatro columnas de tres piezas cada una, coronados por almenas con diseños geométricos, distintos a los de otras fachadas.

Durante este período suponemos que los mayas también desmantelaron los mascarones de la parte inferior de la fachada oriente de los cuartos 1 y 14, a excepción de las esquinas, y en su lugar colocaron paños de celosías enmarcados por guilloches y un diseño trenzado.

Posteriormente, la plataforma de 2C6/1°B fue ampliada hacia el oriente con un adosamiento que desentona totalmente con el refinamiento de la primera, ya que su muro fue elaborado con piedras de factura burda y numerosas cuñas en las junturas, por lo que fue necesario utilizar un grueso aplanado de estuco para darle su apariencia final. Esta etapa fue designada 2C6/1°C y

Figura 11. Plataforma y escalinata de 2C6/1°E.

aunque no pudimos definir sus dimensiones, notamos que su construcción incluyó el desmantelamiento parcial de la plataforma anterior.

El siguiente período corresponde a la construcción de toda el Ala Oriente (cuartos 17-25) (Figura 8b). En este período, denominado 2C6/1°D, los arquitectos adosaron un cuerpo rectangular ornamentado con módulos formados por guiloches, grecas escalonadas, y flores de cuatro pétalos (ver Pollock 1980) (Figura 9), que extendió la plataforma basal de 2C6/1°C hacia el oriente. Sobre este basamento construyeron una hilada de nueve cuartos organizados en eje con fachadas decoradas con diseños distintos al resto del edificio: su parte inferior está formada por un zócalo sencillo y paramento ricamente decorado, pero no con mascarones, sino con grupos de tres columnas con triple atadura en las esquinas y paños con módulos de celosías flanqueados por guiloches, formando el diseño de un petatillo.

El friso del Ala Oriente está dividido en tres sectores, el central (que abarca los cuartos 20-22) estaba ornamentado con siete esculturas antropomorfas en bulto, aparentemente del mismo individuo, con elaborados tocados de plumas que recubren toda la superficie del friso (Figura 10); este personaje fue identificado como el rey de Kabah y se le asocia con el personaje representado en las dos jambas esculpidas del recinto 21, ambas esculpidas con relieves que representan dos escenas de celebración de victoria y otras dos de sacrificio de vencidos (Carrasco 1991).

En los otros cuartos del Ala Oriente (17-19 y 23-25) el friso tenía cascadas de mascarones en las esquinas y sobre los accesos rematados con piezas circulares y almenas triangulares, enmarcados por módulos elaborados con motivos geométricos (Toscano et al. 2007).

El último momento que registramos es 2C6/1°E. Durante esta etapa los mayas adosaron un basamento y una escalinata de cuatro peldaños frente al pórtico del cuarto 15

que cubrieron el costado sur de la plataforma de 2C6/1°D (Figura 11). Llama la atención que en esta modificación los constructores utilizaron dos tipos de elementos: sillares de recubrimiento en la escalinata y piedras de factura burda en el muro de la plataforma, estas últimas que contrastan con el delicado labrado de períodos anteriores.

Aunque no sabemos cuánto tiempo pasó entre la última etapa de modificación y el abandono del Codz Pop, las evidencias indican que los habitantes de Kabah realizaron varias acciones que marcaron el fin de la ocupación formal del edificio (ver Toscano y Huchim en este volumen). Estos eventos aparentemente no causaron mayores problemas estructurales, ya que la construcción presenta un patrón de deterioro similar al de los edificios de la región Puuc que carecen de mantenimiento (ver Toscano y Pérez 2002).

Comentarios finales

Sin duda alguna, el Codz Pop es el edificio dominante del Patio Poniente y del Grupo Este. Su elaborada arquitectura y compleja iconografía, aunada a la ausencia de elementos asociados a actividades domésticas, indican que debió tener funciones relacionadas al ejercicio del poder político e incluso de carácter ritual y administrativo. Esta idea se ve reforzada por su ubicación en el extremo este del Patio Poniente, frente al altar con inscripciones jeroglíficas, y a un amplio espacio abierto en donde posiblemente se efectuaban actividades púbicas, posiblemente con un gran número de personas.

Los trabajos en el Codz Pop, además de contribuir a su conservación, muestran que el edificio cuenta con una historia compleja e interesante. Si bien tenemos una secuencia de construcción muy completa, nos falta analizar la fuerte carga iconográfica de las fachadas e interiores para lograr entender, en la medida de lo posible, el discurso ideológico ahí plasmado. Pensamos que este estudio, conforme avance, contribuirá a entender al edificio e incluso podría ayudar a interpretar la situación sociopolítica de Kabah (Toscano 2009).

Estamos conscientes de que la investigación está en proceso y aún falta mucho por hacer, pero pensamos que vamos por buen camino, ya que estamos conjuntando las interpretaciones de otros autores con los datos recuperados, esperando que su análisis nos proporcione un retrato más profundo del complejo espacio arquitectónico que representa el Codz Pop.

Referencias Citadas

Andrews, George F.

1986 *Los estilos arquitectónicos del Puuc. Una nueva apreciación*. Colección Científica No. 150, Instituto Nacional de Antropología e Historia, México, D. F.

1990 Architectural Survey at Kabah, Archivo de la Sección de Arqueología del Centro INAH Yucatán, Mérida, 1990.

Carrasco Vargas, Ramón, Josep Ligorred Perramón, y Eduardo Pérez de Heredia

1991 *Proyecto Kabah CRY-INAH Informe de los trabajos realizados en la temporada 1990*, Archivo Técnico del Consejo Nacional de Arqueología del INAH, México.

Molina M., Augusto

1975 *La restauración arquitectónica de edificios arqueológicos*. Colección Científica No. 21, Instituto Nacional de Antropología e Historia, México, D. F.

Prem, Hanns

1995 Consideraciones sobre la técnica constructiva de la arquitectura Puuc. En *Cuadernos de Arquitectura Mesoamericana* 29:29-38.

Pollock, Harry E. D.

1980 *The Puuc: An Architectural Survey of the Hill Country of Yucatan and Northern Campeche, Mexico*. Peabody Museum of Archaeology and Ethnology, Cambridge.

Toscano Hernández, Lourdes

2009 *Proyecto Kabah. Investigación y conservación del Codz Pop*. Archivo de la Sección de Arqueología, Centro INAH Yucatán, Mérida.

Toscano Hernández, Lourdes, y Sonia Pérez G.

2002 *Informe de la restauración del edificio 1C1 de Kabah, Yucatán*. Archivo de la Sección de Arqueología, Centro INAH Yucatán, Mérida.

Toscano Hernández, Lourdes, Gustavo Novelo Rincón, y David Ortegón Zapata

2004 Informe de la restauración de lasa estructuras 1A3, 1A9 y 1A12 y Propuesta para la Temporada de campo 2004, Archivo de la Sección de Arqueología, Centro INAH Yucatán, Mérida.

Toscano Hernández, Lourdes, Gustavo Novelo Rincón, y Arturo Valle Uicab

2007 Restauración arquitectónica del Codz Pop. Informe de la Temporada 2006, Archivo de la Sección de Arqueología, Centro INAH Yucatán, Mérida.

Toscano Hernández, Lourdes, y Gustavo Novelo Rincón

2012 La cocina real de Kabah, Yucatán. Ponencia presentada en el XXVI Simposio de investigaciones arqueológicas en Guatemala, Ciudad de Guatemala.

Toscano Hernández, Lourdes, Gustavo Novelo Rincón, David Ortegón Zapata, Oyuki García Salas, y David Palomino Yam

2014 Proyecto investigación y restauración arquitectónica en Kabah, Yucatán. Informe preliminar de la temporada 2011 y Propuesta para la temporada 2012, Archivo de la Sección de Arqueología, Centro INAH Yucatán, Mérida.

Toscano Hernández, Lourdes, y José Huchim Herrera

2014 Terminaciones rituales en los principales edificios de la región Puuc. Ponencia presentada en la 79th Annual Meeting of the Society for American Archaeology, Austin.

Terminaciones Rituales en los Principales Edificios de la Región Puuc

Lourdes Toscano Hernández y José Huchim Herrera

Los restos de cultura material hallados en contextos arqueológicos son susceptibles de múltiples interpretaciones; en la región del Puuc tradicionalmente se había pensado que la acumulación de cerámica y otros utensilios aparentemente domésticos localizados en las cercanías de los edificios considerados como 'Arquitectura de Poder,' eran producidos por actividades cotidianas como la acumulación de basura. Al mismo tiempo, partes incompletas de los edificios fueron interpretadas como destrucciones producto del proceso natural del deterioro. Sin embargo, la aparición constante de accesos incompletos y 'basureros' nos hizo replantear la evidencia recuperada por más de 20 años en la región Puuc de Yucatán. En este trabajo exponemos los restos de cultura material, así como sus asociaciones, que nos han permitido proponer que se trata de complejas ceremonias de abandono, que los mayas realizaron durante el período Clásico Terminal.

The remains of material culture found in archaeological contexts are susceptible to multiple interpretations; traditionally in the Puuc region the accumulation of ceramics and other apparently domestic utensils located near buildings considered 'Architecture of Power' were thought to have been produced by everyday activities, such as the accumulation of waste. At the same time, incomplete parts of the buildings were interpreted as destruction produced by the natural deterioration. However, the regular appearance of incomplete accesses and 'trash heaps' made us reconsider the evidence recovered for more than 20 years in the Puuc region of Yucatán. In this paper, we present the artifacts of material culture, as well as their associations, which have enabled us to propose that these are complex Maya abandonment ceremonies that took place during the Terminal Classic period.

Durante los últimos 30 años, la interpretación de las evidencias de cultura material halladas por los arqueólogos del área Maya se han visto beneficiadas con los avances logrados en la lectura de los textos epigráficos y la interpretación de la iconografía. Estos estudios hicieron más palpables el complejo mundo ideológico, las estructuras de poder y, por supuesto, la vida religiosa de los antiguos habitantes del Mayab. Asimismo, la aplicación de nuevos enfoques en la interpretación del dato arqueológico ha enriquecido el conocimiento de aspectos abstractos como la percepción del espacio o el significado de las elaboradas pinturas o fachadas que adornan los edificios provocando que los ojos de los investigadores se vuelquen hacia el extenso universo ritual de esas sociedades.

Últimamente se han reportado evidencias de rituales asociados a la arquitectura en numerosos sitios, sobre todo de la región del Petén (Craig 2005; Farr y Arroyave 2007, 2008; Iglesias y Ciudad 2009; Pendergast 1998; Walker 1998). Los objetos enterrados en las entrañas de los edificios, basamentos, y plazas, así como acumulaciones de cerámica rota y otros artefactos colocado sobre la superficie de las plazas patios o en el interior de los recintos son evidencias de estas conductas. Su reiterada aparición en el contexto arqueológico nos indica que la ejecución de rituales fue más común de lo que se había supuesto hace algunos años, por lo tanto, pensamos que es factible encontrar pruebas de su práctica en la mayoría de los sitios.

Ante este panorama hemos replanteado la interpretación que antaño dábamos a algunos objetos de cultura material tales como concentraciones de cerámica o elementos arquitectónicos aparentemente fuera de contexto o incluso algunos sectores destruidos de edificios, qué considerábamos como producto de actividades cotidianas o deterioros ocasionados por el tiempo y la falta de mantenimiento. Es así que presentamos, en este trabajo, este tipo de evidencias recuperadas a lo largo de más de 20 años de excavaciones en varios sitios de la Región Puuc de Yucatán, las más antiguas datan del año 1991 y las más recientes del 2013. La información procede de edificios que pertenecen a la denominada 'Arquitectura de Poder' y son: el Palacio de Labná, el Palacio Norte de Sayil, los grupos Temprano y Este de Kabah, y el Cuadrángulo de los Pájaros y el Palomar de Uxmal. Varios de estos edificios fueron residencias de familias gobernantes al menos durante el Clásico Tardío/Terminal.

En los rellenos constructivos de estos edificios hemos encontrado objetos que identificados como parte de rituales reverenciales, pero nuestro objetivo en esta ocasión es abordar contextos mucho más frágiles, que suponemos se formaron en corto tiempo y quedaron depositados en lugares específicos de los edificios, de ahí la importancia de documentar con precisión las evidencias que encontramos durante la excavación de las construcciones o de los espacios de circulación.

Si bien el término *ritual* invita a una rica discusión de corte teórico, que sobrepasa con mucho las intenciones de este trabajo, pensamos que es necesario resaltar sus cualidades retomando la definición de Conrad Kottak, para quien el ritual es un

'...comportamiento formal, estilizado, repetitivo y estereotipado, realizado de forma seria como un acto

Lourdes Toscano Hernández - Instituto Nacional de Antropología e Historia (INAH), Mérida, Yucatán (mtoscanoh@gmail.com);
José Huchim Herrera - Instituto Nacional de Antropología e Historia (INAH), Mérida, Yucatán (uaxak810@gmail.com).

social; los rituales se realizan en momentos y lugares establecidos y tienen un orden litúrgico' (Kottak 2002:414 en Iglesias y Ciudad 2009:33).

Indudablemente el tipo de cualidades mencionadas por Kottak son difíciles de observar en los rituales prehispánicos y solo las podemos inferir a través de los restos de los objetos utilizados y de la impronta que los comportamientos rituales han dejado en los espacios construidos.

La evidencia

Consideramos necesario explicar que la información que se presenta en este trabajo proviene de excavaciones que se hicieron con fines de restaurar los edificios, por lo tanto fueron exploraciones extensivas durante las cuales removimos las partes derrumbadas de las estructuras con el propósito de hallar órdenes de caída que nos permitirán reintegrar algunas partes a su posición original.

Durante estas exploraciones también realizamos el análisis de las causas que originaron el deterioro e identificamos fallas estructurales, así como la secuencia del colapso. Esto nos permite identificar cuándo una construcción fue destruida intencionalmente y cuándo se derrumbó por causas naturales. En algunos casos los edificios fueron explorados con anterioridad y no tenemos los registros completos, por tal razón, retomamos esa información no como una prueba contundente sino como una posibilidad, tal es el caso de varias escalinatas que carecen de piedras de revestimiento.

A continuación presentamos las evidencias localizadas en los sitios de la Ruta Puuc.

Uxmal

Durante las exploraciones efectuadas en 1986-87, se restauró el paramento norte de la Gran Plataforma del Gobernador, en donde se encuentran dos escalinatas, una que conduce a la plaza principal y otra que lleva al Edificio de las Tortugas. Estas fueron desmanteladas quitando casi la totalidad del recubrimiento, ya que solo se encontraron completas las primeras hiladas. El núcleo estaba casi completo y en algunos sectores se observaba la impronta de los sillares (Barrera y Huchim 1990).

La estructura que corona la Pirámide del Adivino, carece de peldaños en su costado oriente. Así mismo, los aposentos carecen de jambas y dinteles. En el lado poniente de este mismo edificio también falta la escalinata.

La Escalinata Sur del Cuadrángulo de las Monjas fue explorada también en 1986-87 y presenta un patrón de destrucción similar al que se documentó en La Gran Plataforma del Gobernador, donde se desprendieron los sillares de los peldaños superiores, dejando el núcleo intacto (Barrera y Huchim 1990).

La estructura M12-9 es una sala hipóstila que se encuentra hacia el oriente del Juego de Pelota, durante los trabajos

de restauración llamó la atención el hecho de que a pesar de haber recuperado los cerca de un 90% de elementos, inclusive los del friso, con caídas ordenadas la mayoría de ellos, las escalinatas estaban desmanteladas.

El Cuadrángulo de los Pájaros fue explorado en su totalidad y las evidencia que aquí se recuperaron se relacionan más con la mutilación de los elementos decorativos de frisos, tal es el caso de dos esculturas que representan a un gobernante en posición sedente. El primero de ellos fue excavado durante la temporada 1993 cuando se restauró el costado poniente, el cual está formado por dos edificios similares en planta y decoración. La escultura fue hallada en buen estado de conservación, junto con el derrumbe del friso y presentaba un golpe en la mandíbula inferior que provocó un desprendimiento. La segunda escultura no se encontró durante la exploración del edificio Poniente-sur. Fue hasta 1996, cuando se exploró la estructura del Dios Pájaro, cuando hallamos el personaje faltante colocado como parte del relleno del patio y si bien el cuerpo estaba en buen estado de conservación, la cara estaba totalmente desfigurada.[1]

El Juego de Pelota se intervino en 1975 y a pesar de haberse aplicado un método de exploración usado para excavar contextos prehistóricos, no se encontraron los elementos de las escalinatas. De tal modo que solamente se pudieron recuperar *in situ* las dos primeras hiladas de los escalones y el núcleo que da volumen al cuerpo de las escalinatas.

Kabah

Los depósitos rituales fueron hallados en la estructura 1A10 del Grupo Temprano y en el Grupo Este en los edificios conocidos como El Codz Pop y El Teocalli.

En la estructura 1A10 encontramos una de las evidencias más complejas ya que estos depósitos fueron localizados en cuatro sectores del edificio, tres en el perímetro inferior del basamento general y uno en el interior del cuarto 2.[2] Todos estos fueron colocados sobre la superficie y estuvieron expuestos hasta que se derrumbaron el basamento y el edificio.

En el interior del cuarto 2, en el sector sur del recinto, abajo del derrumbe de la bóveda, encontramos una mancha de ceniza y algunas piedras quemadas de tamaño pequeño, esta capa tenía un espesor cercano a los 10 cm y estaba directamente sobre el nivel de piso, el cual había sido roto de manera intencional y cuidadosa para excavar una oquedad de forma cuadrada, de casi 1 m por lado (esta intrusión afectó solamente el relleno del zócalo, ya que encontramos intacto el piso del basamento general), posteriormente los mayas rellenaron el hoyo y nivelaron la superficie hasta enrasarlo con el piso. Bajo la capa de ceniza, a nivel de piso y distribuidos en un área aproximada de 1.30 m², hallamos restos de huesos de animales, cinco

[1] Otros elementos escultóricos que se encontraron en rellenos constructivos fueron las representaciones de dos tepezcuintles, también mutilados en las extremidades superiores y el hocico.
[2] La información sobre 1A10 que aquí se presenta fue retomada casi textual de la ponencia 'Rituales de abandono en la estructura 1A10 de Kabah' (Toscano, Novelo, y Zapata 2005).

agujas de hueso, un punzón del mismo material, dos fragmentos de navajillas de obsidiana, y fragmentos de cerámica. Aunque no es fácil reconocer el orden en que fueron colocados estos objetos, resulta evidente que no fueron puestos ahí de manera arbitraria.

A juzgar por la posición en que se encontraron los huesos, el animal debió ser destazado y colocado en trozos en distintas partes de la zona. En este contexto hallamos también los restos de tres vasijas fragmentadas y semicompletas: un vaso de paredes rectas del tipo Kilikan Compuesto perteneciente al grupo de Naranja Fina Silho, característico de Chichén Itzá; un cuenco de soporte anular del tipo Sacalum negro sobre pizarra y un cajete trípode Muna pizarra. Los tiestos fueron encontrados tanto en la superficie como en el relleno de la oquedad antes mencionada, lo que sugiere que ambas acciones se efectuaron durante el mismo evento. En Palenque se han reportado este tipo de conductas, en donde se extraen ofrendas del relleno de los edificios.

Al pie del desplante del basamento, en los costados este, sur, y oeste, encontramos 11 vasijas colocadas sobre el nivel del piso. En el frente meridional los mayas pusieron dos pares de vasijas, integrados por cazuelas de los tipos Muna pizarra y Chumayel rojo sobre pizarra y cajetes trípodes a manera de 'tapa' de los tipos Sahcaba modelado y Nohcacab compuesto. Cada una de las cazuelas contenía un entierro infantil cuyos huesos estaban en mal estado de conservación.

En el sector oeste, a ambos lados del acceso fueron colocadas tres ollas chultuneras de tipo Chumayel rojo sobre pizarra, así como dos cazuelas sobrepuestas, una de las cuales sirvió como 'tapa,' y la otra contenía los restos de otro infante. La cazuela que contenía el entierro es del tipo Chemax negro sobre prepizarra y la 'tapa' es Sacalum negro sobre pizarra.

En el costado este, cercanas al acceso, hallamos una cazuela y un vaso, ambos del tipo Muna pizarra, este último asociado a un elemento decorativo en forma de mazorca de maíz.

En la estructura conocida como El Teocalli, en el Grupo Este, encontramos dos depósitos, cubiertos por el derrumbe del edificio. Uno de ellos estaba en el interior del recinto 23. Después de retirar la bóveda colapsada detectamos una gran mancha de ceniza sobre el piso, la cual tenía entre 8 cm y 10 cm de espesor. En ella se encontraron algunos fragmentos de cerámica doméstica quemada y un perforador de hueso también quemado, una navajilla de obsidiana, así como pequeños fragmentos de hueso no trabajados. La ceniza hace suponer que se utilizó fuego controlado en el ritual, ya que a pesar de encontrarla en gran cantidad, las piedras circundantes no estaban quemadas, al igual que los fragmentos de hueso no trabajados.

El segundo depósito fue hallado al pie de la escalera norte, que encontramos desmantelada parcialmente; estaba formado por otra mancha de ceniza y dos elementos

arquitectónicos procedentes de otros edificios, ellos fueron un clavo de mascarón fragmentado, similar a los de las orejeras del Codz Pop, así como un sillar con decoraciones de plumas, cuya procedencia desconocemos, se recuperaron escasos fragmentos de cerámica doméstica.

Es posible que como parte de la destrucción intencional del edificio también se hayan arrancado los sillares del revestimiento de las escalinatas que se encuentran al norte y al oriente y que permitían la circulación entre los dos niveles del edificio ya que en la actualidad lucen incompletas, pero este no es un dato seguro.

En el Codz Pop, también en el Grupo Este, la evidencia ha sido abundante pues hemos localizado seis depósitos, que al igual que los anteriores estaban cubiertos por derrumbe. Se ubican en los accesos de los recintos 1, 13, y 26, así como en el interior de los recintos 13 y 14 y en la esquina suroeste del cuarto 14. Hemos explorado los depósitos que se encontraron en los accesos y todos tienen como común denominador la destrucción de las escalinatas, así como el remate del zócalo en el área que ocupa el acceso, esta destrucción fue cuidadosa, ya que desmantelaron las piedras de revestimiento de los peldaños, pero dejaron el núcleo, excepto en la escalera del cuarto 26, en donde retiraron solo las filas de listeles y dejaron los junquillos que la recubrían.

En el perímetro de las escalinatas y sobre lo que quedó de sus núcleos hallamos algunos elementos arquitectónicos que pertenecieron a otros edificios, tales como junquillos, piedras en forma de C (cuarto 13) y posibles colmillos de portadas zoomorfas (cuarto 1). Así mismo, enfrente de ambos recintos hallamos varios fragmentos de narices de mascarones, que evidentemente no pertenecieron a ese sector del edificio. Lo anterior, junto con la evidencia hallada por el Arqlgo. Ramón Carrasco en el interior de la tumba del cuarto 8, nos hace suponer que durante este ritual se mutilaron los apéndices nasales de varios mascarones. En todos los contextos hemos encontrado cenizas, pero en la mayoría de los casos el fuego no llegó a quemar las piedras del edificio.

En la esquina sureste del cuarto 14 hallamos también una capa de ceniza, y una gran cantidad de elementos de la ornamentación del edificio, tales como clavos de orejeras, ojos, y fragmentos de narices de mascarón. Todos estaban manchados de ceniza, pero no quemados. Se encontraron algunos fragmentos de cerámica doméstica, pero no formaron parte de la misma vasija. Este hallazgo refuerza la idea de que algunos elementos de la fachada fueron desmantelados o en el caso de las narices, fracturadas.

Sayil

En el año 2007, como parte de los trabajos de mantenimiento mayor realizados en la Ruta Puuc, impermeabilizamos el techo del segundo piso. El derrumbe del basamento del tercer piso yacía sobre la cubierta, por lo que fue necesario explorarlo y consolidar el basamento. Durante estos trabajos encontramos en la esquina noreste una acumulación de ceniza y tierra quemada entre la que había una gran cantidad de pequeños elemento circulares de estuco modelado, posiblemente representando cuentas de jade, así partes de esculturas antropomorfas, que evidentemente fueron depositadas allí. La cerámica era de carácter doméstico y no eran piezas completas.

Otro sector excavado en ese mismo año fue la esquina sureste de los niveles 1 y 2 formado por los cuarto 29-31 y 67. Los recintos estaban colapsados y el derrumbe de los sectores superiores del edificio había caído sobre ellos. Una vez que llegamos al acceso del recinto 67, formado por un pórtico columnado, notamos la presencia de huellas de fuego, que se extendían casi a todo lo largo del pórtico, cuyas piezas presentaban la típica caída ordenada ocasionada por una falla en el desplante. En este caso, acompañando la manipulación de fuego controlado notamos que algunos tamborcillos y listeles del zócalo fueron retirados cuidadosamente, destruyendo parcialmente el acceso. La cerámica fue escasa y no se menciona en el informe que estuviera quemada.

Labná

La información de Labná fue recuperada principalmente durante las temporadas 1991 y 1992, cuando se efectuó la restauración del primer nivel del Palacio. En ese entonces llamó nuestra atención que la escalera al segundo nivel que se encuentra en el Patio Este no estuviera completa y que incluso le faltara el núcleo de la parte superior, tampoco encontramos la escalinata del recinto central y la mayoría de las escalera de los otros cuartos no estaban completas, cómo no hallamos las piedras de recubrimiento consolidamos los núcleos y en algunas ocasiones les dimos forma de peldaños, pero sin colocar el revestimiento, por eso en la actualidad son claramente distinguibles. Una mirada detallada a las piedras cercanas a los accesos nos permite ver que algunos sillares están quemados, pero eso pudo ocurrir en épocas modernas, ya que no estuvieron cubiertas por derrumbe, pues muchos de los recintos permanecieron en pie hasta nuestros días.

En los informes no se reporta la presencia de evidencias de fuego y en los rincones formados por la unión del basamento y las escaleras encontramos los restos de lo que interpretamos como basureros, en donde hallamos fragmentos de cerámica y algunos elementos arquitectónicos del mismo edificio. Sin embargo, durante la restauración de la escalinata que se une con el Sacbé encontramos varias piedras de gran tamaño, que no pertenecen a ningún edificio conocido de Labná y no son típicas de la decoración Puuc, pues semejan grandes hojas, que a juzgar por su espiga, debieron ir colocadas en la parte inferior de un muro.

Hasta aquí hemos expuesto la información que hemos ido acumulando a lo largo de varios años; a diferencia de lo que sucede en la arqueología de las Tierras Bajas, en la región Puuc es poca la evidencia documentada sobre este tema, aunque en Yaxuná, han registrado evidencia abundante (Freidel, Schuler, y Cobos 1998).

Análisis comparativo de la evidencia

Un análisis comparativo entre los distintos contextos documentados en los sitios de la Ruta Puuc nos permiten establecer los siguientes patrones: 1) Todos ellos están en edificios que debieron ser los más importantes dentro de cada asentamiento; 2) En todos los casos hubo destrucción intencional de accesos, ya fueran escalinatas o entradas;[3] 3) Los restos materiales se encuentran en áreas de tránsito intenso, la mayoría de ellos en exteriores; 4) En los mejor documentados se encontraron evidencias de uso de fuego controlado, es posible que estas hayan estado presentes en todos los casos, pero hubo un error en el registro.

Los depósitos de la muestra difieren en: 1) la utilización de vasijas completas, algunas de ellas conteniendo entierros infantiles, esto solo ocurrió en la estructura 1A10 de Kabah; 2) la extracción de objetos que suponemos fueron depositados inicialmente como ofrendas de dedicación; 3) la destrucción parcial de fachadas; 4) la mutilación de elementos escultóricos de la fachada; 5) la colocación de elementos arquitectónicos de otros edificios.

Para tipificar los depósitos del Puuc usamos la taxonomía propuesta por Pagliaro, Garber, y Stanton (2003) para el Área Maya, quienes los clasifican en: 1) de consagración o dedicación; 2) de terminación reverencial; y 3) de terminación de desacralización. En la evidencia arqueológica, estos dos últimos presentan características similares, sin embargo difieren en el grado de la conducta destructiva que presentan, ya que los reverenciales no tienen la intención de profanar, en tanto que los de desacralización muestran una conducta devastadora.

Consideramos que las evidencias halladas en los sitios de Kabah, Sayil, y Labná son los restos de conductas rituales reverenciales y están reflejando prácticas muy semejantes en sitios distintos, pero que se encuentran dentro de la misma región. Por el lugar en donde hallamos los depósitos rituales podemos considerarlos como de abandono más que de terminación, pues como ya mencionamos, las evidencias fueron dejadas en áreas de tránsito intenso, las cuales no hubieran sobrevivido hasta nuestros días si los edificios hubieran seguido en uso.

En el caso de Uxmal, es posible que algunos de los eventos narrados sean el resultado de conductas reverenciales, pero sin duda el caso documentado en las esculturas del Cuadrángulo de los Pájaros difiere grandemente, pues además de mutilar las representaciones del gobernante, una de ellas fue brutalmente desfigurada y enterrada como un objeto inservible en el basamento de una unidad habitacional de tamaño modesto, con características constructivas y decorativas del estilo Chenes.

Rituales actuales

Indudablemente este tipo de contextos abren la posibilidad de interpretarlos de múltiples formas, pero en la medida en que tengamos una idea más completa de las prácticas rituales de los antiguos habitantes del Puuc, estaremos en mejores condiciones de reconocer sus manifestaciones en la evidencia arqueológica.

---

3 Así también logramos distinguir un patrón de destrucción, que consistió en quitar gran parte de las piedras de revestimiento de las escalinatas y en el caso de las entradas, desmantelar el remate del zócalo.

Para poder entender mejor este comportamiento, hemos buscado en la documentación etnográfica sobre la ritualidad maya actual, información que nos ayude a entenderla de mejor manera. En ese sentido, comulgamos con las ideas de Johana Broda, quien propone

...concebir las formas culturales indígenas no como continuidad directa e ininterrumpida del pasado prehispánico, ni como arcaísmos, sino visualizarlas en un proceso creativo de relaboración constante que, a la vez, se sustenta en raíces remotas. La cultura indígena debe estudiarse en su proceso de transformación continua, en el cual las antiguas estructuras y creencias se han articulado de manera dinámica y creativa, con nuevas formas y contenidos (Broda 2001:19).

Es así que nos dimos a la tarea de investigar cuáles son los rituales que aún se practican en la región, detectando que son 13 los más comunes, de entre ellos destacaremos cuatro que están relacionados con aspectos territoriales: dos de ellos se practican antes de ocupar un espacio, ya sea casa o milpa y son denominados *Ki'ilich Ka'ak Otoch* y *Loj* y otros dos cuando se da por terminada la ocupación y son *Jedz'lu'um* y *Makjol*. De acuerdo con el *J'men* Antonio Mukul, los rituales territoriales están íntimamente relacionados, pues son parte de un mismo ciclo, se pide permiso para ocupar un lugar y se dan las gracias cuando se tienen que retirar, esto hace que el lugar quede limpio de cualquier compromiso o si es un lugar sagrado continué con esta vocación.

Consideraciones finales

Como hemos visto, cada vez son más las evidencias de la ritualidad de los antiguos habitantes del Puuc, esta pequeña muestra nos indica que un mejor registro y exploración de los escenarios en donde se desarrollaban las complejas ceremonias que los mayas celebraban, nos conducirá a proponer mejores interpretaciones de los restos materiales, que en la mayoría de los casos hemos interpretado como huellas de acciones cotidianas y comunes.

La prolija actividad litúrgica de los mayas contemporáneos, plasmada en la practica de múltiples ceremonias nos permite vislumbrar la complejidad de la vida ritual prehispánica y si bien es cierto que muchos de los elementos importantes de estas acciones no dejan huellas que podamos obtener a través de los métodos tradicionales de la arqueología, cada vez contamos con otro tipo de estudios cómo los análisis químicos o polínicos, que permiten recuperar información sutil que permitirá armar las piezas de este complejo rompocabezas.

Referencias Citadas

Barrera Rubio Alfredo, y José Huchim Herrera
1990 *Restauración arquitectónica en Uxmal 1986-1987.* Latin American Archaeology Reports No. 1. University of Pittsburgh, Pittsburg.

Broda Johanna y Félix Báez-Jorge (Coordinadores)
2001 Introducción. En *Cosmovisión, ritual e identidad de los pueblos indígenas de México,* editado por Broda Johanna y Félix Báez-Jorge, pp. 15-43. Fondo de Cultura Económica, México, D.F.

Craig, Jessica H.
2005 Dedicación, terminación y perpetuación: un santuario Clásico Tardío en San Bartolo, Petén. En *XVIII Simposio de Investigaciones Arqueológicas en Guatemala 2004,* editado por Juan Pedro Laporte, Bárbara Arroyo, y Héctor Mejía, pp. 275-282. Museo Nacional de Arqueología y Etnología, Guatemala.

Farr, Olivia Navarro, y Ana Lucía Arroyave
2007 Un final macabro: La terminación ritual de la Estructura M13-1 de El Perú-*Waka'.* En *XX Simposio de Investigaciones Arqueológicas en Guatemala, 2006,* editado por Juan Pedro Laporte, Bárbara Arroyo, y Héctor Mejía, pp. 699-719. Museo Nacional de Arqueología y Etnología, Guatemala.

Farr, Olivia, Keith Eppich, y Ana Lucía Arroyave
2008 Ceremonias, conducta y sentido: Una exploración de los rituales de terminación y dedicación en las Estructuras M13-1 y N14-2 de El Perú-*Waka'.* En *XXI Simposio de Investigaciones Arqueológicas en Guatemala, 2007,* editado por Juan Pedro Laporte, Bárbara Arroyo y Héctor Mejía, pp.730-746. Museo Nacional de Arqueología y Etnología, Guatemala.

Freidel, David A., Charles K. Schuler, y Rafael Cobos Palma
1998 Termination Ritual Deposits at Yaxuna: Detecting the Historical in Archaeological Contexts. En *The Sowing and the Dawning: Termination, Dedication and Transformation in the Archaeological and Ethnographic Record of Mesoamerica,* editado por Shirley Boteler-Mock, pp. 135-144. University of New Mexico Press, Albuquerque.

Iglesias Ponce de León, Ma. Josefa, y Andrés Ciudad Ruiz
2009 Rituales del Clásico Terminal en Machaquilá, Petén, En *Península Vol. IV. Núm. 1. Primavera de 2009.* Universidad Complutense de Madrid.

Pagliaro, Jonathan B, James F. Garber, y Travis Stanton
2003 Evaluating the Archaeological Signatures of Maya Rituals and Conflict. En *Ancient Mesoamerican Warfare,* editado por M. Kathryn Brown y Travis Stanton, pp.75-89. Altamira Press, Walnut Creek, CA.

Pendergast, David M.
1998 Intercessions with the Gods: Caches and Their Significance at Altun Ha and Lamanai, Belize. En *The Sowing and the Dawning: Termination, Dedication and Transformation in the Archaeological and Ethnographic Record of Mesoamerica,* editado por Shirley Boteler-Mock, pp. 55-63. University of New Mexico Press, Albuquerque.

Toscano Hernández, Lourdes, Gustavo Novelo Rincón., y David Ortegón Zapata
2005 Rituales de abandono en la Estructura 1A10 de Kabah. Ponencia presentada en el Segundo Congreso Internacional de Cultura Maya, Mérida, Yucatán, del 13 al 19 de marzo.

Walker, Debra S.
1998 Smashed Pots and Shattered Dreams: The Material Evidence for an Early Classic Maya Site Termination at Cerros, Belize. En *The Sowing and the Dawning: Termination, Dedication and Transformation in the Archaeological and Ethnographic Record of Mesoamerica,* editado por Shirley Boteler-Mock, pp. 81-99. University of New Mexico Press, Albuquerque.

Archaeological Fieldwork in the Transitional Zone Between Puuc and Chenes (Campeche, Mexico)

Iken Paap

After the peak of settlement activity on the peninsula of Yucatán during the Late to Terminal Classic period (8th and 9th centuries A.D.), there was an abrupt end to all typical construction activities, followed by a change in the function and use of buildings, the introduction of new architectural concepts, and–eventually–the final abandonment of the settlements. Archaeological finds and features that indicate a drastic upheaval for the elites are found alongside evidence that suggests continuity in parts of the remaining, non-elite population. However, this continuity existed within radically changed sociocultural and environmental contexts. A major part of the discussion on these sudden changes focuses on the 'C-shaped' or 'L-shaped' structures, so named after their characteristic floor plans. These structures are deemed indicators for Epi- to Postclassic activities in the Puuc and neighboring regions. The preliminary results of recent excavations conducted by the Ibero-American Institute in Dzehkabtún (Campeche, Mexico) support the hypothesis that parts of the local population constructed and used the new building forms after the end of the Classic period.

El auge de las actividades durante el Clásico Tardío hasta el Clásico Terminal temprano (siglos VIII y IX d.C.) en muchos de los sitios en la península Yucatán fue seguido de un fin abrupto de toda construcción representativa. A continuación se puede observar una 'reutilización' de edificios abandonados, la erección de nuevas formas de edificios sencillos y –finalmente– el abandono definitivo de la mayoría de los asentamientos. Hallazgos arqueológicos que indican un cambio drástico para las élites se encuentran juntos con evidencias en favor de una continuidad en partes de la población local, non-élite. Sin embargo se trata de una continuidad bajo nuevas condiciones básicas socioculturales y ecológicas. Parte de esta discusión se centra en las llamadas 'estructuras en forma de C' o 'en forma de L', nombradas así por sus plantas características, que sirven como indicadores de actividades epi- y postclásicas para el Puuc y las regiones adyacentes. Los resultados preliminares de las recientes excavaciones del Instituto Ibero-Americano en Dzehkabtún (Campeche, México) apoyan la hipótesis de que partes de la población local construyeron y utilizaron las nuevas formas de construcción después del final del Clásico Maya.

In Dzehkabtún, a Maya site in the north of the Mexican state of Campeche (Figure 1), the Ibero-American Institute is conducting an archaeological research project on the sociopolitical context for the transition from the Late Classic to the Epiclassic period (A.D. 850-1100).[1] Through surface mapping and excavation, the Dzehkabtún Archaeological Project aims to examine the causes and consequences of change for the inhabitants of this settlement at the end of the Classic period, as well as their strategies for crisis management during the sociopolitical and ecologic upheaval that took place during that time. Additionally, we plan to explore the previously little-known archaeological transitional zone between the architectural style-regions of the Puuc and the Chenes in the northern half of present-day state of Campeche.

Dzehkabtún is located in the north of the municipality of Hopelchén, Campeche, on the lands of the now abandoned hacienda Holcatzín. The visible archaeological remains of the ancient settlement center lie on a terrain that slightly slopes to the southeast. The remains are dominated by two 16 and 14 meter high pyramids that are surrounded by an area of dense patio constructions of architecture mainly typical of the region. The whole settlement once covered an area of at least four square kilometers (Figure 2).

This architecture, as well as the known monuments and sculptures from Dzehkabtún, demonstrate that the site was occupied from the Middle Preclassic period (500-250 B.C.) to the Epiclassic or Postclassic (c. A.D. 1100) at the latest. The known architecture of the settlement center–once rich in vaulted buildings, elaborate façades, and sculptured monuments–combines features of the Classic Maya Puuc and Chenes architectural styles (Andrews 1985:31-34). A ceramic survey in the Chenes region revealed a striking accumulation of Terminal Classic materials for Dzehkabtún (Williams-Beck 1994:145-150), but neither the method nor the data source on which this survey is based have been published. During the 19th and 20th centuries, the 'palace' area of Dzehkabtún was severely damaged due to stone robbery (Figure 3). Apart from large quantities of plain stones for building or road construction, a large number of monuments have been removed from the site. Some of them can be found in museums and private collections worldwide (Grube 2009).

---

[1] The Dzehkabtún Archaeological Project (Terminal Classic and Postclassic in northern Campeche, Mexico: Continuities and Disruptions) has been funded by the German Research Foundation (DFG) since 2011. The project is carried out in cooperation with the Instituto Nacional de Antropología e Historia in Mexico. Work would be unthinkable without the support from the Mexican colleagues, in particular from the co-director of the project, Antonio Benavides Castillo. The website with up-to-date information on the project in Spanish and German is http://www.dzk-online.de.

Iken Paap – Ibero-American Institute (IAI) – Prussian Cultural Heritage Foundation, Berlin, Germany (paap@iai.spk-berlin.de).

Research History to 2007

Teobert Maler visited the 'ruined city of Dsekatun' on May 4, 1887. Most of his sketches, photographs, and descriptions are kept with his estate at the Ibero-American Institute in Berlin. Maler's documentation forms the basis for the study of the elite architecture of the archaeological site, since the remaining buildings have been severely damaged since his visit in 1887 (Maler 1997:97-99, Tables 35-39).

Until the 1980s, Dzehkabtún was visited by various archaeologists, including Alberto Ruz Lhuiller (1945:38-41), H. E. D. Pollock (1970:40-41), George F. Andrews (1985:31-36), Nicholas Dunning (1987), and Dominique Michelet with Pierre Becquelin (2001:224). They published descriptions of individual buildings and monuments from the settlement center, but did not examine or record the site as a whole. Already in the 1980s, Andrews (1985:35) emphasized the key role of Dzehkabtún for the understanding of the temporal and spatial relations between the Puuc and Chenes architectural spheres. Nevertheless, Dzehkabtún remained unstudied until the author visited the site in 2007.

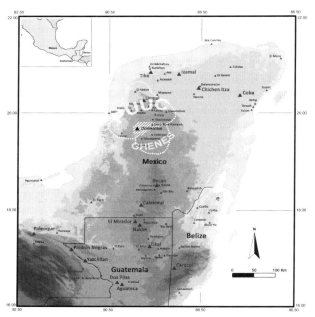

FIGURE 1. YUCATÁN PENINSULA. THE TRANSITIONAL ZONE BETWEEN PUUC AND CHENES ARCHITECTURAL STYLE PROVINCES IS MARKED WITH HATCHED LINES (BASED ON BROWN AND WITSCHEY [2008:MAP 7] AND GENDROP [1988:6, FIG. 9]).

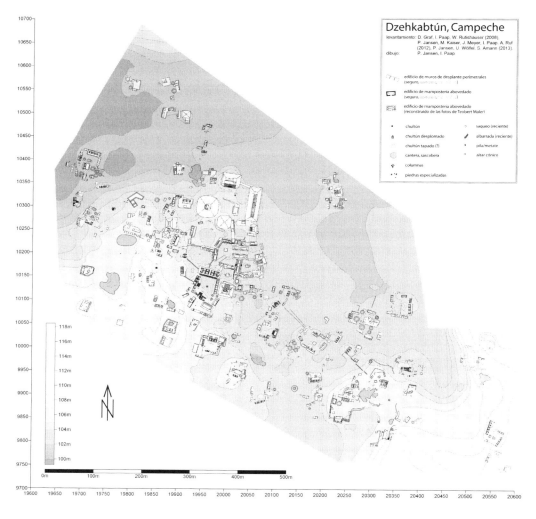

FIGURE 2. DZEHKABTÚN. 2D MAP, JANUARY 2014. ELABORATION BY PHILIPP SEBASTIAN JANSEN AND IKEN PAAP.

a

b

FIGURE 3 A-B. SOUTHWEST CORNER OF THE PALACE PATIO.
(A) PHOTOGRAPH FROM TEOBERT MALER IN 1887 (LEGACY TEOBERT
MALER, IBERO-AMERICAN INSTITUTE, BERLIN); (B) THE SAME VIEW
IN 2012. PHOTOGRAPH BY IKEN PAAP.

Research Questions

In addition to a notable corpus of late sculptures and monuments (Grube 2009), large-scale construction activities from the Epiclassic or Postclassic periods have been documented in Dzehkabtún since 2008. Documentation shows that whole patio groups in the center of the settlement seem to have been transformed and covered with the characteristic 'C-shaped' or 'L-shaped' buildings, often by reusing older stones that were removed from collapsed Classic buildings (Paap 2008). If this is to be interpreted as a sign of a post-monumental peak at this settlement, questions arise as to the processes at the end of the Classic period in Dzehkabtún and the regional integration of this phenomenon.

While the so-called 'collapse' in the southern Maya lowlands (the Mexican and Guatemalan Petén) is relatively well understood, we still know little about the fundamental political and cultural changes in the transition from Classic to Postclassic on the central and northern Yucatán Peninsula. Although, the question of the impact of these changes on the lives of the non-elite inhabitants of the Maya cities of Yucatán has been raised as an important research issue since the late 1990s, only some isolated studies on this topic have so far been carried out. After the peak of settlement activities during the Late Classic

period (c. A.D. 600-900) archaeologists observed a sudden end of all elite construction activities, a subsequent change in the use of function of existing buildings as well as the construction of new building forms, followed by the final abandonment of the settlements during the Terminal and Epiclassic periods (c. A.D. 900-1100) (Prem 2006; Reindel 2003).

A major part of the discussion on this topic are the so-called 'C-shaped' or 'L-shaped' structures, which are seen as indicators for Epi- and Postclassic activities in the Puuc and adjacent regions (Shaw and Johnstone 2006:268-269). Buildings of this type–named after their C-shaped or L-shaped floor plans – were usually built on low platforms. Often a long banquette ran along the inside of their three low walls (the fourth side was left open). The upper walls and roofs were made of perishable materials. We prefer an alternative term for this building type, namely a bench-type building. This term is more variable in relation to the possible layout of these buildings, and refers appropriately to their characteristic banquette.

Bench-type buildings are often found arranged in groups in the central areas of the settlements, where they were built inside existing courtyards or in open spaces, interfering with their original conception of space. The reuse of smooth and sculptured façade elements (e.g. *columnillas* and *tamborcillos*) from older buildings to shape the platform edges and the inner sides of the banquettes is characteristic of this building type.

Bench-type buildings were first recognized as an independent and chronologically relevant feature of architectural typology during the 1990s (Bey, Hanson, and Ringle 1997:239). Since then, they have been recognized and, in part, consolidated at several sites, for example, at Uxmal (Barrera and Huchím 1989; Huchim and García 2000:Lam. 6-10), Sayil (Dunning 1992:109; Tourtellot and Sabloff 1994:16), Huntichmul (personal communication, Rebeca E. Hill, Tulane University, October 2010), Labná (Gallareta 2003:127) and Xkipché (Paap 2006, 2010).

A comprehensive study on the occurrence and variability of this building type as well as an attempt to its classification–as Bey and May (2014) undertook it for the related *popol nah* buildings–is still pending. Until twenty years ago, bench-type buildings were often not even considered when mapping ancient Maya sites (for example, in Edzná, on the Acropolis at the foot of the main pyramid (Andrews 1984:Map 3).

Interpretations of the function of bench-type buildings differ. Archaeologists at first saw no reason to interpret them differently from the Classic residential platforms (Barrera and Huchím 1989:32-37, figs. 30-36; Huchím and García 2000:139) but later on, interpretations as market places or meeting and reception rooms have been proposed (Tourtellot and Sabloff 1994:88). However, these interpretations were based on surface mappings and not on excavations. As with Tourtellot, Sabloff, and

Carmean (1992:97), the underlying conception was that of a hiatus at the end of the Classic period with a subsequent Postclassic occupation by conquering and/or immigrating Maya under Toltec influence from the Gulf Coast region. This model would imply an interpretation of the bench-type buildings as an expression of cultural discontinuity, a fact that should be reflected in archaeological materials associated with the buildings.

Bench-Type Buildings at Xkipché (Yucatán)

At Xkipché, some nine kilometers southwest of Uxmal, six of these buildings (B23-29) were scientifically excavated in 2002 within the framework of the Xkipché Archaeological Project under the direction of Hanns J. Prem (Paap 2006, 2010:73-81). B23-29 belong to a group of nine buildings of this type, situated in the northwest of the main pyramid of Xkipché (Figure 4).

Stratigraphical analysis confirms the assumption of the late chronological position of the Xkipché bench-type buildings. They form the end of a long succession of construction phases (see Figures 5-7) in this area. After several graves that had been dug into the virgin soil, a large platform was erected with at least one building on top. A nearby cistern (chultún Ch23) ensured water supply. Later this construction was demolished and it appears that at least two low rectangular platforms were erected in its place. Finally, several rectangular elongated platforms were built above the already existing structures, with narrow structures in two parallel rows of three or four buildings– bench-type buildings B23-29. Chultún Ch23 had been left open and seemed to have still been accessible. The same was the case for chultunes Ch31, Ch32, and Ch92 in the neighborhood. Various modifications at the platforms indicate that they were in use over a prolonged period; however, absolute dating so far has not been possible, due to the destruction of the remains by milpa farming.

Although the excavated bench-type buildings differ in the type of architecture from Classic buildings, they follow the orientation and spatial layout of the previous buildings. The fact that they were placed directly on the exposed and well-preserved stucco floor of phases 2 and 3 makes a longer interruption of activities in this area unlikely.

The amount of ceramic debris, silex, and obsidian around the platforms was considerable; for the last two phases covering the erection and use of the bench-type buildings we counted 43,847 sherds that are mostly debris from the local tradition (Cehpech). Contrary to earlier statements (Prem 2003:296), several cisterns (chultunes) have been registered in the immediate vicinity of the platforms as well as the directly associated metates. All this reflects the usual scope of features and finds usually encountered in excavations of household platforms and supports an interpretation of these special buildings as habitational.

Nevertheless, although the results from Ek' Balam (Bey, Hanson, and Ringle 1997) already anticipated the Xkipché

FIGURE 4. XKIPCHÉ. MAP OF THE BENCH-TYPE BUILDING GROUP B23-29 (PAAP 2006:FIG. 4).

findings, we had expected to encounter some more explicit friction or discontinuity in the ceramic repertoire starting after the second construction phase. However, the ceramic and lithic features contrarily support a strong continuity from Late Classic times into the latest levels (Figure 7). Pottery of clear 'outside' Postclassic connotation such as Dzibiac, Dzitas, or Mama ceramic groups do only occur in very small quantities and directly on the surface. For Xkipché we therefore assume a continuity of parts of the local population that inhabited the bench-type buildings, even though the specific reasons for this are still poorly understood. Nor is it clear whether the conclusions from the Xkipché materials may be applied to the entire Puuc or even beyond this region.

The assumption of a population-continuity from Classic to Epiclassic times in northern Yucatán is consistent with the earlier results from Ek' Balam (Bey, Hanson, and Ringle 1997). It is basically supported by analysis of surface pottery at other sites such as Nohcacab (Shaw and Johnstone 2006) or Uxmal, where the ceramic materials, which have been unearthed in the context of consolidation works, were summarily counted and analyzed (Barrera Rubio 2003:23).

The results of the important excavations in the bench-type buildings of the Grupo Chanchich at Huntichmul (northern Campeche) in 2009 and 2010 within the framework of the Labná-Kiuic Regional Archaeology Project have so far not been published.

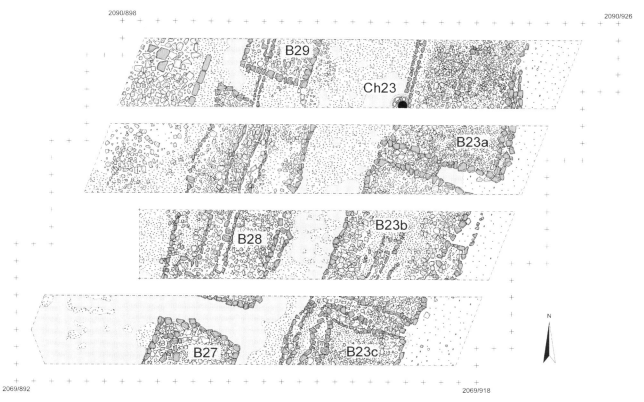

FIGURE 5. XKIPCHÉ. PLANUM OF B23-29, PHASES 4 TO 6 [SEE FIGURES 6 AND 7] (PAAP 2006:FIG. 5).

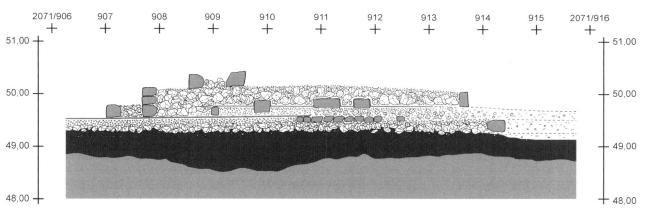

FIGURE 6. XKIPCHÉ. SCHEMATIC PROFILE OF BENCH-TYPE BUILDING B23C, AS EXAMPLE FOR THE B23-29 GROUP (PAAP 2006:FIG. 9).

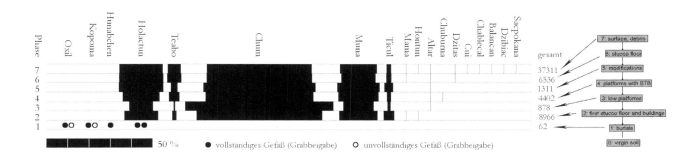

FIGURE 7. XKIPCHÉ. B23-29: LEFT, NUMBER OF CERAMIC SHERDS IN %; RIGHT, ASSOCIATED CONSTRUCTION PHASES (BASED ON PAAP 2006:FIGS. 6 AND 12).

Dzehkabtún: Survey and Mapping

Currently we have completed 40 hectares of surface mapping representing about 10% of the total settlement area. In addition to general and detailed 2D maps, a 3D virtual model was developed to analyze and represent the settlement in its spatial dimension. This includes a cautious virtual reconstruction based on the data from surface surveys and excavation.

The scientific quality and validity of a 3D reconstruction in archaeology depends mainly on the density and on the quality of the available data. Begand (2008) discussed in detail the opportunities and risks of virtual 3D reconstructions and alluded to the threat for scientific validity posed by a speculative database in favor of handsome and attractive models. As in the case of Dzehkabtún, only a very small amount of buildings have so far been excavated, and the majority of the data

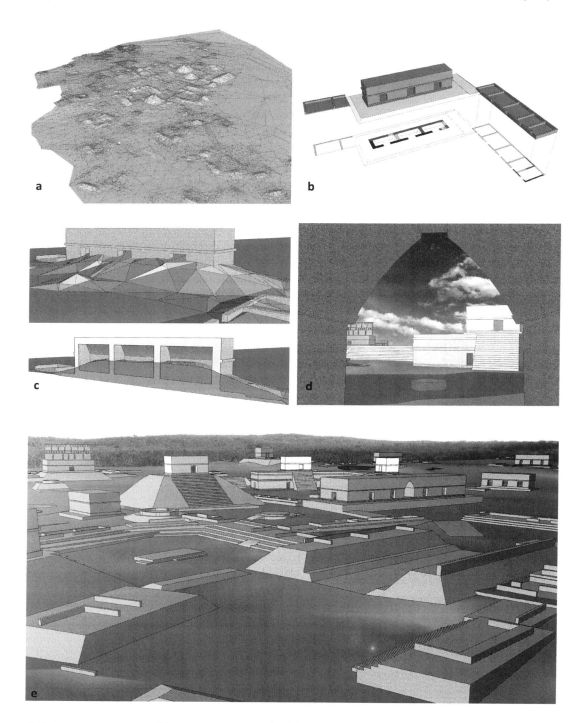

FIGURE 8. MAKING OF THE VIRTUAL 3D MODEL OF DZEHKABTÚN: (A) MESHED ELEVATION POINTS; (B) FLOOR PLAN WITH THE STATE OF PRESERVATION MARKED BY DIFFERENT LEVELS OF GRAY AND SUPERIMPOSED RECONSTRUCTION; (C) CALCULATION OF BUILDINGS' HEIGHT FROM THE GROUND FLOOR AND THE VOLUME OF THE DEBRIS FROM THE COLLAPSED STRUCTURE; (D) RECONSTRUCTED VIEW AT THE PALACE'S SOUTH WING; (E) DETAIL OF THE MODEL, LOOKING TO THE SOUTHWEST. ELABORATION BY PHILLIP SEBASTIAN JANSEN.

have been collected during surveys and mappings of the visible architectural remains on the surface. The risk of misinterpretations from data of this kind was demonstrated impressively by Arnauld, Becquelin, and Michelet in 1989.

Despite the known risks, we do not want to forego the advantages of a virtual reconstruction. We therefore try to make clear and visible the quality of the data in the model itself and simultaneously to achieve an aesthetic result, to allow non-experts access to the archeology of this Maya settlement (Jansen and Paap 2014).

The database of the virtual model of Dzehkabtún is formed by a digital terrain model (DTM), developed from a grid of geodetic points from the surface mapping (Figure 8). On this terrain model, the floor plans of the building were superimposed and reconstructed with the software Google SketchUp from Trimble. This step is based on a detailed 2D map of the site, with all architectural remains marked from light gray (poor preservation, tentative reconstruction) to black (good preservation, confident reconstruction), following the results of our surveys and mappings.

Due to the quality of the available data, the virtual reconstruction in its current version does not take into account a possible time sequence of buildings but rather summarizes all recorded architectural remains in only one model. A detailed reconstruction of individual façades as well as the design of open spaces between buildings was omitted. Both will be gradually completed once we have data from further excavations.

The scientific standards in Dzehkabtún, and our capacities of technical implementation, make the virtual model based on the current state of research look somewhat 'sober' and less detailed than do the results of comparable current visualization projects (Schwerin et al. 2013).

Notwithstanding the aforementioned knowledge gaps, such a virtual model supports the analysis of the settlement structure and internal organization. It also helps to convey a more vivid impression to the wider public than using two-dimensional maps, sectional drawings, and scientific reports.

Excavation

In 2008, we were able to survey the massive and large-scale construction activities in the center of the settlement that were stylistically assigned to its post-monumental occupation (Figure 9). Whole patio groups seem to have been overlaid with bench-type buildings, often by reusing older façade stones. Differences in the design and conception of space to the investigated bench-type buildings in the Puuc–as in Xkipché or in Uxmal–are obvious. In the center of Dzehkabtún three bench-type buildings, parts of the ball court, and a round platform have been excavated in addition to several stratigraphic test pits. In the following section, we briefly present two of these excavations.

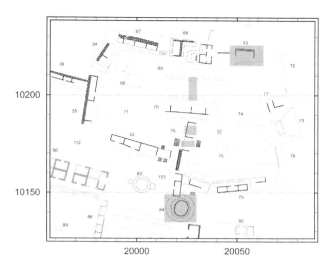

FIGURE 9. CENTRAL PART OF DZEHKABTÚN (DETAIL WITH BALL COURT) WITH REMODELED PATIO GROUPS. BENCH-TYPE BUILDINGS AND LATE ROUND STRUCTURES ARE MARKED IN BLACK; 2013 AND 2014 EXCAVATION AREAS HIGHLIGHTED IN GRAY (GRID: 50 M).

Platform 84

Circular Platform 84 has a diameter of 13 meters and a height of about 2.10 meters (Figure 10). With regard to its location and type of construction it corresponds to a Postclassic platform from Edzná, excavated in 2011 (Estructura 425, Benavides Castillo 2014:170-173) and a similar one from Uxmal, excavated in 1992 (Kowalski et al. 1996). Round, high platforms of this type are generally addressed as a late introduction to peninsular Maya architecture (Benavides and Paap 2016; Kowalski et al. 1996:281).

The remains of the last phase of occupation of Platform 84 in Dzehkabtún were completely excavated in 2013, and a stratigraphic trench of 9 square meters has been dug from the surface down to the natural soil.

In terms of architectural stratigraphy, this platform is clearly a post-monumental construction. It was built directly above the platform edges of adjacent Late Classic buildings. Beneath its northern edge, we found the remains of what stylistically might be an Early Classic building.

The structure could have been reconstructed as rising in three concentric steps to the upper surface that was accessible via a broad staircase on its west side. Its surface was originally covered by a stucco floor and was enclosed by a low circular wall, open towards the stairway. High quality carved façade stones from earlier buildings were reused for the first stage of the platform and for the stairs. The two upper levels and the wall on top had been built from quarry stones and covered with a thick layer of stucco. Unlike in Edzná, we have not been able to identify further remains of buildings on the surface of the platform. No offerings were encountered during the excavation.

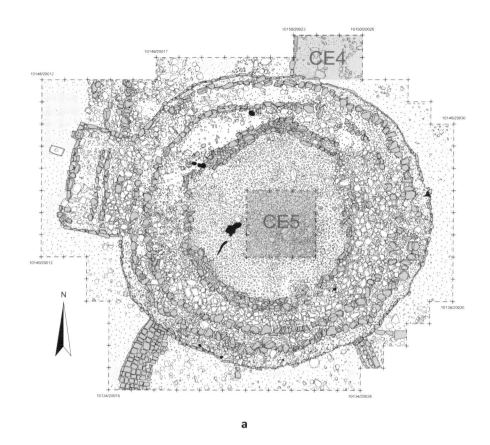

a

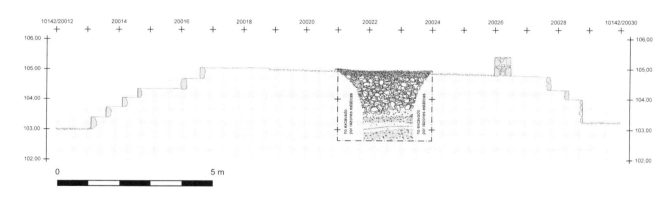

b

FIGURE 10 A-B. PLATFORM 84. (A) SURFACE OF THE LAST PHASE OF OCCUPATION OF THE BUILDING; (B) SCHEMATIC CROSS SECTION WITH THE NORTHERN PROFILE OF THE STRATIGRAPHIC TRENCH INSCRIBED. FOR STATIC REASONS IT WAS REDUCED FROM A SURFACE OF 3 M X 3 M TO 2 M X 2 M AT THE BOTTOM.

The analysis of the ceramic and lithic finds has currently not been completed. However, it is already clear that the platform fill–unlike in the case of structure 425 in Edzná–contained mainly decontextualized Late and Terminal Classic materials. We noted a remarkably large number of obsidian blades and imported pottery from the Petén, which are both indicators for long distance connections during the Classic. Postclassic diagnostic archaeological materials have been found only in very small quantities on the surface. No waste depositions were detected in the immediate vicinity of the platform. The shape of the building and the associated findings clearly indicate a representative or religious function of this platform, without permitting a more detailed statement.

Building 76

Building 76 was erected on top of a 2.30 meters high platform located between two courtyards. It is a bench type building, characteristic of Dzehkabtún, with a series of

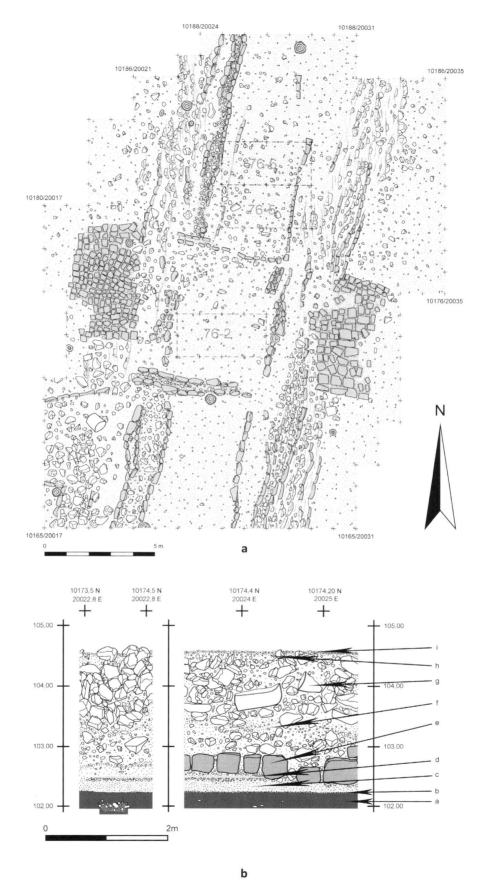

FIGURE 11 A-B. BUILDING 76. (A) SURFACE OF THE LAST PHASE OF OCCUPATION OF THE BENCH-TYPE BUILDING; (B) EASTERN AND NORTHERN PROFILE OF TRENCH 76-2 IN THE CENTRAL ROOM OF THE BUILDING.

rooms formed by low foundation walls and wide banquets along the back wall (Figure 11a). Stairs and ramps made from recycled older façade stones on both long sides of the platform lead down to the ground level of the adjacent patios.

Directly on the surface of the former building (Figure 11b [h, i], we found a few sherds clearly identifiable as Postclassic. In the underlying platform, the filling material was obviously shifted from a Late Classic context (Figure 11b [f]). In addition to ceramics, also spolia (e.g., fragments of columns and two capitals) and a remarkable amount of obsidian blades were found in the platform filling. Remains of an Early Classic substructure (Figure 11b [e]) with an associated floor (Figure 11b [d]) and its *ch'ich* base (Figure 11b [c]) have been excavated at the base of the platform. About 30 centimeters deeper another eroded extensive floor (Figure 11b [b]) covered a level (Figure 11b [a]) with Preclassic ceramics and remains of two stone-covered fireplaces.

Although, the building seems to have been in use for some years (in one of the rooms there were two floors constructed on top of each other), neither a significant Postclassic component nor a clear break with the Late Classic can so far be detected in the associated archaeological materials, as the architecture of the building and the stratigraphic features might suggest. This confirms the results from Xkipché (see above) and from other sites in the northern lowland that–at least outside the major centers–changes in sociopolitical organization that are manifest in a preference for new architectural forms must have been based in the local population. This is also confirmed by the results from the excavation of Platform 84.

Preliminary Results

In this article, we only presented two excavations from Dzehkabtún. Nevertheless, the results are substantially consistent with the results from other excavated areas within and outside the center of the settlement:

- Dzehkabtún was already extensively inhabited during the Late Preclassic period. Some of the 'megalithic style' buildings in the center date back to the Middle Preclassic. There are ceramic finds from the Early Preclassic, but no associated architecture could be detected so far.

- At the latest from the Late Classic, Dzehkabtún was involved in the long-distance trade networks of the Yucatán Peninsula, with the Petén (ceramics) and the present-day Guatemalan Highlands (obsidian).

- According to the current results, it can be assumed that a part of the resident population inhabiting the site during the Classic is responsible for the massive overbuilding of large parts of the center in the Terminal or Epiclassic. This should be examined in the next excavation campaigns in residential buildings near the center and in the periphery of the settlement.

References Cited

Andrews, George F.
  1984 *Edzna, Campeche, Mexico. Settlement patterns and monumental architecture; Summer Research Project, University of Oregon, Eugene*. Reprint. Foundation for Latin American Anthropological Research, Culver City.
  1985 Chenes-Puuc architecture: Chronology and cultural interaction. In *Arquitectura y arqueología: metodologías en la cronología de Yucatán = Architecture and archaeology: Methodological approaches in Yucatan chronology. Simposio organizado por George F. Andrews y Paul Gendrop, bajo el patrocinio de CEMCA y de la Federación de Alianzas FrancoMexicanas en la ciudad de México, del 28 al 29 de junio de 1984*, edited by George F. Andrews and Paul Gendrop, pp. 10-39. Centre d'Études Mexicaines et Centraméricaines, México, D.F.

Arnauld, Marie-Charlotte, Pierre Becquelin, and Dominique Michelet
  1989 Fiabilidad de las observaciones de superficie en un sector del Puuc occidental? In *Memorias del Segundo Coloquio Internacional de Mayistas*, Vol. 1., edited by Alain Breton, pp. 377-389. Universidad Nacional Autónoma de México, Instituto de Investigaciones Filológicas, México, D.F.

Barrera Rubio, Alfredo
  2003 La arqueología en Yucatán en la última década del siglo XX. In *Escondido en la selva: arqueología en el norte de Yucatán*, edited by Hanns J. Prem, pp. 15-35. Instituto Nacional de Antropología e Historia/Universität Bonn, México D.F./Bonn.

Barrera Rubio, Alfredo and José Huchim Herrera
  1989 Exploraciones recientes en Uxmal (1986-1987). In *Memorias del Segundo Coloquio Internacional de Mayistas*. Vol. 1, edited by Alain Breton, pp. 265-286. Universidad Nacional Autónoma de México, Instituto de Investigaciones Filológicas, México, D.F.

Begand, Christian
  2008 *Virtuelle Gebäuderekonstruktionen. Virtuelle Archäologie: Anwendung und Erstellung von 3D-Rekonstruktionen historischer Gebäude*. VDM Verlag Dr. Müller, Saarbrücken.

Benavides Castillo, Antonio
  2014 *La arquitectura precolombina de Edzná, Campeche, México*. Colección Rafael Rodríguez Barrera. Campeche: Gobierno Municipal.

Benavides Castillo, Antonio and Iken Paap
  2016 Dzehkabtún y Edzná, Campeche: edificios de planta circular. *Mexicon* 37(2):29-33.

Bey, George J., III, and Rossana May Ciau
  2014 The Role and Realities of Popol Nahs in Northern Maya Archaeology. In *The Maya and their Central American Neighbors. Settlement Patterns, Architecture, Hieroglyphic Texts, and Ceramics*, edited by Geoffrey E. Braswell, pp. 335-355. Routledge/Taylor & Francis, London/New York.

Bey, George J., III, Craig A. Hanson, and William M. Ringle
  1997 Classic to Postclassic at Ek Balam, Yucatan: Architectural and Ceramic Evidence for Defining the Transition. *Latin American Antiquity* 8(3):237-254.

Brown, Clifford T. and Walter R. T. Witschey

2008 *The Electronic Atlas of Ancient Maya Sites*. Electronic document, http://mayagis.smv.org, accessed August 28, 2014.

Dunning, Nicholas P.
1987 Monuments in Yucatan and Campeche. *Mexicon* 9:99.
1992 *Lords of the Hills: Ancient Maya Settlement in the Puuc Region, Yucatán, Mexico*. Monographs in World Archaeology Vol. 15. Prehistory Press, Madison.

Gallareta Negrón, Tomás
2003 Análisis de un centro Puuc: el caso de Labná. In *Escondido en la selva: arqueología en el norte de Yucatán*, edited by Hanns J. Prem, pp. 119-136. Instituto Nacional de Antropologia e Historia/Universität Bonn, México D.F./Bonn.

Gendrop, Paul
1988 *Rio Bec, Chenes, and Puuc styles inMaya architecture*. Labyrinthos, Lancaster.

Grube, Nikolai
2009 Los monumentos esculpidos de Dzehkabtun, Campeche: epigrafía e iconografía. *Los investigadores de la cultura maya* 18(2):27-39.

Huchím Herrera, José and Cesar García Ayala
2000 La arquitectura que denota una ocupación tardía en Uxmal, Yuc. *Los investigadores de la cultura maya* 8(1):138-154.

Jansen, Philipp Sebastian and Iken Paap
2014 Dzehkabtún 3D – levantamiento topográfico y reconstrucción virtual de un sitio Maya. *Los investigadores de la cultura maya* 22, in press.

Kowalski, Jeff Karl, Alfredo Barrera Rubio, Heber Ojeda Más, and José Huchim Herrera
1996 Archaeological Excavations of a Round Temple at Uxmal: Summary Discussion and Implications for Northern Maya Culture History. In *Eighth Palenque Round Table, 1993*, edited by Martha J. Macri and Jan McHargue, pp. 281-296. Pre-Columbian Art Research Institute, San Francisco.

Maler, Teobert
1997 *Peninsula Yucatán*, Monumenta Americana Vol. 5, edited by Hanns J. Prem. Berlin: Gebr. Mann Verlag

Michelet, Dominique and Becquelin, Pierre
2001 De Río Bec a Dzibilchaltún. Interrogaciones acerca de la ciudad maya clásica desde la perspectiva del Yucatán central y septentrional. In *Reconstruyendo la ciudad maya. El urbanismo en las sociedades antiguas*. Publicaciones de la S.E.E.M. Vol. 6, edited by Andrés Ciudad Ruiz, María Josefa Iglesias Ponce de León, and María del Carmen Martínez Martínez, pp. 211-251. Sociedad Española de Estudios Mayas, Madrid.

Paap, Iken
2006 *El Epiclásico en el noroeste de Yucatán. Informe de las temporadas 2002, 2003, 2004 en Xkipché (Yucatán, Mexico)*. Report submited to the Consejo de Arqueología. Universidad de Bonn.
2008 Reconocimiento y mapeo de Dzehkabtún (Municipio de Hopelchén, Campeche). *Los Investigadores de la Cultura Maya* 17(2):176-191.
2010 Die Ausgrabungen der Universität Bonn in Xkipché, Yucatán, 2002-2004. In *Götter, Gräber und Globalisierung: Indianisches Leben in Mesoamerika. 40 Jahre Alt- und Mesoamerikanistik an der Universität Hamburg*, edited by Lars Frühsorge, Armin Hinz, Annette I. Kern, and Ulrich Wölfel, pp. 69-90. Kovač, Hamburg.
2011 Erinnern und Vergessen im archäologischen Befund: Xkipché. In *Erinnerungsorte in Mesoamerika: Beiträge der IX. Mesoamerikanistik-Tagung 03.-05. Februar*

2006, Universität Hamburg, edited by Lars Frühsorge, Armin Hinz, Jessica N. Jacob, Annette I. Kern, and Ulrich Wölfel, pp. 69-86. Shaker, Aachen.

Pollock, Harry E. D.
1970 Architectural notes on some Chenes ruins. In *Monographs and Papers in Maya Archaeology*. Papers of the Peabody Museum of Archaeology and Ethnology, Harvard University, Vol. 61, edited by William R. Bullard, pp. 1-87. Peabody Museum, Cambridge, Mass.

Prem, Hanns J.
2003 *Xkipché: una ciudad Maya clásica en el corazón del Puuc. Vol. 1: El asentamiento*. Universität Bonn/Instituto Nacional de Antropología e Historia, Bonn/México D.F.
2006 ¿A dónde se habrán ido todas las piedras? La profanación de edificios del Clásico Terminal. In *Los Mayas de ayer y hoy: memorias del Primer Congreso Internacional de Cultura Maya*, edited by Alfredo Barrera Rubio and Ruth Gubler, pp. 250-274. Instituto de Cultura de Yucatán/Instituto Nacional de Antropología e Historia, Mérida.

Reindel, Markus
2003 El apogeo de la arquitectura Puuc: evolución de una cultura del Clásico Tardío en el norte del área Maya. In *Escondido en la selva: arqueología en el norte de Yucatán*, edited by Hanns J. Prem, pp. 79-96. Instituto Nacional de Antropología e Historia/Universität Bonn, México D.F./Bonn.

Ruz Lhuillier, Alberto
1945 *Campeche en la arqueología maya*. Acta Antropológica Vol. 1. Instituto Nacional de Antropología e Historia, México, D.F.

Schwerin, Jennifer von, Heather Richards-Rissetto, Fabio Remondino, Giorgio Agugiaro, and Gabrio Girardi
2013 The MayaArch3D project. A 3D WebGIS for analyzing ancient architecture and landscapes. *Literary and Linguistic Computing* 28(4):736-753.

Shaw, Justine M. and Dave Johnstone
2006 El papel de la arquitectura postmonumental en el norte de Yucatán. *Los investigadores de la cultura maya* 14(1):267-278.

Szymański, Jan
2010 Round Structures in Pre-Columbian Maya Architecture. *Contributions in New World Archaeology* NS:35-71.

Tourtellot, Gair and Jeremy A. Sabloff
1994 Community structure at Sayil: A case study of Puuc settlement. In *Hidden Among the Hills: Maya Archaeology of the Northwest Yucatan Peninsula, First Maler Symposium, Bonn 1989*. Acta Mesoamericana, Vol. 7. edited by Hanns J. Prem, pp. 71-92. Von Flemming, Möckmühl.

Tourtellot, Gair, Jeremy A. Sabloff, and Kelli Carmean
1992 'Will the Real Elites Please Stand Up?' An Archaeological Assessment of Maya Elite Behavior in the Terminal Classic Period. In *Mesoamerican Elites: An Archaeological Assessment*, edited by Diane Z. Chase and Arlen F. Chase, pp. 80-98. University of Oklahoma Press, Norman.

Williams-Beck, Lorraine A.
1994 The Chenes Ceramic Sequence: Temporal, Typological, and Cultural Relations within a Regional Framework. In *Hidden Among the Hills: Maya Archaeology of the Northwest Yucatan Peninsula, First Maler Symposium, Bonn*. Acta Mesoamericana 7, edited by Hanns J. Prem, pp. 133-163. Von Fleming, Möckmühl.

Scan the QR code to learn more about the
Dzehkabtún Archaeological Project:

Part II: Art and Writing

The Nunnery Quadrangle at Uxmal: Creation, Captive Sacrifice, Ritual, and Political Authority in a Puuc Maya Palace Complex

Jeff Karl Kowalski

This chapter examines the individual meanings and broader ideological significance of a selection of iconographic motifs of the Nunnery Quadrangle at Uxmal, Yucatán. The quadrangle's sculptural program interweaves references to cosmic creation, ancestral sources of political authority, and more contemporaneous ritual performances and historical events. Motifs associated with originary time include the Feathered Serpents and Pawahtun figures on the West Building. Other façade motifs to more current, though not necessarily more secular, historical events, including ceremonies involving the display of captives, and the performance of a type of torch sacrifice in connection with rituals of accession and/or cyclical renewal of time and agricultural fertility. Such iconography, combined with the quadrangle's monumental scale, superlative stonework, and restricted access, demonstrate that the quadrangle was designed to identify Uxmal as a central place and paramount political capital where the exalted social status of its king, Chan Chahk K'ak'nal Ajaw, and other members of the elite, was affirmed through imagery and social practice.

Este capítulo examina los significados individuales y la significación ideológica más amplia de una selección de motivos iconográficos del Cuadrángulo de las Monjas de Uxmal, Yucatán. La programa escultórico del cuadrángulo entreteje referencias a la creación cósmica, fuentes ancestrales de la autoridad política y actuaciones rituales más contemporáneas y acontecimientos históricos. Motivos relacionados con el tiempo originario incluyen las serpientes emplumadas y Pawahtunes en el edificio oeste. Otros motivos de fachada refieren a eventos históricos más corriente, aunque no necesariamente más secular, incluyendo las ceremonias que implican la presentación de cautivos, y la práctica de un tipo de sacrificio antorcha en relación con los rituales de accesso al trono y/o renovación cíclica del tiempo y la fertilidad agrícola. Dicha iconografía, combinado con la escala del cuadrángulo monumental, mampostería superlativo, y acceso restringido, demuestran que el cuadrángulo fue diseñado para identificar Uxmal como un lugar central y capital político primordial donde el estatus social de su analtecido rey, Chan Chahk K'ak'nal Ajaw, y otros miembros de la elite, se afirmaron a través de imágenes y práctica social.

In this study, I examine selected imagery of the Nunnery Quadrangle (Figure 1), the imposing 'palace' group constructed between about A.D. 895 and 907 during the reign of the ruler Chan Chak K'ak'nal Ajaw ('Lord Chaak'), for whom it may have functioned as an administrative complex and set of council houses, as William Ringle has suggested, serving as a seat of government for a regional state dominated by Uxmal (Figure 2) (Kowalski and Dunning 1999; Kowalski 2003:218-220; Ringle 2012; Ringle and Bey 1999:281-284; Schele and Mathews 1998:259-260). This study is a preliminary report that forms part of a wider examination of the form, function, and meaning of the Nunnery Quadrangle, with special emphasis on the significance of its sculptural facades. To interpret the iconography of the facades I have developed a working conceptual model that focuses on the following themes: (1) origins and creation; (2) ancestral sources of authority and power; and (3) recent events in ritualized frameworks. This paper will outline some aspects of imagery associated with creation mythology, and then discuss imagery related to warfare, captive display, and sacrificial ritual in greater detail.

Claims to political authority, among the Maya kings as for other Mesoamerican rulers, were grounded in and considered part of an existential continuum with acts of creation, sources of supernatural and ancestral power, and periodic ritual performance considered to maintain links between personified forces of nature, the living community, and its sacred past (Freidel, Schele, and Parker 1993; Newsome 2001). References to creation-related time, space, and characters appear in various examples of ancient Mesoamerican architecture, ranging from the quadrangular world-directional patio at the frontier Olmec site of Teopantecuanitlan (Martínez 1985), to the mask-laden radial pyramids of Maya 'E-Groups' (Aimers and Rice 2006), to the central panels of the South Ballcourt at El Tajín, Veracruz (Koontz 2009:55-66). In pre-conquest sources, such as the text of the Tablet of the Cross at Palenque (Schele and Freidel 1990:237-261), or in post-conquest indigenous sources, such as the Quiché Maya *Popol Vuh* (Christenson 2003), creation-related events form the prelude to subsequent accounts of distant divine ancestors, the founding of dynasties, and elite-oriented polity histories (Florescano 2002). Two such creation-related images appear on the West Structure of the Nunnery; feathered serpents and God N or Pawahtun figures.[1]

Two sinuous feathered serpents wind their way across the West Structure of the Nunnery (Figures 3 and 4). These have been associated with the cult of the central Mexican deity Quetzalcoatl, known in the northern Maya area as

---

[1] Sachse and Christenson (2005:1) discuss key concepts and mythic narratives associated with Maya creation mythology, which they consider to be 'the central paradigm in Maya mythology. . .from the Late Preclassic period through the Spanish conquest. . . .'

Jeff Karl Kowalski - Emeritus Professor, Northern Illinois University (jeffkarlkowalski@gmail.com).

FIGURE 1. VIEW OF THE NUNNERY QUADRANGLE AT UXMAL, WITH THE NORTH STRUCTURE ACROSS THE COURTYARD, THE EAST STRUCTURES ON THE RIGHT AND STAIRWAY OF THE WEST STRUCTURE ON THE LEFT. PHOTOGRAPH BY JEFF KOWALSKI.

K'uk'ulcan (Foncerrada 1965:139-140). This imagery is rare in Classic Maya art, leading some to see these snakes as late additions that reflect a conquest of Yucatán by Tula, Hidalgo (Foncerrada 1965:139-140). However, these serpents seem to be an integral part of the Nunnery's original iconographic program. Therefore, we must ask why Chan Chaak K'ak'nal Ajaw, who conserved many Maya traditions and art forms, decided to give this new imagery such prominence in his principal administrative palace complex. While they probably served to identify Uxmal as a 'Toltec' capital city (an exemplary urban center), another important reason hinges on the god Quetzalcoatl's 'primordial role as a creator' (Ringle et al. 1998). According to H. B. Nicholson (1979), among the Late Posctlassic Aztecs this powerful deity's attributes and associations cut across multiple themes—divine creativity, rain and agricultural fertility, and war and sacrifice.[2] The first distinctive representations of the feathered serpent deity in Mesoamerica, dated to about A.D. 150-250, appear on the Old Temple of Quetzalcoatl at Teotihuacan, where the feathered serpent seems to have been associated primarily with water, fertility, divine creativity, and cyclical time (Sugiyama 2004), although connections with war, sacrifice and political authority are also evident (Sugiyama 2004; Taube 1992b). Michael Coe (Coe and Koontz 2008:110), noting the aquatic environment surrounding these serpents, associated them with highland Maya

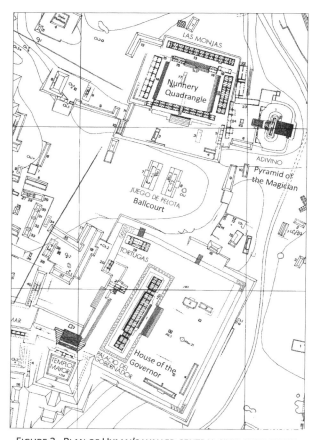

FIGURE 2. PLAN OF UXMAL'S WALLED CENTRAL CIVIC-CEREMONIAL DISTRICT. THE NUNNERY QUADRANGLE, ALONG WITH THE MAIN BALLCOURT AND THE HOUSE OF THE GOVERNOR TO THE SOUTH, EVIDENTLY WAS CONSTRUCTED DURING THE REIGN OF THE RULER CHAN CHAK K'AKNAL AJAW. PLAN ADAPTED AFTER GRAHAM 1992:4:83.

---

[2] According to Michael Smith (2003:206), 'As a prime creator, he was associated with Ometeotl and Tezcatlipoca, and in his guise as Ehecatl, god of wind, he belonged with Tlaloc.' In another manifestation he was the malevolent and warlike deity, Tlahuizcalpantecuhtli, representing Venus as 'lord of the house of dawn.'

FIGURE 3. WEST STRUCTURE OF THE NUNNERY QUADRANGLE. PHOTOGRAPH BY JEFF KOWALSKI.

creation myth, presumably likening these Teotihuacan feathered snakes slithering through shell-filled waters to the movement of Gucumatz, the plumed serpent who gives birth to living things from primordial waters in the creation account in the K'iche' Maya *Popol Vuh*.[3] Therein Gucumatz, accompanied by other deities, embodies the divine principle that introduces light, life, and order into the original waters of darkness and chaos.[4] The creation of cosmic and terrestrial time, space, and creatures, and earlier imperfect races of human beings, is then followed by exploits of the ancestral heroes who defeat forces of death and darkness, then rising to merge their identity with celestial bodies (the sun and moon). Thereafter the present race of humans is created as a prelude to an account of the history and deeds of the K'iche' kings and 'nation.'

In addition to embodying forces of divine creativity, the feathered serpent had a political significance. According to Saburo Sugiyama (2004:121-122) headdresses representing either feathered serpents, or the reticulated reptilian headdress that alternates with the feathered serpent heads on the Feathered Serpent Pyramid, were worn as symbols of rulership at Teotihuacan, thereby demonstrating a paramount's 'divine authorization...to rule the cosmos that was created by the Feathered Serpent' (Sugiyama 2005: 235-236; see also Sugiyama 2004:121-122, 134-138).[5]

After Teotihuacan's decline, the following Epiclassic period (c. A.D. 600-900/1000) witnessed the rise of new political centers, reorganization of interregional elite trade and communication networks, possible population movements, innovative architectural and artistic

FIGURE 4. FEATHERED SERPENT SCULPTURE ON NORTHERN SECTION OF FAÇADE OF THE WEST STRUCTURE OF THE NUNNERY QUADRANGLE. PHOTOGRAPH BY JEFF KOWALSKI.

expressions (Diehl and Berlo 1989), and the spread of a new or revitalized feathered serpent cult (Ringle et al. 1998). Two of these Epiclassic centers, Xochicalco and Cacaxtla, incorporate prominent feathered serpent imagery in their artistic programs, with the great plumed snakes functioning simultaneously as cosmological and dynastic-political symbols (Smith 2000; Brittenham n.d. [2008]).[6]

---

[3] Coe and Koontz (2008:110) specifically note that: 'A legend from the Maya highlands suggests that we have here another version of the first moment of creation, with an opposed pair of serpents, one representing life, greenness, and peace, and the other heat, the desert regions, and war, cavorting or conversing in the primal ocean.'

[4] For one translation of these mythic events see Tedlock (985:72-73).

[5] Sugiyama (2004:135) also associates the imagery on the Feathered Serpent Pyramid at Teotihuacan with primordial time and creation events as a prelude to and validation for legitimate rulership.

[6] At Xochicalco seated human figures in the folds of the snakes' bodies represent rulers, perhaps ancestral kings, whose authority and quasi-divine status is confirmed by the Feathered Serpent, their patron deity who indicates their control over powerful natural forces connected with water, earth, blood, and fertility, as well as their legitimacy as heirs to the urban tradition of Teotihuacan (see Smith 2000:79).

a   b   c

FIGURE 5 A-C. GOD N OR PAWAHTUN FIGURES ON THE WEST STRUCTURE OF THE NUNNERY QUADRANGLE. (A) TURTLE SHELL BODY BENEATH FEATHERED CANOPY, ABOVE CENTRAL DOORWAY; (B) FIGURE WITH SPIDER WEB CARTOUCHE, LOCATED ON FAÇADE SOUTH OF CENTRAL DOORWAY; (C) GOD N/PAWAHTUN FIGURE EMERGING FROM TURTLE SHELL, LOCATED ON NORTH END OF FAÇADES. PHOTOGRAPHS BY JEFF KOWALSKI.

Whereas the feathered serpents of Xochicalco or Cacaxtla may have been inspired more directly from Teotihuacan predecessors, those at Uxmal, and at the slightly later capital city of Chichén Itzá, represent more intrusive iconographic features. These sacred snakes traveled a more circuitous path involving the participation of both cities in long-distance coastal and overland exchange systems that resulted in the dissemination of precious goods and potent ideologies, including what Alfredo López Austín and Leonardo López Luján (2004) have termed the Zuyuán Religion, which provided additional claims to divine authority for rulers striving to survive the rupture caused by the collapse of the Classic Maya cities during the ninth century.

The Uxmal feathered serpents represent the ruler Chan Chaak K'ak'nal Ajaw's effort to identify himself as a 'Toltec,' not as a conquered vassal of Tula, but as a sovereign whose power stems from Tollan, or Tulan as it is called in later highland Maya sources (cf. Coggins 2002; Kowalski 1994a, 2007:261; Ringle 2012:194, 210-213), in which, as Frauke Sachse and Alan Christenson (2005:26) have noted, it refers to 'an otherworldly place of creation' that presaged and breathed life into the world of ordered time, space, and human life.

Indicating the cultural and iconographic hybridity of the Nunnery Quadrangle, while also alluding to world creation and political order, are depictions of the Maya deity known as God N or Pawahtun, an 'old god' who appears associated with turtle shells, water lilies, spider webs, and emerging from flowers on the façade of the West Structure (Figure 5) (Kowalski and Dunning 1999:281-282; Schele and Mathews 1998:281-282).[7] The

relationship between God N and world creation is alluded to in the account of the creation events in Bishop Diego de Landa's *Relación de las Cosas de Yucatán*. In his account of the annual Maya New Year ceremonies, which Karl Taube (1988:13-15, 215, 310-311) has identified as a ritual reenactment of creation, Landa (Tozzer 1941:135) notes that: 'Among the multitudes of gods which this nation worshipped they worshipped four, each of them called Bacab.' These Bacabs are described as four brothers placed at the four cardinal directions to support the sky, thus reconstituting world order following a great flood. Landa (Tozzer 1941:135-137) also mentions two sets of related deities, the Pauahtuns and the Xib Chacs, who also have a fourfold identity corresponding to specific colors and world directions.[8] Comparable descriptions in the *Chilam Balam of Chumayel* and related texts refer to a cosmic flood that occurs when the sky collapses on the earth. The four Bacabs are then 'set up' and 'trees of abundance' with world directional colors and associated birds are placed to mark the four world quarters and central axis (Roys 1967:100).[9]

[7] In several previous works, my interpretation of the Pawahtun figures on the West Structure of the Nunnery focused on that deity's earth/ underworld associations, which were seen as corresponding to the

association of the west with the sun's descent into the underworld and a quadripartite 'world directional' configuration of the Nunnery Quadrangle proper (e.g., Dunning and Kowalski 1994:82; Kowalski 1994a:102-104, 1999:281-282). While it remains clear that Pawahtuns in some cases do have terrestrial and chthonic characteristics (Bassie 1989:6-7, 15, 36-37; Taube 1992a:92-99), and I still feel that there are substantial reasons to see the four-part layout of the Nunnery as embodying a world directional scheme, it now seems more plausible to me that the role of the Bacabs/ Pawahtuns in world creation (that resulted in the establishment of ordered space and time, as well as proper social and political order) was the principal reason for their visual prominence on this building.

[8] As Gabrielle Vail (2000:127) notes: 'These associations are clearly evident in the Maya codices, as first noted by Cyrus Thomas (1882:59-92) and Eduard Seler (1887) with respect to the Dresden Codex and Madrid Codex year bearer pages. Thus, quadripartite deities with directional affiliations seem to form a common component of Postclassic Yucatec religion.'

[9] The relevant passage in the *Chilam Balam of Chumayel* is: 'There would be a sudden rush of water when the theft of the insignia <of Oxlahun-ti-ku> occurred. Then the sky would fall, it would fall down

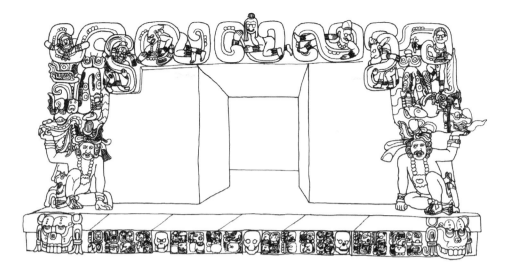

FIGURE 6. TEMPLE 22, COPAN, HONDURAS, DRAWING OF SCULPTURE FRAMING INNER DOORWAY SHOWING KNEELING PAWAHTUNS/BACABS SUPPORTING THE UPPERWORLD, REPRESENTED AS THE COSMIC MONSTER WHOSE OVERARCHING BODY TAKES THE FORM OF A SERIES OF S-SHAPED CLOUD SCROLLS. DRAWING BY LINDA SCHELE, NO. 1048, FAMSI.

In Classic Maya iconography, God N frequently appears as an atlantean figure sustaining the sky above the earth and underworld, merging aspects of the Bacabs and Pawahtuns described above (Taube 1992:figs. 46f-g, 47a). At Copan, Honduras, two kneeling God N or Pawahtun figures frame the inner doorway of Structure 22, lifting up the overarching sky, represented as a reptilian 'cosmic monster' whose serpentine body consists of S-shaped cloud scrolls (*muyal*) (Figure 6). This temple, built to mark the first k'atun anniversary of the accession of Copan's thirteenth ruler, dominates the small East Court of Copan's Acropolis, access to which, like the Nunnery Courtyard, was probably restricted to members of the royal court.[10] The kneeling figures at Copan also represent personified mountains. According to Karen Bassie (1989:36):

In his k'an *turtle form, God N represented the earth. The metaphor that the turtle god invokes is that the rising of the earth's surface from the sea was like*

a turtle surfacing from a pool of water. The four old men marked with the kawak elements were the manifestations of God N as the four great mythological mountains of the directions (Taube 1992[a]92-99).

God N in the guise of a mountain deity appears at Chichén Itzá on the upper panels of pillars of the Lower Temple of the Jaguars. God N deities emerge from the ends of turtle carapaces that are merged with personified mountain *witz* monsters, from which emerge youthful maize gods (Kowalski 1994:106; Schele and Mathews 1998:217, fig. 6.11). God N figures are also portrayed rising from the cleft heads of *witz* monsters seen on pillars from other structures at this site (Schmidt 2007:fig. 8; Taube 1994:214-216, fig. 2a).[11]

God N's creation-related and world directional associations refer not only to the establishment of cosmic order, but also relate to cultural, social, and political order. As Karl Taube (2003) has observed, the establishment of four-sided layouts, although involving natural elements such as trees, mountains, and birds, represents the distinction between ordered human space versus the disordered and threatening wilderness space of untamed nature. He also notes that: 'On a more political level, Pawahtuns also support the corners of celestial thrones, with the seated lord occupying the central place of this four-cornered social world...' (Taube 2003:464).

At the Nunnery Quadrangle such references to cosmic creation are juxtaposed to vivid references to warfare and subsequent ritual accompanied by music and dance

---

upon the earth, when the four gods, the four Bacabs, were set up, who brought about the destruction of the world. Then, after the destruction of the world was completed, they placed <a tree> to set up in its order the yellow cock oriole. Then the white tree of abundance was set up. A pillar of the sky was set up, a sign of the destruction of the world; that was the white tree of abundance of the north. Then the black tree of abundance was set up <in the west> for the black-breasted pixoy to sit upon. Then the yellow tree of abundance was set up <in the south>, as a symbol of the destruction the world, for the yellow-breasted pixoy to sit upon, for the yellow cock oriole to sit upon, the yellow timid mut. Then the green tree of abundance was set up in the center <of the world. As a record of the destruction of the world' (Roys 1967: 100).

[10] Gigantic Bacab or Pawahtun figures also adorned the northwest and northeast corners of Structure 10L-11 (Temple 11) at Copan (Fash 2001:fig. 104). According to Fash (2001:168): 'Proskouriakoff was the first to note that there were dozens of fragments of the body of what must have been a gigantic crocodile. The northern façade of Yax Pahsaj's Structure 10L-11 represented an enormous version of the cosmogram depicted in the inner chamber of Structure 10L-22. Again, the message conveyed was that the ruler was the single individual who could control all the supernatural forces of the universe, and who was uniquely capable of providing for the well-being of his people.'

[11] The figures emerging from the witz/mountain monsters on the pillars of the inner Temple of the Big Tables are identified as maize gods (Schmidt 2007:165, fig. 8), but more closely resemble a similar figure identified as a Pawahtun on cylindrical columns from the North Colonnade (Taube 1994:216, fig. 2a).

FIGURE 7. SEATED AND BOUND CAPTIVE FIGURE FROM WESTERN END OF SOUTH FAÇADE OF THE NORTH STRUCTURE OF THE NUNNERY. PHOTOGRAPH BY JEFF KOWALSKI.

FIGURE 8. MUSICIAN IN ANIMATED (DANCING?) POSE HOLDING DRUM AND RATTLE, ON EASTERN END OF SOUTH FAÇADE OF THE NORTH STRUCTURE OF THE NUNNERY. PHOTOGRAPH BY JEFF KOWALSKI.

(Figures 7, 9-13). These include depictions of captives and warriors, as well as a drummer/percussionist (Figure 8), the latter evoking the importance of music at elite ceremonials also seen in the Bonampak murals (Foncerrada 1965:148-152; Seler 1917:46, 58, 60, 61, abbn. 36, 47a-b, 52-55, tafn. XI-2, XII-1, XV, XVI). Bound and naked captive figures with displayed genitalia appear on the front and back of the North Structure. Sculptural elements stored within the North Structure indicate that several more naked captives were interspersed across this building's facades, as were individuals (probably warriors or warrior/priests) holding torches (Figure 9) (Schele and Mathews 1998:272, 276, 278-279, figs. 7.22, 7.23, 7.25, 7.27, 7.30, 7.33). None of the captives on the North Structure bear personal glyphic names of the sort that appear on some captives in southern Maya art (Marcus 1974:87). They thus recall the general class of prisoners known as *baak*, appearing in a 'count of captives' epithet in royal title phrases, in which the defeated are tallied as a class of goods rather than individuals (Stuart 1985). David Webster observes that in some cases 'statements of royal captive-taking should be understood literally (as personal battlefield exploits)...' while in others they may 'pertain more generally to captives taken by the king's warriors and dedicated to him,' a practice that has been documented at Piedras Negras, Yaxchilan, and related secondary sites, on monuments showing *sajal'ob* or secondary lords offering captives as tribute to the high kings or their representatives (Golden 2003; Webster 2000:94).

The visibility and corporeal presence of the Uxmal captives was designed to attract the eye of a viewer from the courtyard below, to whom they would have signaled the difference between the successful captors, who gathered in this palatial quadrangle, and defeated and demeaned captives, brought into this space anticipating

a future of servitude or sacrifice. Stephen Houston and colleagues have discussed this aspect of the ethos and imagery of Maya warfare and captive display, asserting that 'Maya testimonials to prowess in war operated more as memorials to defend honor and exhortations to future conduct than as crude 'propagandistic' boasting about the past' (Houston et al. 2006:203).

Another set of human figures appears on the West Structure of the Nunnery. Some of them, who seem to be warriors who are protagonists in sacrificial rituals, hold torches or staffs (Figures 12, 13). Others, who may be a special category of captives, wear less than the captors, and have prominently displayed penises pierced by wooden slats or pins (Figures 10, 11) (Schele and Mathews 1998:278-279, figs. 7.30, 7.33). This painful practice is portrayed on Stelae 7 and 4 from Itzimte, Campeche. On both of these monuments the upper panels feature the depiction of a triumphant warrior brutally slaying a prisoner who has pins or slats thrust through his penis (Von Euw 1977:4:13, 4:19). Similar pins pierce the upper arm of the captive on Itzimte Stela 7 (Figure 14). Perhaps also identifying these phallic Uxmal figures as incipient sacrificial victims are special garments in the form of 'winglike' elements marked with such sacrificial pegs, that cover their shoulders and/or hang at their sides. A similar form is attached to the ear of the captive on Itzimte Stelae 7 and 4 (Von Euw 1977:419 and 4:13). Apparently made of flexible cloth or paper, these objects may be counterparts for the strips of cloth that mark captives in southern Classic Maya art (Schele 1984:21; Schele and Miller 1986:212, 226, pl. 86). They also recall the painted paper streamers attached to some sacrificial victims in central Mexico (e.g., such as those attached to prisoners tied to circular 'gladiatorial' stones [*temalacatl*] during the Tlacaxipehualiztli festival celebrated by the Mexica-Aztecs; see de Casas 1970:202-

FIGURE 9. GROUP OF HUMAN FIGURAL SCULPTURES FOUND STORED WITHIN THE NORTH STRUCTURE OF THE NUNNERY QUADRANGLE. PHOTOGRAPH BY JEFF KOWALSKI.

FIGURE 10. CAPTIVE FIGURE WITH PIERCED PHALLUS AND THIGHS. SOUTHERN END OF FAÇADE OF WEST STRUCTURE OF THE NUNNERY. PHOTOGRAPH BY JEFF KOWALSKI.

FIGURE 11. SIDE AND FRONTAL VIEWS OF CAPTIVE FIGURE WITH PIERCED PHALLUS AND THIGHS. NORTHERN END OF FAÇADE OF WEST STRUCTURE OF THE NUNNERY. PHOTOGRAPH BY JEFF KOWALSKI.

FIGURE 12. STANDING FIGURE HOLDING TORCH FROM SOUTHERN END OF FAÇADE OF WEST STRUCTURE OF THE NUNNERY. PHOTOGRAPH BY JEFF KOWALSKI.

FIGURE 13. TORSO OF FIGURE HOLDING TORCH FROM NORTHERN END OF FAÇADE OF WEST STRUCTURE OF THE NUNNERY. PHOTOGRAPH BY JEFF KOWALSKI.

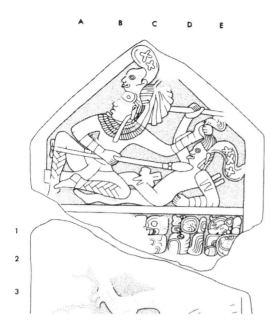

FIGURE 14. TOP PORTION OF STELA 7 FROM ITZIMTE, CAMPECHE
(AFTER VON EUW 1977:4:19)

203 and the Codex Nuttall, page 83, Nuttall 1975).[12]

The identification of these 'winged' figures as captives is complicated, however, by that some figures holding torches wear variants of such specialized garments. Seler (1917:abb. 54) illustrates one such figure that originally adorned the upper frontal façade of the North Structure of the Nunnery, and another torchbearer found stored within the North Structure has pins piercing his upper arms and wears what appears to be wearing a cloth panel holding wooden sacrificial pins as a cape-like garment.

There is also an example of a figure with a pierced penis who holds a torch, suggesting that he may not be a captive (Schele and Mathews 1998:fig. 7.23). He seems more closely related to a scene from North Temple of the Great Ballcourt at Chichén Itzá that depicts a monumental stone penis pierced by two slats (Figure 15). This phallus is approached by an individual who may be piercing his own erect penis in an autosacrificial bloodletting, perhaps performed at a shrine in connection with royal investiture ceremonies. The fact that none of the torchbearers have their wrists bound, and that the 'winged' or 'caped' figures wear more clothing than the captive figures seen on the North Structure might also indicate that they are warriors who are wearing specialized clothing associated with sacrificial ritual. Their pierced penises also resemble

those seen on a Classic Maya polychrome vessel (K3844) illustrated by Looper (2009:75), who notes that it portrays

. . . supernaturals (way) with bound and pierced penises in a procession toward a temple containing an enthroned bundle (Fig. 2.30). On this vase, some of the figures carry rattles, suggesting a musical performance and dance. This image can be compared to the jambs of the Upper Temple of the Jaguars at Chichén Itzá, which depict warriors with bound genitals (Schele and Mathews 1998:Figs. 6.25-28).

At one time, the emphasis on such phallic representations in northern Maya art was taken as evidence for either the introduction of foreign cults and/or the arrival of foreign groups (Foncerrada 1965:151-152). However, Laura Amrhein (2001), as well as Traci Ardren and David Hixon (2006), point out that phallic imagery, particularly taking the form of large phallic columnar altars, is abundant in northern Yucatán. Moreover, the pierced penises seen on these Uxmal figures, whether victors or captives, refer to a long-lived and widespread male penitential practice that involved ritual piercing the penis to draw blood for sacrificial offerings intended to communicate with deities, ancestors, and the otherworld, thereby promoting the welfare of their dynasty and city-state polity. Ardren and Hixon have discussed such self-sacrifice as part of a regimen of bodily practice that shaped an aristocratic male identity and demonstrated a privileged status 'through enactment of ritualized self-violence' as a demonstration of the capacity to bear pain.[13] Noting that the increased emphasis on such phallic imagery in the northern Maya area accompanies period of intensified regional conflict, Ardren (2012:62) states that, 'The placement of these symbols of these symbols on buildings and within elite plazas perhaps marked such areas as sites of male/male social activity where the individual man became one with a larger masculine group.' This interpretation certainly squares with the situation at the Nunnery Quadrangle, constructed during the evident militaristic expansion and consolidation of an Uxmal-dominated state, and clearly housing elite activities, including both council meetings as well as ritual performances whose principal protagonists, at least as portrayed in visual imagery, were men.[14]

---

[12] The similarity of these 'winglike' shoulder coverings to the object adorning the defeated captive on Itzimte Stela 7, along with their prominently displayed penises, supports the identification of these figures on the West Structure of the Nunnery as displayed captives. However, the fact that they are not bound and wear more clothing than the captive figures seen on the North Pruucture might also indicate that they are warriors who are wearing specialized clothing associated with sacrificial ritual.

[13] Ardren and Hixon (2006:22) interpret the practice as demonstrating 'dominant conceptualizations of masculinity through the enactment of ritualized self-violence' thus reinforcing 'the power of such hegemonic values as well as the privileged status of those able to withstand such a performance.' Ardren (2012) elaborates on this argument, examining how masculine imagery and bodily practices served to strengthen and 'naturalize' cultural concepts of male superiority emphasizing aggressive character traits associated with 'manliness' and confirmed through training for and success in warfare.

[14] Ardren (2012:61-62) also observes that the emphasis on phallic imagery in the Northern Maya Lowlands coincides with a period when warfare became more widespread and violent, likely increasing as population growth in the Puuc region intensified 'border conflicts or territorial claims.' (p. 61) In this more militaristic sociopolitical setting the prominent display of phalli (either as larger stone monuments or in other imagery) embodied an 'ethos of militarism' (p. 61) and a 'symbol of idealized masculine aggressiveness and courage.' (p. 62)

FIGURE 15. SECTION OF THE RELIEFS FROM THE NORTH TEMPLE OF THE GREAT BALLCOURT AT CHICHÉN ITZÁ (AFTER WREN AND SCHMIDT 1991:FIG. 9.9)

What is the meaning of the many figures holding torches? Karl Taube (1988a:333-335) observed that torches, and the burning of captives with fire, were important components in specialized types of Maya sacrificial rituals (see also Looper 2009:72-75, fig. 2.29). The so-called Scaffold Vase depicts a large wooden platform supporting a nearly naked captive, his hair gathered in the form of antlers, identifying him as having the status of prey captured by warrior-hunters (Taube 1988a:333, fig. 12.3; Houston et al. 2006:219-222, fig. 6.19). Two warriors touch flaming torches to the prisoner's backside, perhaps to ignite his loincloth, or perhaps to light a bundle of sticks, like those attached to the back of a ceramic captive figurine (Schele and Miller 1986:228, pl. 94). Comparing this Maya scaffold rite to the central Mexican Tlacaxipehualiztli festival honoring Xipe Totec 'the flayed god of spring and earthly renewal,'[15] Taube associated the Maya scaffold rite involving the torching of prisoners with two types events; a recurrent one 'concerned with the vernal renewal of the fields' (Taube 1988a:331), and an intermittent one associated with royal inauguration ceremonies. The first of these may have been a Classic period prototype for the protohistoric 'Tup Kaak rain rituals that occurred in the spring months of Mac and Pax' (Taube 1988a:334-335). During Pax, rain-bringing rituals known as Pacum Chac that honored the rain deity Chaak were held at the conclusion of a five-day long period of war ceremonies dedicated to the god Cit Chac Coh ('Father Red Puma'). These included a military dance known as holcan okot (dance of the warriors) (Tozzer 1941:164-165).[16] Referencing a doorjamb from Tohcok (Figure 16), Karl Taube observes that:

Considering the strongly martial nature of the Pacum Chac *festival, it could well be that this rain offering did not entail the hunting of animals [culminating in a sacrifice of deer during Mac] but the capture and sacrifice of men. At the Campeche site of Tohcok, there is a painted doorjamb that depicts a spiked censer containing a slain victim and burning bundles of wood. Above the victim dances a warrior, painted black and wearing a jaguar-skin skirt, tail, and leggings* (Taube 1988a:334).

The performance of military dance, perhaps cognate to the holcan okot warrior's dance, is depicted at various Terminal Classic northern Maya sites, including Mul-Chic and Kabah. The Mul-Chic murals dramatically portray battle and post-battle ritual sacrifice and dance. Scenes of prominent war captives appear on the north wall, while the south wall depicts stoning and hanging of captives and sacrificial rituals involving masked deity impersonators garbed as Chaaks (rain gods) (Barrera Rubio 1980:173-174, figs. 1-3). Their active poses suggest that they participate in a vigorous dance—whose martial character suggested by its association with the brutal immolation shown on the adjacent wall.

Another military dance is depicted on the carved jambs of the Codz Pop palace at Kabah, Yucatán (Pollock 1980:figs 372-372; Looper 2009:93-94). The upper panels depict two figures, with one wearing a Chaak headdress variant shown in a dynamic dancing pose. The lower register shows two individuals sacrificing a defeated captive (Figure 17).[17] A variant of such scenes may occur on Uxmal Stela 14 (Graham 1992:4:108), on which Matthew Looper (2009:165) has suggested that the ruler 'Lord Chaak' may be 'dancing as he confronts supernatural beings' (Figure 18). The Uxmal king appears as a rain god impersonator, while the sacrificial nature of this event may be signaled by the triple-knot motif that crowns his headdress. Accompanying 'Lord Chaak' is a military captain standing

---

[15] Taube suggested that: '...the sacrifice may represent three distinct agricultural processes: the torching of the victim's back, the milpa burning; the spearing of his flesh, the planting; and the flowing blood, the rains' (Taube 1988a:333).

[16] The holcan okot war dance, along with a related martial dance known as the batel okot was also performed during the five-day 'new year's festival' period associated with Muluc years (Tozzer 1941:144-145). Elsewhere Landa describes the holcan okot as a dance 'in which eight hundred Indians, more or less, dance with little streamers. They dance to a beat with a long war-like step...' (Tozzer 1941:94). The reference to wearing 'little streamers' is interesting in light of the use of the specialized 'wing-like' shoulder coverings seen at Uxmal.

[17] Looper (2009:93-95) writes of the Kabah scene: 'Taking into account the costumes and attributes of these two images, the obvious interpretation of the upper register is simply as a battle scene. Nevertheless, the dancing figure in the upper register has no hip cloth, and a knotted, feathered device covers his crotch. Although the carving is not very clear this appears similar to the fabric bindings that the Maya used in genital bloodletting. Another, more detailed version of this ceremony from a Classic-period vase shows a processional dance of men approaching a temple and holding ceremonial bars (Fig. 2.30). Their penises have been pierced with spines and bound in knotted cloth. The Codz Poop scene may depict a similar collective dance of auto-sacrificial bloodletting. . . Viewed in the context of these pottery paintings, the appearance of bloodletting attributes on the Codz Poop jambs suggests that the rite may have been conceived as a demonstration of bravery among warriors. In fact, in sixteenth-century Yucatán, this particular aspect of bloodletting was emphasized. Landa observed that 'he who did this [genital bloodletting] the most was considered as the bravest; and their sons from the earliest age began to practice it' (Tozzer 1941:114). Moreover, we know that during the Classic period, dance frequently involved bloodletting, especially among groups of men (Fig. 2.19, Plate 11). This is perhaps expressed most dramatically in the Bonampak murals, in the Room 3 sacrificial dance (Plate 2). . . . The program of the Codz Poop jambs is thus structurally similar to the murals at Bonampak, in which the dance and bloodletting rituals in Rooms 1 and 3 complement the scenes of battle and the torture and sacrifice of captives in Room 2.

FIGURE 16. PAINTED DOORJAMB FROM TOHCOK, CAMPECHE (AFTER PROSKOURIAKOFF 1965: FIG. 13B).

FIGURE 17. LOWER HALF OF NORTHERN JAMB FROM ROOM 21 OF THE CODZ POP PALACE AT KABAH. PHOTOGRAPH BY JEFF KOWALSKI.

above a sacrificial victim grievously wounded by a spearthower dart (Kowalski and Dunning 1999:290-291). What may be a bundle of wooden slats is strapped to the captive's midriff, perhaps tinder to be kindled in a torch sacrifice like those alluded to on the Nunnery facades. Alternatively, this may be a type of paper or cloth object of the type seen on the sacrificial victim at the bottom of Piedras Negras Stela 11 (Taube 1988a:343).

Taube (1988a:340-350) has also suggested that the scaffold rite and torching of prisoners may have been associated with royal inauguration ceremonies. It is worth noting that William Ringle (2012:213) has interpreted the feather-framed niches on the façade of the West Structure of the Nunnery as symbolic 'canopies,' described in several highland Guatemalan Maya chronicles (e.g., the *Titulo de Totonicapan*) as constituting one of the principal insignia associated with inauguration into ranked royal or noble offices. Perhaps these Uxmal canopies also correspond conceptually to the elevated scaffolding depicted on Late Classic 'niche' stelae at Piedras Negras, Guatemala (Figure 19). Proskouriakoff (1960) proposed that such monuments portrayed the formal installation into power of historical rulers seated in an elevated space crowned by a cloth canopy adorned with cosmic symbols. According to Stephen Houston, this ceremony, rather than representing accession, can now be identified as part of a first K'atun cyclical time period-ending ritual performed by the reigning king.[18] Given that later sources refer to the installation of the deities presiding over incoming K'atuns as comparable to the seating in office of a king

(Roys 1967:77; 'Katun 11 Ahau is set upon the mat, set upon the throne . . .'),[19] however, it seems possible that the imagery merges aspects of period-ending and accession ritual.[20] The Late Preclassic period murals at San Bartolo, Guatemala indicate that the use of wooden scaffolding as a seat of power has very ancient prototypes, with the elevation of a human ruler (an early *Ajaw*) taking place on a scaffold that is a mirror image for one on which the Maize God is portrayed (Saturno 2009:127-128, fig. 13). This correspondence fits well with Taube's (1988a:343) observation that 'The Piedras Negras accession stelae are virtually dripping with imagery of agricultural fertility of agricultural renewal associated with scaffold sacrifice.' The connection between human sacrifice and royal accession ceremonies is made explicit on Piedras Negras Stelae 11 and 14, both of which depict slain captives lying at the foot of the scaffold's ladder. Taube (1988a:343) notes that the Piedras Negras sacrificed captives are also associated with wood bundles:

Thus, the Piedras Negras examples may also represent a form of the Tup Kaak *in which captives, rather than game, were offered for rain. It is uncertain whether these are the victims slain in the scaffold sacrifice, but given their presence on scaffold monuments, it is a reasonable supposition.*[21]

[18] According to Stephen Houston (personal communication, March, 2014), the identity of the particular K'atun ending is indicated by the presence of the numbered Ajaw day marking its end on the 'copal bag' held by the king.

[19] See also Roys (1967:72, 135 165, 204).

[20] In a discussion of the Principal Bird Deity and the Piedras Negras niche stelae, Karl Taube (1987:5-6) notes that: 'In Classic Maya iconography, the Principal Bird Deity is also associated with human sacrifice and accession to high office.'

[21] Taube's (1988:343) observations also note that: 'Moreover, the Stela 11 victim has an object of paper or cloth on the small of his back. Similar garments are worn by the victim on the Scaffold Vase and the victim on the illustrated figurine (figs. 12.3, 12.4). It appears that, as Piedras Negras, the scaffold sacrifice and a variant of the Tup Kaak were parts of a single renewal ceremony.' The reference to the placement of a paper

FIGURE 18. UXMAL STELA 14, SHOWING THE RULER CHAN CHAK K'AKNAL AJAW STANDING ON A TWO-HEADED JAGUAR PEDESTAL/THRONE. (AFTER GRAHAM 1992: 4:108)

The visual/sculptural evidence discussed here suggests that torch sacrifice, like that also probably associated with the Pax ceremonies and with royal accession and/or with K'atun rituals performed at southern Maya sites, was practiced at Uxmal and indicates that related types of ritual events involving the presentation, display, and sacrifice of prisoners, accompanied by music and dance, occurred within and nearby the Nunnery Quadrangle.

Aspects of the Nunnery Quadrangle's plan and iconographic program embodied the archetypal and primordial time and space associated creation of the present world and its inhabitants, both divine and human. Other façade motifs refer to more current, though not necessarily more secular, events, including possible investiture ceremonies, the display and implied torture and sacrifice of captives in connection with rituals of accession and/or cyclical renewal of time and agricultural fertility.

The Nunnery, Ballcourt, and House of the Governor were constructed by Uxmal's ruler, Chan Chaak K'ak'nal Ajaw, who recently used, or was still using, military force to increase his city's control over the Eastern Puuc region (Kowalski 2003b; Kowalski and Dunning 1999), so such war ritual was related to practical aspects of conquest and perhaps also served to sustain the martial fervor and courage of the dancers. The Nunnery Quadrangle's ambitious scale seems to reflect the king's recently gained control over new sources of labor, while its abundant imagery visually confirmed that Uxmal was fully entitled to be regarded as the paramount polity in the Eastern Puuc region, however short-lived that claim proved to be.

Acknowledgements. I would like to acknowledge the Center for Pre-Columbian Studies at Dumbarton Oaks, where my fellowship during the spring of 2013 provided me with the financial support, library resources, and scholarly contacts that furthered my study of the form, function(s) and meaning(s) of the Nunnery Quadrangle at Uxmal. I also thank William Ringle for feedback provided based on a conference presentation of this study, and Meghan Rubenstein for informing me that a scene of captive scaffold sacrifice appears on one of the recently discovered sculptured jambs from the Codz Pop structure at Kabah.

References Cited

Aimers, John J., and Prudence M. Rice
2006 Astronomy, Ritual, and the Interpretation of Maya 'E-Group' Architectural Assemblages. *Ancient Mesoamerica* 17:79-96.

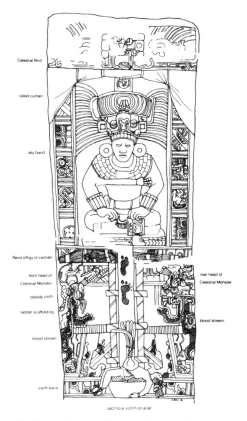

FIGURE 19. STELA 11 FROM PIEDRAS NEGRAS, GUATEMALA, A.D. 731. (DRAWING BY LINDA SCHELE, NO. 6111, COURTESY OF FAMSI).

or cloth object associated with the body of a sacrificed prisoner seems particularly relevant to the 'dressing' of the potential sacrificial victims seen on Itzimte Stela 7 or on the Nunnery at Uxmal.

Amrhein, Laura M.
n.d. [2001] An Iconographic and Historic Analysis of Terminal Classic Maya Phallic Imagery (Yucatán). Ph.D dissertation, Virginia Commonwealth University.

Anawalt, Patricia R.
1981 *Indian Clothing before Cortés: Mesoamerican Costumes from the Codices*. University of Oklahoma Press, Norman.

Ardren, Traci
2012 The Phalli Stones of the Classic Maya Northern Lowlands: Masculine Anxiety and Regional Identity. In *Power and Identity in Archaeological Theory and Practice: Case Studies from Ancient Mesoamerica*, edited by Eleanor Harrison-Buck, pp. 53-62. University of Utah Press, Salt Lake City.

Ardren, Traci, and David R. Hixson
2006 The Unusual Sculptures of Telantunich, Yucatán: Phalli and the Concept of Masculinity among the Ancient Maya. *Cambridge Archaeological Journal* 16 (1):7-25.

Barrera Rubio, Alfredo
1980 Mural Paintings of the Puuc Region of Yucatán. In *Third Palenque Round Table, 1978, Part 2*, edited by Merle Greene Robertson, pp. 173-182. University of Texas Press, Austin.

Bassie, Karen
1989 Maya Creator Gods. Mesoweb Articles (www.mesoweb.com/features/bassie/CreatorGods)

Broda de Casas, Johanna
1970 Tlacaxipehualiztli: a Reconstruction of an Aztec Calendar Festival from 16th Century Sources. *Revista española de antropología americana* 5:197-274.

Brittenham, Claudia Lozoff
n.d. The Cacaxtla Painting Tradition: Art and Identity in Epiclassic Mexico. Ph.D. dissertation, Department of the History of Art, Yale University, New Haven, CT, 2008.

Christenson, Alan
2007 *Popol Vuh: The Sacred Book of the Maya*. University of Oklahoma Press, Norman [originally published 2003].

Coe, Michael D., and Rex Koontz
2008 *Mexico: From the Olmecs to the Aztecs* (6th edition). Thames and Hudson, New York.

Cohodas, Marvin
1978 *The Great Ball Court at Chichen Itza, Yucatan, Mexico*. New York and London: Garland Publishing, Inc.

Coggins, Clemency Chase
2002 Toltec. *RES: Anthropology and Aesthetics* 42:34-85.

Diehl, Richard A., and Janet C. Berlo (editors)
1989 *Mesoamerica after the Decline of Teotihuacan A.D. 700-900*. Dumbarton Oaks Research Library and Collection, Washington, D.C.:

Fash, William L.
2001 *Scribes, Warriors and Kings: The City of Copan and the Ancient Maya* (revised edition). Thames and Hudson, London and New York.

Florescano, Enrique
2002 Los paradigmas mesoamericanos que unificaron la reconstrucción del pasado: el mito de la creación del cosmos; la fundación del reino maravilloso (Tollán), y Quetzalcóatl, el creador de estados y dinastías. *Historia Mexicana* 52 (2):309-359.

Foncerrada de Molina, Marta
1965 *La escultura arquitectónica de Uxmal*. Universidad Nacional Autónoma de México, México, D.F.

Freidel, David, Linda Schele, and Joy Parker
1993 *Maya Cosmos: Three Thousand Years on the Shaman's Path*. William Morrow, New York.

Golden, Charles W.
2003 The Politics of Warfare in the Usumacinta Basin: La Pasadita and the Realm of Bird Jaguar. In *Mesoamerican Warfare*, edited by M. Kathryn Brown and Travis W. Stanton, pp. 31-48. Altamira Press, Lanham.

Graham, Ian
1992 *Corpus of Maya Hieroglyphic Inscriptions, Vol. 4, Pt. 2: Uxmal*. Peabody Museum of Archaeology and Ethnology, Harvard University, Cambridge, MA.

Houston, Stephen D., David Stuart, and Karl A. Taube
2006 *The Memory of Bones: Body, Being, and Experience among the Classic Maya*. University of Texas Press, Austin.

Koontz, Rex
2009 *Lightning Gods and Feathered Serpents: The Public Sculpture of El Tajín*. University of Texas Press, Austin.

Kowalski, Jeff Karl
1994a The Puuc as Seen from Uxmal. In *Hidden among the Hills: Maya Archaeology of the Northwest Yucatan Peninsula*. First Maler Symposium, Bonn, 1989, edited by Hanns J. Prem, pp. 93-120. Verlag Von Flemming, Möckmühl, Germany.

1994b Los mascarones de Tlalóc del Cuadrángulo de la Monjas, Uxmal: Formas Teotihuacanos como símbolos 'Toltecas.' In *Memorias del Primer Congreso International de Mayistas*, pp. 104-156. Universidad Nacional Autónoma de México, México, D.F.

2003a Evidence for the Functions and Meanings of Some Northern Maya Palaces. In *Maya Palaces and Elite Residences: An Interdisciplinary Approach*, edited by Jessica Joyce Christie, pp. 204-252. University of Texas Press, Austin.

2003b Collaboration and Conflict: An Interpretation of the Relationship between Uxmal and Chichén Itzá during the Terminal Classic/Early Postclassic Periods. In *Escondido en la selva: Arqueología en el Norte de Yucatán*, edited by Hanns J. Prem, pp. 235-272. Univeridad de Bonn/Instituto Nacional de Antropología e Historia Bonn/México, D.F.

2007 What's 'Toltec' at Uxmal and Chichén Itzá: Merging Maya and Mesoamerican Worldviews and World Systems in Terminal Classic to Early Postclassic Yucatan. In *Twin Tollans: Chichén Itzá, Tula, and the Epiclassic to Early Postclassic Mesoamerican World*, edited by Jeff Karl Kowalski and Cynthia Kristan-Graham, pp. 277-313. Dumbarton Oaks Research Library and Collection, Washington, D.C.

Kowalski, Jeff Karl, and Nicholas P. Dunning
1999 The Architecture of Uxmal: The Symbolics of Statemaking at a Puuc Maya Regional Capital. In *Mesoamerican Architecture as a Cultural Symbol*, edited by Jeff Karl Kowalski, pp. 274-297. Oxford University Press, New York.

Landa, Diego de (see Tozzer 1941)

López Austin, Alfredo, and Leonardo López Luján
2000 The Myth and Reality of Zuyuá: The Feathered Serpent and Mesoamerican Transformations from the Classic to the Postclassic. In *Mesoamerica's Classic Heritage: From Teotihuacan to the Aztecs,* edited by Davíd Carrasco, Lindsay Jones, and Scott Sessions, pp. 21-84. University Press of Colorado, Boulder.

Looper, Matthew G
2009 *To Be Like Gods: Dance in Ancient Maya Civilization.* University of Texas Press, Austin.

Maler, Teobert
1901 Research in the Central Portion of the Usumatsintla Valley. *Memoirs of the Peabody Museum of American Archaeology and Ethnology*, II (1). Harvard University, Cambridge.

Marcus, Joyce
1974 The Iconography of Power among the Classic Maya. *World Archaeology* 6 (1), Political Systems: 83-94

Martínez Donjuán, Guadalupe
1985. El Sitío Olmec de Teopantecuanitlan en Guerrero. *Anales de Antropología* 22: 215-226.

Miller, Mary Ellen
1986 *The Murals of Bonampak.* Princeton University Press, Princeton, NJ.

Newsome, Elizabeth A.
2001 *Trees of Paradise and Pillars of the World: The Serial Cycle of '18 Rabbit God-K,' King of Copan.* University of Texas Press, Austin.

Nicholson, Henry B.
1979 Ehecatl-Quetzalcoatl vs. Topiltzin Quetzalcoatl of Tollan: A Problem in Mesoamerican Religion and History. *Actes du XLIIe Congrés International des Américanistes* VI: 35-47. Paris: Société des Américanistes.

Nuttall, Zelia (editor)
1975 *The Codex Nuttall: A Picture Manuscript from Ancient Mexico: The Peabody Museum Facsimile.* Vol. 23168, No. 2. Dover Publications, Inc., New York.

Pollock, Harry E. D.
1980 *The Puuc: An Architectural Survey of the Hill Country of Yucatan and Northern Campeche.* Memoirs of the Peabody Museum of Archaeology and Ethnology, Harvard University, Vol. 19. Harvard University, Cambridge, MA.

Proskouriakoff, Tatiana
1960 A Historical Implications of a Pattern of Dates at Piedras Negras, Guatemala. *American Antiquity* 25 (4):454-475.
1965 Sculpture and Major Arts of the Maya Lowlands. In *Handbook of Middle American Indians*, Vol 2, edited by Gordon R. Willey, pp. 469-497. University of Texas Press, Austin.

Ringle, William M.
2012 The Nunnery Quadrangle of Uxmal. In *The Ancient Maya of Mexico: Reinterpreting the Past of the Northern Maya Lowlands*, edited by Geoff Braswell, pp. 189-226. Equinox Press, London.

Ringle, William M., Gallareta Negrón, Tomás, and George J. Bey, III
1998 The Return of Quetzalcoatl: Evidence for the Second Spread of a World Religion during the Epiclassic Period. *Ancient Mesoamerica* 9:183-232.

Roys, Ralph L.
1967 *The Chilam Balam of Chumayel.* University of Oklahoma Press, Norman.

Sachse, Frauke, and Allen J. Christenson
2005 Tulan and the Other Side of the Sea: Unraveling a Metaphorical Concept from Colonial Guatemalan Highland Sources. Mesoweb Publications (*www.mesoweb.com/articles/tulan/tulan.html*)

Saturno, William
2009 Centering the Kingdom, Centering the King: Maya Creation and Legitimization at San Bartolo. In *The Art of Urbanism: How Mesoamerican Kingdoms Represented Themselves in Architecture and Imagery*, edited by William L. Fash and Leonardo López Luján, pp. 111-131. Dumbarton Oaks Research Library and Collection, Washington, D.C.

Schele, Linda
1984 Human Sacrifice Among the Classic Maya. In *Ritual Sacrifice in Mesoamerica,* edited by Elizabeth P. Benson and Elizabeth H. Boone, pp. 6-48. Dumbarton Oaks Research Library and Collection, Washington, D.C.

Schele, Linda, and Mary Ellen Miller
1986 *The Blood of Kings: Dynasty and Ritual in Maya Art.* Kimbell Art Museum, Fort Worth, in association with George Braziller, New York.

Schele, Linda, and David Freidel
1990 *A Forest of Kings: The Untold Story of the Ancient Maya.* William Morrow, New York.

Schele, Linda, and Peter Mathews
1998 *The Code of Kings: The Language of Seven Sacred Maya Temples and Tombs.* Scribner, New York.

Schmidt, Peter
2007. Birds, Ceramics, and Cacao: New Excavations at Chichén Itzá. In *Twin Tollans: Chichén Itzá, Tula, and the Epiclassic to Early Postclassic World*, edited by Jeff Karl Kowalski and Cynthia Kristan-Graham, pp. 151-204. Dumbarton Oaks Research Library and Collection, Washington, D.C.

Seler, Eduard
1917 *Die Ruinen von Uxmal.* Abhandlungen der Königlich Preussichen Akademie der Wissenschaften, Philosophisch-historische Klasse 2. Verlag der Königl. Akademie der wissenschaften in commission bei Georg Reimer, Berlin.

Smith, Michael E.
2003 *The Aztecs* (2nd Edition). Blackwell Publishing, Malden, MA.

Smith, Virginia
2000 The Iconography of Power at Xochicalco: The Pyramid of the Plumed Serpents. In The *Xochicalco Mapping Project: Archaeological Research at Xochicalco*, Volume II, edited by Kenneth Hirth, pp. 57-82. The University of Utah Press, Salt Lake City.

Stuart, David
1985 The 'Count-of Captives' Epithet in Classic Maya Writing. In *Fifth Palenque Round Table, 1983,* edited by Virginia M. Fields, general editor Merle Greene Robertson, pp. 97-101. Pre-Columbian Art Research Institute, San Francisco.

2005 Ideology and Classic Maya Kingship. In *A Catalyst for Ideas: Anthropological Archaeology and the Legacy of Douglas Schwartz*, edited by Vernon L. Scarborough, pp.257-286. School of American Research Press, Santa Fe.

Sugiyama, Saburo

2004 Teotihuacan as an origin for Postclassic Feathered Serpent Symbolism. In *Mesoamerica's Classic Heritage: From Teotihuacan to the Aztecs,* edited by Davíd Carrasco, Lindsay Jones, and Scott Sessions, pp. 117-144. University Press of Colorado, Boulder.

2005 *Human Sacrifice, Militarism, and Rulership: Materialization of State Ideology at the Feathered Serpent Pyramid, Teotihuacan*. Cambridge University Press, New York.

Taube, Karl

1987 A Representation of the Principal Bird Deity in the Paris Codex. *Research Reports on Ancient Maya Writing* 6: 1-10. Center for Maya Research, Washington, D.C.

1988a A Study of Classic Maya Scaffold Sacrifice. In *Maya Iconography,* edited by Elizabeth P. Benson and Gillett G. Griffin, pp. 331-351. Princeton University Press, Princeton.

1988b The Ancient Yucatec New Year Festival: The Liminal Period in Maya Ritual and Cosmology. Ph. D. dissertation, Department of Anthropology, Yale University.

1992a *The Major Gods of Yucatan: Schellhas Revisited*. Studies in Pre-Columbian Art and Archaeology 32. Dumbarton Oaks Research Library and Collection, Washington, D.C.

1992b The Temple of Quetzalcoatl and the Cult of Sacred War at Teotihuacan. *RES: Anthropology and Aesthetics* 21: 58-87.

1994 The Iconography of Toltec Period Chichen Itza. In *Hidden Among the Hills: Maya Archaeology of the Northwest Yucatan Peninsula*, edited by Hanns J. Prem, pp. 212-246. Acta Mesoamericana 7. Verlag Von Flemming, Möckmühl, Germany.

2003 Ancient and Contemporary Maya Conceptions about Field and Forest. In *Lowland Maya Area: Three Millennia as the Human-Wildland Interface*, edited by Arturo Gómez-Pompa, Michael F. Allen, Scott L. Fedick, and Juan J. Jimenez-Osornio, pp. 461-492. Food Products Press, New York.

Tedlock, Dennis

1985 *Popol Vuh: The Definitive Edition of the Mayan Book of the Dawn of Life and the Glories of the Gods and Kings*. Simon and Schuster, New York.

Tozzer, Alfred M. (translator and editor)

1941 *Landa's Relación de las Cosas de Yucatán, a Translation*. Papers of the Peabody Museum of American Archaeology and Ethnology 18. Harvard University, Cambridge, MA.

Vail, Gabrielle

2000 Pre-Hispanic Maya Religion: Conceptions of Divinity in the Postclassic. *Ancient Mesoamerica* 11 (1):123-147.

Von Euw, Eric

1977 *Corpus of Maya Hieroglyphic Inscriptions, Volume 4: Part 1: Itzimte, Pixoy, Tzum*. Peabody Museum of Archaeology and Ethnology, Harvard University, Cambridge, MA.

Webster, David

2000 The Not So Peaceful Civilization: A Review of Maya War. *Journal of World Prehistory* 14 (1):65-119.

Wren, Linnea, and Peter Schmidt

1991 Elite Interaction During the Terminal Classic Period of the Northern Maya Lowlands: Evidence from the Reliefs of the North Temple of the Great Ball Court. In *Classic Maya Political History: Hieroglyphic and Archaeological Evidence*, edited by T. Patrick Culbert, p. 199-225. School of American Research and Cambridge University Press, Cambridge.

The Hieroglyphic Platform at Kabah

Meghan Rubenstein and Philipp Galeev

In front of the western façade of the Codz Pop at Kabah is a low, four-sided platform. Once faced with two courses of stones carved with hieroglyphs, only about half of the blocks remain on the monument; the rest lie scattered in the rubble. Due to the condition of the stones and the disorder of the inscription, little progress has been made on the decipherment of the Hieroglyphic Platform. Our fieldwork in 2013 resulted in a new catalog of the monuments and its associated blocks, which allowed us to build upon previous interpretations. In this paper, we present our initial findings and place the hieroglyphic monument within the larger corpus of Terminal Classic inscriptions from the Northern Lowlands. We offer a discussion of stylistic variation and suggest the text fragments record royal authority, military activity, and calendric activity at Kabah.

Al frente de la fachada occidental del Codz Pop en Kabah hay una plataforma baja de cuatro lados. Originalmente bordeada con dos filas de piedras talladas con jeroglíficos, sólo una mitad de los bloques aún permanecen en el monumento; el resto está esparcido por los escombros. Debido a la condición de las piedras y al desorden de la inscripción, el progreso en el desciframiento de la Plataforma Jeroglífica ha sido lento. Nuestra investigación en el 2013 resultó en un nuevo catálogo de los bloques jeroglíficos asociados con esta estructura, lo que nos permitió aumentar y complementar las interpretaciones anteriores. En este capítulo, presentamos nuestros hallazgos iniciales y colocamos el monumento jeroglífico dentro del corpus más amplio de las inscripciones del Clásico Terminal de las tierras bajas del norte. Ofrecemos una discusión sobre la variación estilística y sugerimos que los fragmentos de texto registran la autoridad real, la actividad militar, y la actividad relacionada al calendario en Kabah.

The Puuc region in Yucatán, Mexico, is known for its elaborately sculpted stone buildings. Among the most familiar is the Codz Pop at Kabah, an ornate structure prominently situated on a large platform in the East Group (Pollock 1980:174, fig. 335). The adjacent plaza is bordered with monumental architecture, multistory buildings marking its eastern and southern boundaries. To the immediate north is a royal kitchen, exposed by a recent archaeological investigation (Toscano et al. 2014). It is likely that these structures were part of an important administrative center during the Terminal Classic period (c. A.D. 800-950).

In the East Group, the Codz Pop stands apart not only physically, but also visually (Figure 1). Its façade is among the most complex in ancient Mesoamerica; no two sides are alike. The iconographic program incorporates images of both a religious and historical nature, including the repeated depiction of an individual, referred to in the literature as the King of Kabah. We associate the final construction phase of the Codz Pop with his reign (Carrasco 1994; Carrasco and Pérez de Heredia 1996; Ligorred 1993; Rubenstein 2015). The hieroglyphic inscriptions on the carved doorjambs help us to place this building in the 9th century (Stuart and Rubenstein 2014).

Centered at the base of the steps in front of the Codz Pop's infamous western façade is the Hieroglyphic Platform, known also as 2B2, Structure D, and the Hieroglyphic Altar. The low, four-sided structure consists of a solid rubble core with two courses of facing stones carved with a lengthy hieroglyphic inscription (Figure 2a-d and Figure 3a-d). If the content is similar to other texts in the Maya area, decipherment of this monument would add to our historical knowledge of Kabah and the Puuc region by providing names, places, and events associated with the site.

Unfortunately, only 54 blocks remain on the monument and their placement dates to the mid-twentieth century. Nearly 100 additional blocks lie scattered in the rubble, unknown to most scholars. Further complicating the matter, many of the stones associated with this structure are badly damaged or worn. These conditions have made decipherment of the Hieroglyphic Platform challenging.

In 2013, we renewed efforts in the decipherment of this monument. Rubenstein was studying the art and architecture of the Codz Pop while Galeev was working on the hieroglyphic inscriptions in the Puuc region. Since our two areas of research overlapped at this platform, we joined forces to create a catalog that recorded the hieroglyphic blocks both on and off the monument. This collaboration permitted a more in-depth analysis of the hieroglyphic content, part of which we present below. While our treatment of the material in this format is by no means exhaustive, we share a brief history of research on this monument as well as our process of documentation and preliminary findings.

History of Documentation and Research

By the mid-nineteenth century, the Hieroglyphic Platform was already in a state of disrepair. Explorer John Lloyd Stephens, who visited Kabah in 1842, was the first to note the monument's poor condition—which he emphasized

Meghan Rubenstein - Colorado College (meghan.rubenstein@coloradocollege.edu); **Philipp Galeev** - Knorozov Center for Mesoamerican Studies, RSUH (f.galeev@gmail.com).

FIGURE 1. VIEW OF THE HIEROGLYPHIC PLATFORM (2B2) FROM THE SOUTHWEST WITH THE WESTERN FACADE OF THE CODZ POP IN THE BACKGROUND. KABAH, YUCATÁN, MEXICO. PHOTOGRAPH BY MEGHAN RUBENSTEIN.

by giving it only a cursory mention in his text. According to Stephens, 'Mr. Catherwood made drawings of these [hieroglyphic blocks] as they lay scattered about, but as I cannot present them in the order in which they stood, they are omitted altogether' (Stephens 1843, Vol 1:388; see illustration opposite page 387). The structure that once supported the facing stones is not mentioned at all, suggesting that most of the façade was detached by this time. Photographs of the western façade of the Codz Pop from the late nineteenth and early twentieth century confirm this level of destruction, showing little more than a raised area of stone rubble (Teobert Maler 1997:fig. 72; Carnegie Institution of Washington, Peabody Museum of Archaeology and Ethnology archive number 58-34-20/28273).

The monument visible at the site today is a mid-twentieth century reconstruction. In 1951, Instituto Nacional de Antropologia e Historia (INAH) archaeologist Raúl Pavón Abreu and his team began the first controlled excavations at the Codz Pop (Pavón et al. 1951a, 1951b). This work was focused on the western façade and the associated Hieroglyphic Platform. The INAH field report echoes Stephens's earlier observations, remarking that the monument was destroyed and the stones from the structure were strewn about the platform, which they attributed to an earlier, non-scientific exploration.[1] Pavón's project moved forward to try to identify the use of the structure,

which they called the Hieroglyphic Altar, alluding to the presumed function. In 1952, a project under the direction of Ponciano Salazar Orgegón excavated into the center of the mound, however, the results were inconclusive (Salazar 1953:124).

At the end of the 1951 field season, Pavón reset the blocks on the platform. His hope was that this action would preserve the carved stones for future scholars, who might be able to read the text (Pavón et al. 1951a). The loose blocks were grouped together and placed face down about 10 meters from the monument.[2] Without a doubt their work protected stones from looters and slowed the inevitable erosion. Although Salazar continued Pavón's work at and around the Codz Pop in the following year (Salazar et al. 1952; Salazar 1953), since that time there has been no further excavation of the Hieroglyphic Platform, only regular cleaning.[3]

The first attempts to decipher the monument followed in 1986, when Nikolai Grube published a set of drawings of the platform in *Mexicon*. In the accompanying analysis, he proposed a reading order, suggesting that the text begins and ends on the west side of the platform. Grube also noted that there were no calendric blocks from which to ascertain a date. The exception was a glyph block with numeric

[1] 'Se encontraba totalmente destruido. Pudiéndose observar que había sido explorado no científicamente, incluso usando explosivos por lo que las piedras con jeroglíficos se encontraban diseminados en toda el área de dicha plaza' (Pavón et al. 1951a).

[2] For a more complete summary of archaeological work related to the platform in the early 1950s, see Moedano 1952; Pavón et al. 1951a, 1951b; Salazar et al. 1952; and Salazar 1953.
[3] Ramón Carrasco Vargas' project revisited the monument in the early 1990s and produced new illustrations of the platform (Carrasco et al. 1992).

a

b

c

d

FIGURE 2 A-D. HIEROGLYPHIC PLATFORM (2B2), KABAH, YUCATÁN, MEXICO. (A) WEST FACADE, (B) SOUTH FACADE; (C) EAST FACADE; (D) NORTH FACADE. PHOTOGRAPHS BY MEGHAN RUBENSTEIN.

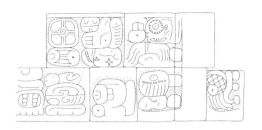
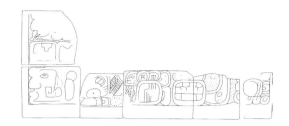

a

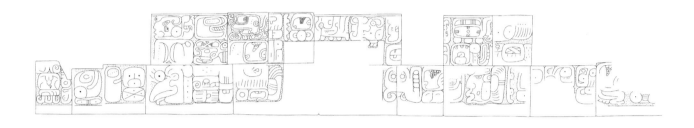

b

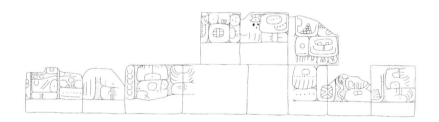

c

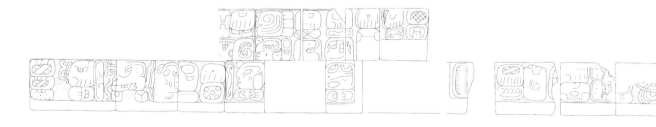

d

FIGURE 3 A-D. HIEROGLYPHIC PLATFORM (2B2), KABAH, YUCATÁN, MEXICO. (A) WEST FACADE, (B) SOUTH FACADE; (C) EAST FACADE; (D) NORTH FACADE. DRAWINGS BY MEGHAN RUBENSTEIN AFTER ERIC VON EUW'S UNPUBLISHED FIELD NOTES.

a   b

FIGURE 4 A-B. EXAMPLES OF CARVED STONES INCLUDED IN ERIC VON EUW'S CATALOG DETERMINED NOT TO BE PART OF THE HIEROGLYPHIC PLATFORM. (A) BLOCK 3; (B) BLOCK 6. PHOTOGRAPHS BY MEGHAN RUBENSTEIN.

content (see Figure 8e), which he reproduced from Hugo Moedano (1952), who published this loose stone in a short summary of the 1951 field season. Although this block contained the type of information for which Grube was looking, he was unable to locate it at the site during his visit.

Few scholars working on Puuc inscriptions have referenced the Hieroglyphic Platform. Often, they cite a lack of a reading order and incomplete text, or the platform is left out of their analysis (Graña-Berhrens 2002; Ligorred 1993:70-71). Kowalski (1985) discussed the platform in relation to a hieroglyphic altar at Uxmal. He drew attention to several glyph blocks on the monument, pointing out emblem glyphs similar to the ones found at the neighboring site (Kowalski 1985:figs. 24 and 28), and several glyphs that might represent noblewomen, which he proposed demonstrate an interest in dynastic lineage at Kabah (Kowalski 1985:figs. 24-27).

While analysis has been limited, good documentation of the Hieroglyphic Platform has greatly assisted the present work. In addition to Maler's late nineteenth century images, several other individuals and institutions photographed the monument in the nineteenth and twentieth centuries, most notably the Carnegie Institution of Washington.[4] The CIW visited the site during the excavation and reconstruction in the early 1950s and were able to photograph a number of stones before they ended up in the rubble. There are also two nearly complete sets of drawings of the associated blocks. In the 1970s, Eric von Euw, on behalf of the Corpus of Maya Hieroglyphic Inscriptions at the Peabody

Museum at Harvard, visited the site and created a catalog of the monument and the loose stones. All of his images were drawn to scale and checked with light. In the 1990s, an INAH project under the direction of Ramón Carrasco Vargas did the same. The results from Carrasco's work can be found in an INAH report (Carrasco et al. 1992), while those of von Euw remain unpublished.

In 2013, we began creating our own record of the Hieroglyphic Platform. The intention was to record the currently accounted for stones for the ongoing INAH archaeological project, under the direction of Lourdes Toscano Herández, and to revisit the inscription 65 years after Pavón's work.

We started by mapping, numbering, and photographing the monument and the associated fragments. In addition to the blocks on the platform, of which there are 54 cemented in place, approximately 90 carved stones were located nearby. We used Eric von Euw's field sketches and numbering system to form the basis for our own system.[5] The original drawings by von Euw included the four sides of the platform and 76 fragments. We determined that two of those fragments were not from the Hieroglyphic Platform, but rather from the eastern facade of the Codz Pop (Figure 4a). Another oddly shaped stone is likely from a different type of monument, although we cannot discount its possible relationship to this one (Figure 4b). Several additional fragments are rather small, which makes it difficult to extract any information from them.[6]

---

[4] Digitized photographs from the Carnegie Institution of Washington excavations (held by the Peabody Museum of Archaeology and Ethnology) are available through the Visial Information Access database at Harvard University: http://via.lib.harvard.edu/via.

[5] A preliminary version of our catalog is included in the appendix of Meghan Rubenstein's 2015 dissertation. The catalog numbers used in this chapter, which are based on von Euw's numbering system, refer back to this document.

[6] Since there are uncarved sections of the platform, the original catalog and map includes smooth stones, which were later removed.

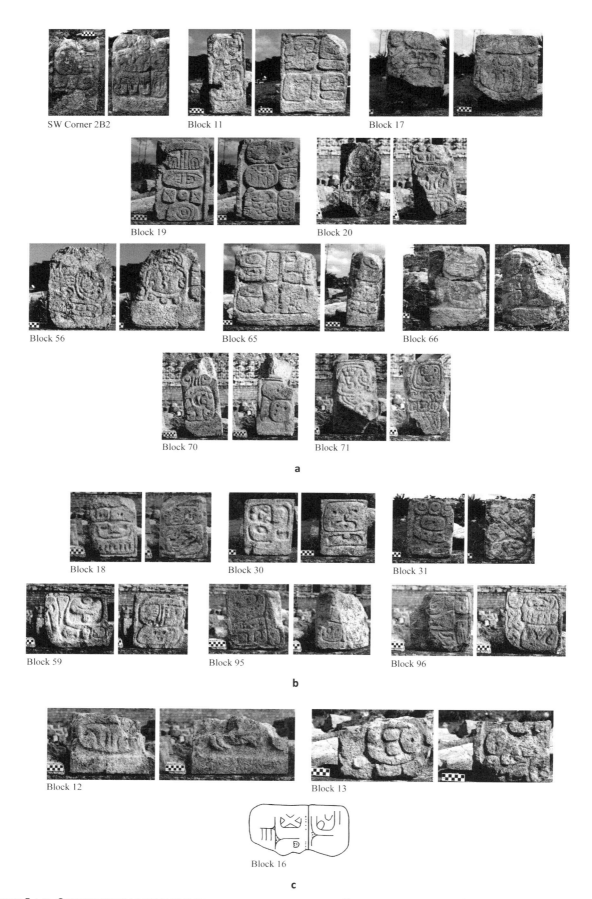

Figure 5 a-c. Cornerstones located in the rubble associated with the Hieroglyphic Platform. (a) large cornerstones; (b) small cornerstones; (c) uncategorized cornerstones. Photographs by Meghan Rubenstein. Drawing by Meghan Rubenstein after Eric von Euw's unpublished field notes.

The stones were cleaned by the archaeological project at Kabah in October 2013 and were re-photographed in December 2013.

Form and Function

While hieroglyphic decipherment is the primary aim of our project, we also wanted to study the form of the structure itself and speculate on its original function. The monument is equal in length on each of its four sides, however the design on the facing stones varies slightly. The central portion on each side is uncarved (see Figures 2 and 3). While the uncarved portions of the north, east, and south sides measure the same, the smooth portion of the west side of the monument, which faces the main access stairs to the Codz Pop, is considerably longer—almost twice the width.

On this western edge (see Figures 2a and 3a), one other stone projects at a right angle. Based on an early CIW photo (58-34-20/56130.1), a second block also projected from this edge at the other side of the uncarved surface. While these records date to the period following Pavón's reconstruction, he must have seen some evidence for stairs on the western portion of the Hieroglyphic Platform.

Our own work confirms that there are at least 19 additional cornerstones associated with this structure, far more than the seven missing from the reconstructed monument (Figure 5a-c). Furthermore, the cornerstones are two different heights. One set is equal to the remaining corner stone on the platform, varying between 39 and 52 cm (Figure 5a).[7] Within this set there are narrow corners and corners whose widths are the same dimension as the height. The second set is approximately two-thirds the height, between 19 and 26 cm, and all of them are nearly cubic (Figure 5b). Two additional cornerstone are fragmented, although Blocks 12 and 13 are likely part of the first category based on the scale of the carving, and a third uncategorized corner was illustrated by von Euw, but not relocated during our search (Figure 5c).

Based on this evidence, there are a few explanations for the extra cornerstones. The first possibility is that the platform contained a third level of stones. However, the border along the top of the glyphs on the second course indicates otherwise. Another possibility—hinted at in the 1950s reconstruction—is that this platform had steps on the western side (Figure 6). Examples of the radial platform are found throughout the Puuc region, including on the south side of the House of the Governor at nearby Uxmal. In fact, radial platforms appear throughout ancient Mesoamerica. Still, even with three levels of steps on the western side of the platform, which would be possible if built from the small blocks in Figure 5b, there are additional cornerstones.

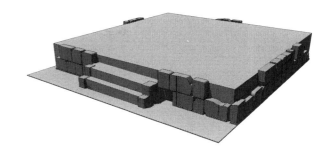

FIGURE 6. RECONSTRUCTION OF THE HIEROGLYPHIC PLATFORM SHOWING STEPS ON THE WEST SIDE. RENDERING BY PHILIP GALEEV.

Another option that we would like to propose is that the Hieroglyphic Platform was only two courses of stones, as it is now, but that hieroglyphic steps were part of each side. We think it is a possibility that these steps might not have been built into the structure, but were free standing—in front of the areas with smooth, uncarved surfaces.

The possible placement of steps around the monument suggests that it functioned as a platform rather than an altar, as originally labeled by Pavón. The steps would have allowed for one to ascend the monument and stand in front of the Codz Pop, as a figurehead, orator, or performer. The raised height of the person on the platform would have made someone more visible to those below the larger building platform that supports the Codz Pop.[8]

Hieroglyphic Text

There is no doubt a degree of accuracy in the placement of the stones reset by Pavón's project in the 1950s. Many of the blocks are connected by continuous lines and shared writing style. Yet, while some of the carved blocks relate to each other, the original reading order is largely unknown, thus providing a limited context for the hieroglyphic inscription.

The aim of the preliminary analysis of the inscription, which we offer here, is not to reconstruct a complete sequence nor make sense of the whole text. Instead, we focus on the paleography, or style, of the carving and the individual readings for the glyphs depicted, which allows us to propose some new ideas about the monument.

The glyphic blocks, both on and off the monument, are carved in three styles, which we have identified by comparing three examples of the name of the deity *K'awiil* on the Hieroglyphic Platform (Figure 7a-c). These styles are not unusual for the region; they are similar to texts from

---

[7] Some size variation in the stones is due to damage.

[8] For an extended analysis of the relationship between the platform and the Codz Pop, see Rubenstein 2015, Chapter 6.

a   b   c

FIGURE 7 A-C. EXAMPLES OF K'AWIIL (**K'AWIL-WI-LA**) WRITTEN IN THREE SEPARATE WRITING STYLES ON THE HIEROGLYPHIC PLATFORM. (A) SOUTH FACADE; (B) SOUTH FACADE; (C) NORTH FACADE. PHOTOGRAPHS BY MEGHAN RUBENSTEIN. DRAWINGS BY PHILIPP GALEEV.

neighboring sites. For this paper we want to focus on the style that we find most interesting, that is the presence of the Xcalumkin style, first noted by Grube (1986). Writing from Xcalumkin, a site located about 30 km west of Kabah, is set apart by its double-line carving. As the name suggests, the style is found only at Xcalumkin; Kabah is an exception.

The Xcalumkin style appears on both the west and south sides of the Hieroglyphic Platform. In addition, it is found among the loose stones. Examples from the rubble include two of the cornerstones pictured in Figure 5a: Block 56, which reads **SIHO'M** (Figure 8c) and *[yu]-xu-ul-le* (Figure 9d), and Block 71 (Figure 5a), which reads *IK'... tz'ap...* (Figure 9f).

The appearance of this style of hieroglyphic writing on the monument at Kabah allows us to consider the following possibilities:

1. There were several scribes.
2. More than one text might be present on this monument.
3. The shared style might demonstrate some kind of relationship between Kabah and Xcalumkin.
4. If there is a relationship between Kabah and Xcalumkin, we might be able to narrow the dates for the monument. The recorded history of Xcalumkin covers a very short period of time (9.14.17.00–9.16.10.0.0), thus the appearance of its

paleographic style on the platform at Kabah might indicate that it was carved during this period, which translates in our calendar to the second half of 8th century.

While we are on the topic of dates, we also want to note that the platform text includes calendric entries, but unfortunately none of them are preserved completely. For example, we have two *tzolk'in* days '**AJAW**day (Figure 8a) and '**IK'**day (Figure 8b). Yet, without numbers we cannot calculate the dates. There are also two examples of months from the 365-day calendar (*haab*), but they too are incomplete. One is the month **SIHO'M**, previously mentioned (Figure 8c). The other is part of Block 52 (Figure 8e), discussed below.

Even though we cannot pinpoint a date with the tzolk'in and haab examples, the presence of these glyphs confirms the use of the Classic calendar system, which was distributed throughout the Maya Lowlands during the Classic period. However, we are not only viewing a Classic use of the calendar but also a local example, the *tuun-'ajaw* dating system (Proskouriakoff and Thompson 1947).

For example, in Block 15 (Figure 8d) we can see a sequence that could be analyzed as **ti-WAL-la 'u-4-...**, *ti-wal 'u-4-... 'during the 4th...'*. A similar expression is found at Ek' Balam and some other sites in Northern Yucatán, where *ti-wal* introduces the *tuun* dating. Thus, we can assume that after the number followed by *tuun* 'year' translates to 'during the 4th year.'

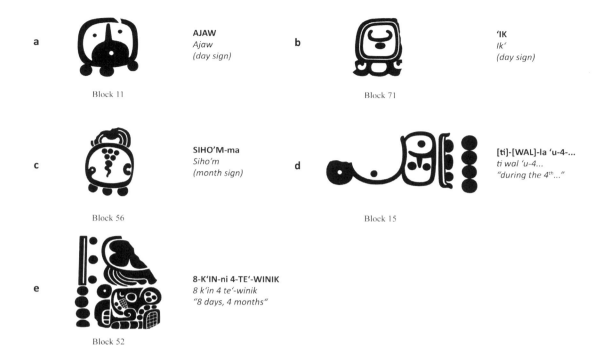

a — **AJAW** *Ajaw* (day sign) — Block 11

b — **'IK** *Ik'* (day sign) — Block 71

c — **SIHO'M-ma** *Siho'm* (month sign) — Block 56

d — **[ti]-[WAL]-la 'u-4-...** *ti wal 'u-4-...* "during the 4th..." — Block 15

e — **8-K'IN-ni 4-TE'-WINIK** *8 k'in 4 te'-winik* "8 days, 4 months" — Block 52

FIGURE 8. CALENDRICS/NUMBERS ON THE HIEROGLYPHIC PLATFORM. DRAWINGS BY PHILIPP GALEEV.

We also want to return attention to Block 52 (Figure 8e), the stone Grube thought was missing.[9] The reading order is unclear, as the numerals before **K'IN-ni** ('day') are written mirrored, but the whole sequence, **8-K'IN-ni 4-TE'-WINIK** ('8 days, 4 months'), is similar to a Long Count or Distance number. Based on presence of examples from the Classic period and the Northern Yucatecan calendars, we suggest that the platform was created during the transition period, when both calendric systems were in use.

As we mentioned earlier, the reading order of the majority of the glyphic blocks is unclear, but we have extracted some interesting examples that can help us understand the contents of the text.

First of all, we can identify some verbal expressions:

1. In Block 1' on the south side of the monument, we see the sequence **CHUM-wa-ni**, *chum-waan-Ø* 'he sat' (Figure 9a). The appearance of this positional verb is surprising, as we have no other examples in the texts from the Puuc region or Northern Yucatan. In Classic Maya texts, this expression is used in the context of accession and often relates to the lord 'ajaw.' Therefore, we suggest that this block references the accession of a noble person, maybe a king or another high-ranking individual.

2. In Block 7 on the south side of the monument, we have the sequence **'u-KAB-ji-ya**, *'u-kab-[i]j-iiy-Ø* 'he ordered it' (Figure 10a). Like *chumwaan*, this verb is also rare in this region. During the Classic period, *ukabjiiy* was used in various contexts, for example the military order or the order for the erection of a monument. Unfortunately, we cannot identify the context in which it appears in the text of the Hieroglyphic Platform. But it is important to note that this verb belongs to the category of the expressions that introduce high-ranking persons (hence its inclusion in Figure 10, titles and marks of authority).

3. With regard to military context, we should also note that we have one example of the verb **CH'AK-ka-ja**, *ch'a[h]k-aj-Ø* 'it was chopped' (Figure 9b). This expression is usually confined to a military context. In our case, *ch'ahkaj* follows the unclear sequence **ch'a?-la-ka**, which could be an unknown toponym. Thus, we suggest that this text is relaying successful military activity at Kabah.

4. The inscription also contains some examples of the constructive expressions, like *'uxul* 'carving' (Figures 9c-e), and *tz'ap* 'to erect' (Figure 9f). Because we have three examples of the *'uxul* expression, it is possible that the text of the platform refers to either three different monuments or describes several different stages of the carving of the Hieroglyphic Platform. These examples also seem to confirm the use of a local variation of the

---
[9] Grube (1986) looked for Block 52 during his visit to Kabah, which was reproduced by Moedano in 1952. Not able to find the stone, he speculated that it might not exist. We relocated it in the rubble in 2013.

123

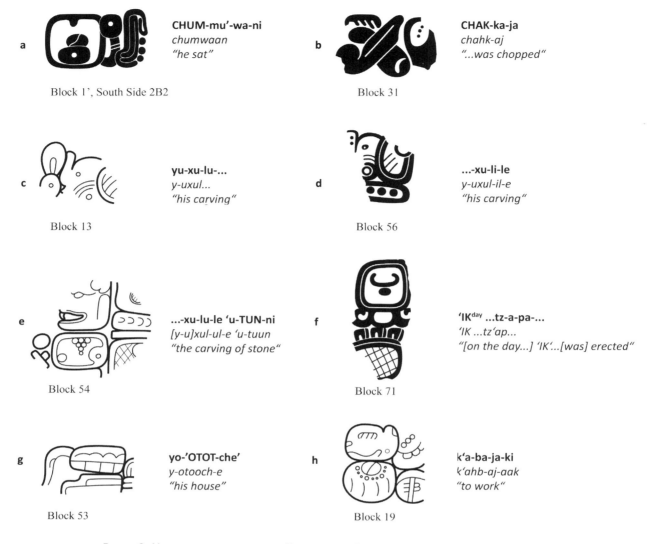

a CHUM-mu'-wa-ni
chumwaan
"he sat"

Block 1', South Side 2B2

b CHAK-ka-ja
chahk-aj
"...was chopped"

Block 31

c yu-xu-lu-...
y-uxul...
"his carving"

Block 13

d ...-xu-li-le
y-uxul-il-e
"his carving"

Block 56

e ...-xu-lu-le 'u-TUN-ni
[y-u]xul-ul-e 'u-tuun
"the carving of stone"

Block 54

f 'IK^day ...tz-a-pa-...
'IK ...tz'ap...
"[on the day...] 'IK'...[was] erected"

Block 71

g yo-'OTOT-che'
y-otooch-e
"his house"

Block 53

h k'a-ba-ja-ki
k'ahb-aj-aak
"to work"

Block 19

FIGURE 9. VERBAL EXPRESSIONS ON THE HIEROGLYPHIC PLATFORM. DRAWINGS BY PHILIP GALEEV.

language. Block 56 (Figure 9d) **...-xu-ul-le**, *[y-u] xul-ul-e'* contains the final *–e'* vowel, which is good evidence for Yucatecan influence. This is probably the same feature we have in Block 54 (Figure 9e). The appearance of the *tz'ap* expression (Figure 9f) is surprising, because this verb is not used to refer to platforms or other kinds of flat objects, thus we can assume that this verb was used to describe the erection of another monument. In this case, it is likely that there was something like a stela either on, or near, the Hieroglyphic Platform.

5. In Block 53 (Figure 9g), we can see **yo-'OTOT-ti**? *y-'otoot-Ø* 'his house.' We suggest that some of the constructive expressions on the altar could be related to the construction of a building in Kabah, probably the Codz Pop or another structure in the East Group, based on proximity.

6. Finally, in Block 19 (Figure 9h) we have the sequence **k'a-ba-ja-ki**, derived from the word

k'ab 'the hand,' and the suffix *-aj* and an unclear suffix *–aak*. It likely corresponds to the examples from Chichén Itzá, such as *y-uxul-naj-aak* from the Temple of the Four Lintels (Lnt.1, blocks A4-B4). We also should note that in Yucatecan languages we find the expressions *k'abtah* 'hacer alguna obra de manos/to do work by hand' or *k'abte a kol* 'haz tu milpa/tend to your milpa' (Barrera and Rendón 1980:362), which represent the applicative form with the sense 'to work (with one's hands).' In this case, we suggest that in our example the word *k'ab* could also signify 'to work.'

In addition to verbal expression there are some other important sequences related to titles and marks of authority we want to highlight.

1. First, we have the title *'ajaw* 'lord.' Since this appears on the same monument as the verbs *chumwaan*, 'he sat' (Fig. 9a), and *'u-k'abjiiy*, 'he ordered it' (Fig 10a), this appears to confirm

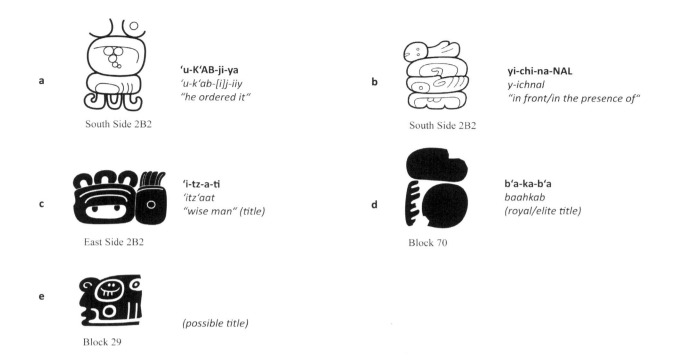

a 'u-K'AB-ji-ya
'u-k'ab-[i]j-iiy
"he ordered it"

South Side 2B2

b yi-chi-na-NAL
y-ichnal
"in front/in the presence of"

South Side 2B2

c 'i-tz-a-ti
'itz'aat
"wise man" (title)

East Side 2B2

d b'a-ka-b'a
baahkab
(royal/elite title)

Block 70

e (possible title)

Block 29

FIGURE 10. TITLES AND MARKS OF AUTHORITY ON THE HIEROGLYPHIC PLATFORM. DRAWINGS BY PHILIP GALEEV.

royal authority at Kabah, an idea that has been assumed in the past based on the iconography associated with the Codz Pop. Moreover, the sixth block on the west side of the platform (Figure 10b) is carved with the sequence **yi-chi-na-NAL**, *y-ichnal*-Ø 'in the presence of,' which introduces high-ranking person, usually an *'ajaw*, in Classic Maya inscriptions.

2. In addition to the *'ajaw* title, there are also examples of lower ranking titles, such as *'itzaat* on the third block on the east side platform (Figure 10c), *baahkab* on Block 70 (Figure 10d), and a rare glyph on Block 29 (Figure 10e), a possible title that depicts a head with a tamal inside the eye. This same glyph also appears on an Early Classic vessel from Ucanal.

Conclusion

Although in the early stage of our analysis, we can draw some conclusions based on our examination of the hieroglyphic stones associated with the monument. We have suggested that the monument, in the past referred to as an altar, is more likely a platform. The abundance of cornerstones, which vary in size, led us to propose that the Hieroglyphic Platform originally had steps on one or more of its sides.

The interpretation of the text, while still inconclusive, offers a number of clues to its content and meaning. We propose that the text confirms that there was royal authority at Kabah, and that the text might record the accession of one of the site's lords. We also found evidence of military activity in the inscription, a claim supported by the iconography of the building with which the Hieroglyphic Platform is associated, the Codz Pop. Finally, we found evidence of ritual/calendric activity, such as the erection of monuments and the celebration of important calendar cycles. This proposal is based on the presence of the tzolk'in day *'Ajaw, tuun-'ajaw* dating, and *ti-wal* expressions.

Other hieroglyphic inscriptions in the Puuc region and across ancient Mesoamerica have similar foci. The Hieroglyphic Platform at Kabah combines authority, ritual activity—including accessioning—and tracking the calendar. What makes this monument unique is the possible addition of several events over time; the various styles might be indicative of the evolving nature of the structure. The paleographic relationship to Xcalumkin is suggestive, and the varied hands hint at the layered text, or perhaps text that was added to at different periods, or at least assembled by several authors.

The questions left unanswered are the specifics of the dates and the meaning behind the rituals and accession(s). Learning more about how the monument functioned might also help understand more about the importance of the Hieroglyphic Platform at Kabah.

Aknowledgments. We wish to thank several institutions for providing permission to complete and funding for this research. Rubenstein's fieldwork at Kabah was carried out under Consejo de Arqueología del Instituto Nacional de Antropología e Historia, Mexico, permit number 401.B(4)19.2013/36/1879 and supported by a Fulbright-García Robles fellowship from La Comisión

México-Estados Unidos para el Intercambio Educativo y Cultural and the U.S. Department of State's Bureau of Education and Cultural Affairs, and an E. D. Farmer grant from the Mexican Center at the University of Texas at Austin. Galeev's 2013 fieldwork was supported by the Ministry of Education and Science of the Russian Federation, and from 2009 to 2013 by the Federal special-purpose program 'Scientific and academic personnel of innovative Russia' (project No. 14.740.12.1356 'Epigraphic heritage of the pre-Columbian cultures of America: new approaches to the study of the ancient civilizations'). We also thank Lourdes Toscano Hernández and Gustavo Novelo Rincón for their support of this project and our work at Kabah.

References Cited

Barrera Vásquez, Alfredo, and Silvia Rendón (editors)

1980 *Diccionario Maya Cordemex*. Ediciones Cordemex, Mérida, Yucatán.

Carrasco Vargas, Ramón et al.

1992 *Informe de los trabajos realizados en la temporada 1992, Proyecto Kabah*. Instituto Nacional de Antropología e Historia, Centro Regional Yucatán. December, Archivo de la Dirección de Monumentos Prehispánicos del I.N.A.H. Informe 30-62.

Carrasco Vargas, Ramón

1994 El gobernante de rostro escarificado de Kabah. *Arqueología Mexicana* 5(I):75-77.

Carrasco Vargas, Ramón, and Eduardo Pérez de Heredia

1996 Los últimos gobernadores de Kabah. In *Eighth Palenque Round Table, 1993*. M. Macri and J. McHargue, eds. pp. 297-307. San Francisco: The Pre-Columbian Art Research Institute.

Graña-Behrens, Daniel

2002 *Die Maya-Inschriften aus Nordwestyukatan, Mexiko*, Fakultät der Rheinischen-Friedrich-Wilhelms, University of Bonn.

Grube, Nikolai

1986 Die Hieroglyphenplattform von Kabah, Yucatán, México. *Mexicon* VIII(1):13-17.

Kowalski, Jeff Karl

1985 The Historical Interpretations of the Inscriptions of Uxmal. In *Fourth Palenque Round Table, 1980*. E.P. Benson, ed. pp. 235-247. Pre-Columbian Art Research Institute, San Francisco.

Ligorred Perramon, José de Calasanz

1993 La escultura Puuc: Análisis iconológico del Codz Pop de Kabah, Archaeology thesis, Escuela Nacional de Antropología e Historia, Mexico.

Maler, Teobert

1997 *Península Yucatán*. Berlin: Gebr. Mann.

Moedano Kóer, Hugo

1952 Un adoratorio jeroglífico en Kaba'. In *Tlatoani; boletín de la Sociedad de Alumnos de la Escuela Nacional de Antropología e Historia*. 1:21-22.

Pavón Abreu, Raúl et.al.

1951a Compendio de los trabajos efectuados durante el año de 1951, por el INAH en las Zonas Arquelógicas de Kabah, Yucatán y Tacah, Hopelchen, Campeche. Instituto Nacional de Antropología e Historia, Centro Regional Yucatán. Archivo de la Dirección de Monumentos Prehispánicos del I.N.A.H. Informe 1134-5.

1951b Informe general de los trabajos en la Zona Arqueológica de Kabah., Yucatán, desde junio 10 hasta julio 28 de 1951. Temporada I. Instituto Nacional de Antropología

e Historia, Centro Regional Yucatán. Archivo de la Dirección de Monumentos Prehispánicos del I.N.A.H. Informe 1134-6.

Pollock, Harry E. D.

1980 *The Puuc: An Architectural Survey of the Hill Country of Yucatan and Northern Campeche, Mexico*. Peabody Museum of Archaeology and Ethnology, Cambridge.

Proskouriakoff, Tatiana Avenirova, and J. E. S. Thompson

1947 Maya Calendar Round Dates such as 9 Ahau 17 Mol. In *Carnegie Institution of Washington, Notes on Middle American Archaeology and Ethnology* 79:143-150.

Rubenstein, Meghan

2015 *Animate Architecture at Kabah: Art and Politics in the Puuc Region of Yucatán, Mexico*. Ph.D. dissertation, University of Texas at Austin.

Salazar Ortegón, Ponciano et al.

1952 *Informe de la II Temporada de Exploraciones Arqueológicas efectuada en la zona de Kabah, Yucatán, durante el año de 1952*. Instituto Nacional de Antropología e Historia, Centro Regional Yucatán. Archivo de la Dirección de Monumentos Prehispánicos del I.N.A.H. Informe 1136-1.

Salazar Ortegón, Ponciano

1953 Exploraciones y problemas de reconstrucción del Codz Pop y del Sistema I de la Zona Arqueológica de Kabah, Yuc., Tesis de Maestria en Ciencias Antropológicas, Escuela Nacional de Antropología e Historia, Mexico.

Stephens, John Lloyd

1843 *Incidents of Travel in Yucatan*. 2 Volumes. New York: Harper.

Stuart, David and Meghan Rubenstein.

2015 The Reading of Two Dates from the Codz Pop at Kabah, Yucatan. *Maya Decipherment*, October 30, 2014. http://decipherment.wordpress.com/2014/10/30/the-reading-of-two-dates-from-the-codz-pop-at-kabah-yucatan/

Toscano Hernández, Lourdes, Gustavo Novelo Rincón, David Ortegón Zapata, Oyuki García Salas, y David Palomino Yam

2014 Proyecto investigación y restauración arquitectónica en Kabah, Yucatán. Informe preliminar de la temporada 2011 y Propuesta para la temporada 2012, Archivo de la Sección de Arqueología, Centro INAH Yucatán, Mérida.

Making it a Date: Positioning the Chocholá Style in Time and Space

Maline D. Werness-Rude

Working in northern Yucatan during the Late Classic period, Maya potters created a subset of vessels exhibiting deeply carved iconographic panels alongside incised texts. Their fine craftsmanship and nuanced use of word and image speak to contexts of elite production and consumption. Now called the Chocholá style, these luxury goods name northern political actors and provide insight into the regional interactions in which they engaged. As recent work continues to expand the corpus, its mention of specific dates and its accordant ties to northern sociopolitical development in the eighth century have only become clearer. I begin this chapter with a brief update regarding the Chocholá version of the standard inscription that was often used to dedicate elite ceramic wares. As part of this overview, I suggest that ceramicists working in the style used pattern recognition to signal sociopolitical affiliation. I then move on to focus on recurrent titles and their statistical frequency. Finally, a close look at Chocholá dates indicates just how important this trope was to the style as a whole. In further examining this material, I identify some clear links to the monumental record as well as several other more tentative connections before exploring the ideological associations carried by such literal and metaphorical positioning.

Trabajando en el norte de Yucatán durante del periodo Clásico Tardío, los alfareros mayas crearon un subconjunto de vasos que exhiben paneles iconográficos elaborados con grabados profundos, acompañados por textos jeroglíficos incisos. Su fino trabajo artesanal y matizada uso de la palabra e de la imagen habla de contextos de producción y consumo asociados con la élite. Adscritos al ahora llamado estilo Chocholá, esas vasijas de lujo nombran actores políticos del norte de la península de Yucatán y proporcionan una idea sobre las interacciones regionales en las que participaban. Conforme el trabajo reciente continúa ampliando el corpus de este tipo de cerámica, la mención de fechas específicas y su lazo concomitante al desarrollo sociopolítico del norte peninsular durante del siglo VIII se han convertido en asuntos más claros. Inicio este capítulo con una breve actualización sobre la versión chocholá de la inscripción estándar que los escribas utilizan con frecuencia para dedicar objetos de cerámica de élite. Como parte de este resumen, sugiero que los ceramistas asociados con el estilo utilizaron el reconocimiento de determinadas pautas para indicar su afiliación sociopolítica. Luego me enfoco en la mención de títulos recurrentes en las inscripciones y su frecuencia estadística. Finalmente, una mirada cercana a las fechas chocholá indica lo importante que era este tema para el estilo en su conjunto. Al examinar más detenimiento este material, identifico enlaces con los registros monumentos, así como varias otras conexiones tentativas antes de explorar las asociaciones ideológicas implicadas en los posicionamientos literales y metafóricos declarados en las vasijas.

When John Lloyd Stephens (1843) first published accounts of his explorations illustrated by his traveling companion Frederick Catherwood, they introduced modern, western readers to the ancient art and architecture of the Yucatán Peninsula. Stephens and Catherwood's work augmented and reflected a fascination with this part of the Maya world as demonstrated by the many archaeological projects and intensive anthropological and art historical studies that have since flourished, not to mention an ever-burgeoning tourist trade and the illicit trafficking in antiquities that often accompanies such prolonged interest.[1] Despite this scholarly attention, many of the actors who peopled northern courts, and the spectacles and successes that captivated them, remain shadowy at best. In the ongoing effort to understand northern cultural development, it is thus important to analyze new texts as they come to light, with particular attention paid to examples that provide specific historical data, insights into poetics, and nuanced aspects of word choice and usage.

Chocholá style ceramics provide a window into Late Classic Puuc political development and it is in this context that the present work contributes to Puuc archaeology. The corpus of Chocholá vessels has recently expanded, which warrants an updated overview of the inscriptions they carry. In addition to briefly identifying pattern recognition and attendant signals regarding sociopolitical affiliation, focusing analysis on dates and titled individuals helps us explore the extent of the influence exerted by northern Maya nobles. It also allows us to temporally and spatially re-locate a corpus that has been heavily (though thankfully not completely) looted due to an ever-expanding interest in the Yucatán and its archaeological remains.

Introducing the Chocholá Style

Potters working in the Yucatán Peninsula in the Late Classic (c. A.D. 700-800) began producing vessels with deeply carved panels for their elite patrons (Figure 1).[2]

---

[1] While time constraints and the focus of this chapter prevent a full enumeration of the scholarly work focused on Northern Yucatecan pottery, early and/or formative projects include Herbert Spinden's (1913) and Harry Pollock's (1980) groundbreaking studies, George Brainerd's (1958) and George Vaillant's (1927) respective efforts to analyze ceramics, as well as the formal reports of Robert Smith's (1971) excavations at Mayapan and those of E. Wyllys Andrews IV and E. Wyllys Andrews V (1980) at Dzibilchaltun.

[2] For previous considerations focused on the style, see Traci Ardren (1996), Erik Boot (1997, 2006, 2008), Michael Coe (1973), José Miguel García Campillo (1992), Judith Strupp Green (1997), Nikolai Grube (1990), Carolyn Tate (1985), Ricardo Velázquez Valadés and colleagues (2005), and Maline Werness-Rude (Werness 2010; Werness-Rude 2015). For the analysis that allows us to restrict its production to a one hundred year period of time focused in Late Classic Yucatán, especially see Garciá Campillo (1992) and Werness-Rude (Werness 2010).

Maline D. Werness-Rude - Ventura College (mwernessrude@vcccd.edu).

A

B

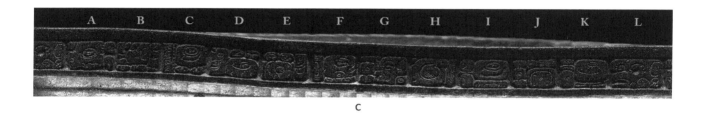

C

FIGURE 1 A-C. ISOLATED BUST SCENE. CHOCHOLÁ STYLE CERAMIC VESSEL, PUUC REGION, YUCATÁN, MEXICO, C. A.D. 700-800. (A) VIEW OF ICONOGRAPHIC PANEL; (B) VIEW OF DIAGONAL TEXT OPPOSITE THE ICONOGRAPHIC PANEL; (C) ROLL-OUT PHOTOGRAPH OF RIM TEXT (IMAGES © ETHNOLOGISCHES MUSEUM, STAATLICHE MUSEEN ZU BERLIN. PHOTOGRAPHS BY CLAUDIA OBROCKI.)

Largely taking the form of cups with rounded and/or slightly flaring sides or gourd-shaped profiles (Figures 2a and 7), these objects undoubtedly were used as high-end serving dishes that, along with other aspects of elite material culture, provided a backdrop for the many-faceted interactions between aligned and/or competing polities.[3] These vessels, and other luxury items like them, acted as much more than just accessories, however. Chocholá artists developed objects that carried nuanced messages designed to support elite prerogatives during their dissemination and use in feasting events or as gifts.[4] The style has continued to enjoy popularity with collectors in the modern period and many have commented upon the sophistication such ceramic wares display. Indeed, one of the earliest published examples can be found in Stephens's (1843:275) travel account.[5]

The depth of carving, trickle (post fire) paint, and consistent formatting all help to visually define the Chocholá corpus, which is otherwise characterized by a fair degree of visual range. Images are always set off from the vessel wall by a deeply carved frame that is kept rigidly separate from the rim and the base. Potters also typically constructed single scene panels that could be viewed at a glance with little or no turning of the cup. The specific images they created can also be sorted into types, most of which revolve (often literally) around the body (or bodies) of beautiful elites or supernatural entities. As a result, Chocholá images and/or vessel shapes can be grouped in the following way:[6]

1. Imagery: Human figures[7]
    a. Isolated Bust Scene
    b. Lone Lords
    c. Conference and Multiple Figures Scene

---

[3] For an overview of the connection between ceramics and elite political control see Maline Werness-Rude and Kaylee Spencer (2015:especially 47-49 and 98-100).

[4] Most of the aforementioned scholarly attention given to the Chocholá style (see footnote 2) has acknowledged its connection with, and support of, the elite apparatus. For more explicit, extended examinations of the ways in which the Chocholá style participated in, and supported, such power structures, see Boot (2008), García Campillo (1992), and Werness-Rude (Werness 2010; Werness-Rude 2015).

[5] Stephens is not alone; almost every scholar to discuss this body of

material (see footnote 2) acknowledges it as one of the pinnacles of Maya ceramic production.

[6] In what follows I provide a brief overview of the Chocholá style definition. For a fuller development of such material, see Werness (2010) and footnote 2.

[7] While there are some examples that show female dignitaries, most of the human characters to grace the sides of Chocholá vessels are male, so I will use the male pronoun throughout unless otherwise warranted.

d. Ballplayers
2. Imagery: Supernaturals/Non-Humans
    a. God L
    b. K'awiil/God K
    c. Disembodied Heads
    d. Serpents and Other Watery Beings
    e. GI and the Paddler Gods
    f. Miscellaneous Deities
    g. Miscellaneous Animals and Animal
      Supernaturals
3. Devoid of imagery: Gourd-shaped vessels with rim
bands
    a. With completely three dimensional, modeled/
      molded profiles
    b. With stylized, carved profiles

While all of these groups are statistically significant, images focused on human leaders by far outweigh the other categories.

The idiosyncratic dedicatory texts that appear as rim, vertical, or diagonal inscriptions also help define the style, both in the way they look and in what they say. In conjunction with a major period of epigraphic advancement, Nikolai Grube (1990), Barbara MacLeod (1990), David Stuart (1989), and others turned to portable media, especially pottery, with an eye to deciphering the texts they display (see also Houston and Taube 1987). These hieroglyphic strings have long been recognized as quintessentially different from their typically stationary, monumental counterparts despite overlaps in historical and ritual subject matter.[8] Because of its looting and subsequent dissemination to public and private collections around the world, the Chocholá style offered a well published, already identified corpus at a time when large-scale, easily accessible ceramic databases basically did not exist.[9] It was also selected for extended analysis because of the repetition it displays across vessels. While the formulaic nature of rim texts had already been widely acknowledged by scholars, the Chocholá style offered an extreme case of such replication.[10] Indeed, Chocholá examples are so emphatically repetitive, both in what they say and how they say it, that these glyphic strings factor into definitions of the style (García Campillo 1992; Green 1997; Grube

1990; Werness 2010). I have argued elsewhere (Werness 2010; Werness-Rude 2015) that such visual and textual continuity indicates highly intentional, conscious efforts to create a cohesive body of portable goods. According to this model, one piece, when seen during isolated moments of consumption, would automatically be connected with the corpus—and its sociopolitical affiliations—in the eyes of educated, contemporary viewers.

The epigraphic advances of the late twentieth century have clearly identified the main components of the Dedicatory Formula (or Primary Standard Sequence).[11] The common rim text found on all types of elite Maya ceramic wares, regardless of region, typically includes an opening dedicatory segment followed by more specific description and naming of vessel content and type, as well as mention of the person for (or by) whom it was made. In the case of the Chocholá style, the Dedicatory Formula frequently follows standard patterns of placement at the vessel's rim, but it can also occur, in truncated form, as a diagonal or vertical text either as a replacement for, or in conjunction with the rim band sequence (Figure 1).[12] Scribes began the sequence with the requisite dedicatory/creation statement followed by terms that designate the cups as carved clay drinking cups/bowls for holding liquids, like chocolate or *atole* (a corn based drink), meant for titled individuals.[13]

Beyond these shared traits dictated by the formulaic nature of the dedicatory sequence, potters working in the style created idiosyncratic forms for some of the standard inclusions. Diagnostic examples include the use of a complete bird—rather than just its wing—to signify the **k'i** syllable, and an anthropomorphized variant of the **lu** sign, both of which occur exclusively on Chocholá wares.[14] What is more, when they occur, the introductory

---

[8] For early recognition of the standardized, formulaic nature of rim texts, and their specific tie to the ceramic medium, see Coe (1973).

[9] Justin and Barbara Kerr published the first *Maya Vase Book* in 1989 (the Kerrs ended the printed series after six volumes, at which point they turned to an online forum; now thousands of images, with more added regularly, make up the Maya Vase Database, which is accessible and searchable online: www.mayavase.com). In doing so, the Kerrs began the work of compiling a far-reaching database of ancient Maya ceramics characterized both by its depth and breadth as well as by its consistently high quality roll-out images (a technology developed by Justin Kerr himself). Their work continues to this day despite Barbara Kerr's death in 2014. In this context, it is important to note that when Grube, MacLeod, Stuart, and others were beginning to analyze ceramic texts, they did not have easy access to the vast body of material now available due in large part to the Kerrs' efforts.

[10] Coe (1973) discussed and began to codify such formulaic rim texts in the same publication in which he introduced and defined the Chocholá style, presumably due in part to the marked repetition these vessels display.

[11] The Dedicatory Formula was first called the Primary Standard Sequence (PSS for short) because scholars did not yet know what it said (see Coe 1973). Now that we have a better understanding of its content I, following others (Stuart 2005:114), prefer the descriptive title Dedicatory Formula.

[12] Indeed, this diagonal or vertical orientation, unusual in other ceramic traditions, is so frequent in the style as to act as another of its diagnostic features (Werness 2010).

[13] I have provided the barest overview of Chocholá Dedicatory Formulae here. The specific references vary from container to container and some terms are still not completely deciphered. There continue to be questions regarding the translation of the carving phrase as *y-uxul*, for instance, despite almost universal agreement that it does indeed refer to the carved medium. Similarly, debate continues regarding the exact English translation of another term, *u-jaay*, with most recent interpretations suggesting that it marks the ceramics on which it is featured as clay cups or bowls in place of the original reading emphasizing thin walls (Grube 1990; Hull 2012; Kettunen and Helmke 2014; MacLeod 1990). Of the liquid contents recorded in such inscriptions, fresh chocolate and atole are often mentioned. When diagonal or vertical textual orientations are chosen over horizontal rim bands, scribes had to shorten the Dedicatory Formula and often did so by omitting the initial, dedicatory glyph (likely understood as implicit in such circumstances; see figs. 1b, and 6).

[14] While many examples of full-figured birds appear in Maya script these are logographic in nature (i.e. the word *yaxun*, translated as bird). The **k'i** syllable used repeatedly as part of the *y-uk'ib* phrase (his drinking vessel), ubiquitous in the Dedicatory Formula, can only be found in full-figure form in the Chocholá corpus; it is only ever rendered as a bird wing in non-Chocholá examples, regardless of the specific word it helps form. The **lu** syllable is likewise altered in unusual ways that are almost completely restricted to the Chocholá corpus (Erik Boot 2007,

phrases that open the text take on distinctive (though still poorly understood) forms (e.g. glyph blocks D-E and A-C in Figures 1c and 7 respectively).[15] Logographic references to complimentary dualities (e.g. glyph block B, Figure 7) are often inserted.[16] Scribes also frequently incorporated a distinctive *ajaw* superfix when writing the introductory glyph (see glyph blocks D and A in Figures 1c and 7 respectively), though it remains unclear if it should actually be read as *ajaw* in this context. Because of their uniqueness, these features seem to have been intentionally created in part to separate the associated vessels from other ceramic traditions, thereby introducing a specific, immediately recognizable visual identity tied to the style and the political actors responsible for its creation (Werness 2010).

Chocholá Titles

It is not surprising, given the Chocholá style's intentional connection with the political superstructure, that it incorporates even more explicit geopolitical references, including textual allusions to the people who would have used such vessels. In the vast majority of instances that make mention of the vessel's owner/patron, the scribe favored using titles—of which *Sajal* (Figure 1c, glyph block C; Figure 5, block F; Figure 7, block J), *Bakab* (Figure 2b, block A5; Figure 5, block H), *Chak Ch'ok* (Figure 2b, block B4; Figure 3, blocks A and A'5; Figure 4b, block C1; Figure 5, block D), *Kelem* (Figure 5, block E), *Kalomte'* (Figure 6, block 2), and *Cholom* (Figure 7, block I) were most repeated—rather than (and/or in addition to) personal monikers. While *chak ch'ok* and *kelem* refer to the youth and vitality of the character so named, *sajal*, *bakab*, *kalomte'*, and *cholom* are particularly linked with political office even though their exact meaning remains illusive. What is more, some of the titles, like *sajal* and *kalomte'*, required official seating or investiture similar to the way a paramount ruler would be seated in *Ajaw*-ship (e.g. kingship), and such honors, at least in the case of a *sajal*, likely reflected personal accomplishment as well as birthright (Zender 2004:154, 300).

Sajal (Figure 1c, block C; Figure 5, block F; Figure 7, block J) in particular suggests a direct, if subordinate connection with royalty and has been tentatively translated as "feared one," (making it a rather pointed title for figures

who acted as regional governors, although "one who fears" has also been proposed).[17] Other possible interpretations of this common, courtly designation include "war captain" (Schele 1991:10) and "regional governor" (Schele 1991:7; Stuart 1985:17-18 as cited in Jackson 2013:12). The title could occasionally be associated with priestly office and identified the bearer as having a sociopolitical status elevated beyond that of many other titled lords (Zender 2004). While it is unclear if it was a universal duty of the office, monumental inscriptions indicate that *sajal'ob* managed war campaigns and were responsible for presenting the resultant prisoners to their kings (Zender 2004:203).[18]

Bakab likely creates an even more explicit connection between political office and specific spaces. While *bakab* is typically spelled syllabically as **ba-ka-ba**, in the spirit of idiosyncratic variation in which Chocholá artists delighted, they frequently wrote **ba-ka-KAB**, using the logograph for earth as the main sign in the title (Figure 2b, block A5). As a result, *bakab* may refer to a "literal 'hilltop' that supported the sky (a reference to elevated palace dwellings and temples controlled by lords?) or someone in charge, ultimately, of agricultural terrain" (Houston, Stuart, and Taube 2006:63).[19] Conversely, the *ajaw* designation and other common titles like *aj tz'ib* and *k'inich* are not emphasized. Even though such terms do appear as clear titles in the corpus, they are rarely used, and then only in conjunction with, and modified by, other formal designations (like *y-ajaw* and *aj uxul*[?], see footnote 22).

Of the various titles they employed, Chocholá artists selected *sajal* the most frequently, using it just over half of the time (approximately 54%) when including mention of human agents in the Dedicatory Formula (Figure 15).[20] Only slightly less frequently chosen, *ch'ok* or *chak ch'ok* (35%; Figure 2b, block B4; Figure 3, blocks A and A'5; Figure 4B, block C1; Figure 5, block D) and *bakab* (23%; Figure 2b, block A5; Figure 5, block H) were also popular, while *kelem* (Figure 1c, block B; Figure 5, block E), *kalomte'* (Figure 6, block 2), and *cholom* (Figure 7, block I) were used in roughly 18%, 12%, and 14% of all

---

pers. comm.; David Stuart 2008, pers. comm.; for further discussion see García Campillo 1992; Werness 2010)

[15] The common epigraphic shorthand of labeling glyphs by letters and numbers is employed here for ease of reference. Lettering starts with the first full, visible glyph block and letters are used to designated each column moving from left to right such that the letter A marks the first column, B the second, C the third, and so on. Conversely, numbers are used to designate the rows of text, increasing as they move from top to bottom. Thus, the first glyph block appearing in the upper left corner of a text string would be designated block A1. When only one line of text occurs, then only letters (if the text is oriented horizontally, as is the case in both figs. 1c and 7) or numbers (if the text is oriented vertically) will be used. In examples containing two distinct areas of text, the second text will be labeled using A', B', and so on.

[16] The particular root found in glyph B (fig. 7) has been tentatively translated as the logograph for *k'al*, 'close' or 'fasten', marking the completion of the vessel (Grube 1990: 323f; Macri and Looper 2003:225).

[17] Many scholars have discussed the connections between the *sajal* title and royalty (for representative examples, see Houston and Stuart 2001:61-64; Houston and Inomata 2009; Jackson 2013; Villela 1993:esp. 40-43; Zender 2004:3-5). Based on the root *sa* (*sah*), "to fear," Nikolai Grube and Werner Nahm (1991, as cited in Jackson [2013:12]; see also Villela [1993:40-41]) have proposed a reading of "feared one," while Stephen Houston and David Stuart (2001:61) have tentatively suggested "one who fears."

[18] The *'ob* ending used here pluralizes the affected term.

[19] Stephen Houston, David Stuart, and Karl Taube (2006) developed this interpretation specifically through their analysis of the spelling variant offered by the Chocholá style.

[20] All statistics are approximations and will continue to shift as new material comes to light. Currently the sampling size reflects a corpus of approximately 157 pieces. Just over half of those 157 examples include glyphs of one form or another. Furthermore, about 40% of all vessels name people, either through the sole inclusion of titles (most commonly), or in a combination of titles and personal names. Put a different way, when artists elected to include writing, they chose to incorporate titles roughly three quarters of the time. Such nominal phrases index the amount of effort expended in intentionally tying these vessels to the historical record.

A

B

FIGURE 2 A-B. CALENDRICAL GROUP. CHOCHOLÁ STYLE CERAMIC VESSEL, PUUC REGION, YUCATÁN, MEXICO, C. A.D. 700-800. (A) VIEW OF 13 AJAW DATE; (B) ROLL-OUT VIEW OF 13 AJAW DATE AND THE DIAGONAL TEXT ON THE OPPOSITE SIDE OF THE VESSEL (PHOTOGRAPH © JUSTIN KERR, MAYA VASE DATABASE: K4466)

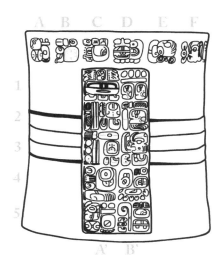

FIGURE 3. CALENDRICAL GROUP. CHOCHOLÁ STYLE CERAMIC VESSEL, PUUC REGION, YUCATÁN, MEXICO, A.D. 736 (DRAWING BY MALINE WERNESS-RUDE FROM SOTHEBY'S, INC. [2004:LOT 290])

dedicatory statements respectively.[21] Conversely, *k'inich*, *ah tz'ib*, and other terms like the *ajaw* designation, can only be found in one, two, or, at the most, three examples in the current sampling.[22]

Seemingly significant patterns can also be discerned when titular isolation or combination is considered. For instance, while *bakab* is one of the most selected titles, it only occurs by itself in 6% of examples that contain titular referents, in contrast with *ch'ok/chak ch'ok* (Figure 4, block C1) or *sajal*, which individually occur approximately 12% and 14% of the time.[23] Even though *bakab* appears about twice as often, overall, as *kalomte'*, scribes selected *kalomte'* somewhat more frequently than the popular *bakab* when ending a dedicatory statement with a single title rather than a titular string.[24]

Other examples of titular combinations can be codified in similar ways. Many combinations, like *bakab chak ch'ok sajal kalomte'* and *sajal cholom y-ajaw* only appear once in the corpus as it stands.[25] Even some of the titular strings that only focus on combining the more frequently selected titles, like *bakab kelem sajal*, occur but once. Indeed, despite the extreme repetition found in the Chocholá Dedicatory Formula, scribes developed unique combinations 15% of the time. Upon expanding this number to include instances that

[21] *Chak ch'ok* can and is frequently abbreviated to the simpler *ch'ok* phrase, especially when it is included with other titles in a glyphic string.
[22] The root *tz'ib* refers to writing, so *ah tz'ib* becomes 'he of the writing,' i.e., a scribe. In the context of image making, when possessed, *tz'ib* applies specifically to the painted medium, while carved examples are identified using the **lu**-bat phrase (Stuart 1987). The Chocholá style is no exception, and one of the standard components of the Chocholá Dedicatory Formula (the collocation **yu-[lu-bat] lu**; his/her/its carving) designates the vessels in question as carved wares belonging to the historical figures they then name either in titular and/or personal form. Outside of the corpus, *tz'ib* can be abstracted through additional suffixing (*u tz'ibnalnajal*) and can thus refer to "drawing/decoration" more generally (Kettunen and Helmke 2014:31/151). In the more focused Chocholá case study, the *ah tz'ib* marker must likely be understood in this sense as well. Although trickle (post-fire) paint has been applied to some Chocholá examples, there is no apparent correlation between its use and the inclusion of *ah tz'ib*; the emphasis (in both text and artistic technique) remains rooted in the deep carving for which the style is known. In the rare incorporation of *ah tz'ib*, the owner/creator's designation likely reflects the more general understanding of the term as connected with visual/written communication while also providing the opportunity for a nice visual coupling—*ah tz'ib ah uxul* (?), 'he of the writing, he of the carving' (see Kerr Maya Vase Database: K9092). Thus, the carving expression is a smaller, medium-specific sub-category, while the writing expression can both refer to the specific painted medium or, in this case, the art of writing more generally. Alternately, of course, the *ah tz'ib* may be a scribe who does both but identifies as a painter, or in still another possible scenario, the object thus labeled was gifted to, and names, another scribe—a painter—who owned, but did not create, it (these are less likely scenarios given that, in the case of northern ceramic production, carving was the predominant medium by the Late Classic).
[23] Because the discussion shifts focus here to the use of titular phrases and their spread, all of the more specific statistics regarding title selection that follow are calculated only in relation to the subset of Chocholá vessels that display titles of one kind or another rather than in relation to the corpus as a whole.
[24] An isolated *kalomte'* is named in roughly 8% of the cases that include mention of titles in contrast to *bakab* (6%), even though *bakab* references trump *kalomte'* ones when strings that combine titles are considered (these two titles account for 23% and 12% of all title usage, respectively, including cases when the title reference occurs in isolation and/or in combination with other names).
[25] Outside of the Chocholá body of material, it is not unusual for scribes to supplement *sajal* (or some of the other official designations metioned here) with additional titles (Zender 2004:202-204, 223, 297).

131

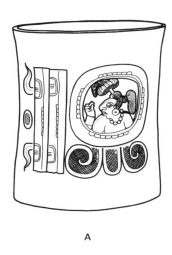

A

B

FIGURE 4 A-B. CALENDRICAL GROUP. CHOCHOLÁ STYLE CERAMIC VESSEL, PUUC REGION, YUCATÁN, MEXICO, C. A.D. 700-800. (A) VIEW OF 11 AJAW DATE; (B) VIEW OF T-SHAPED TEXT ON THE OPPOSITE SIDE OF THE CONTAINER (DRAWINGS BY MALINE WERNESS-RUDE FROM COE AND KERR [1997:99, 100])

can only be found on two examples, that percentage jumps to 25%. Such a focus on visual and textual variation in titular phrases suggests a degree of intentionality. If the sociopolitical implications of the style are taken into consideration, the emphasis on variety likely reflects a desire to link elites with overarching power structures while simultaneously alluding to individuality and a large number of distinct participants without providing even more specific personal names.

Only three phrases that combine two titles repeat with any significant statistical frequency. *Cholom sajal* (Figure 7, blocks I and J), *chak ch'ok sajal*, and *kelem sajal* (Figure 1c, blocks B and C) collocations each account for approximately 8% of nominal examples, making them the most popular of the various name combinations.[26] Despite the variability seen in title choice, one can often discern a general order, apparently reflecting internal hierarchies. In the frequent cases where *bakab* is included, it invariably ends the naming sequence, for instance, while *chak ch'ok* typically initiates name phrases when it occurs (Figure 5, blocks D-H).[27]

Image and Text, Text and Place

The statistical analysis of Cholholá titles reveals that such information varies relative to vessel imagery. Artists

frequently chose *sajal* when they elected to create cups with imagery focused on youthful lordly visages (Figures 1 and 5). This trend also partially explains the popularity of this title as the Young Lord image type acts as the most frequently chosen motif in the corpus. In this more specific context, not only is it often included, *sajal* is typically modified by other formal designations. It can appear in conjunction with *bakab, chak ch'ok, kalomte'*, and *kelem* either singly or in various combinations, which seems to indicate the desire to emphasize the extended status of these subsidiary lords (Figure 1c, blocks B-C; Figure 5, blocks D-H). Conversely, while *sajal* can also occur in non-image contexts, neither *cholom* nor *ah tz'ib* labels complement imagery focused on human elites even when they co-occur with *sajal* (Figure 7, blocks I-L).

When potters decided to carve depictions of the watery deity GI into their cups, they also chose to include a sole *chak ch'ok* title in the associated glyphic strings. In contrast, vessels showing ballplayers typically include *chak ch'ok kelem* phrases, with further additions possible, while commonly featuring *bakab* in the image 'captions' that also show up in that scene category. It thus seems as if scribes emphasized the state of play by accompanying images of ballplayers diving before a ball with texts carrying conceptual associations of youth and vitality. While the current evidence suggests such trends, artists working in the style also consistently demonstrated their ability to combine features in innovative ways. Like the broader young lord umbrella motif of which it is a part, for instance, cups showing the ballgame could also create much longer strings, as when one acclaimed owner is named as a *chak ch'ok kelem sajal u-yul bakab* (Figure 5, blocks D-H).[28]

---

[26] Despite the extreme repetition that characterizes much of the Cholholá Dedicatory Formula, scribes could and did occasionally change the order of some pairings or otherwise manipulate them. One vessel (Kerr Maya Vase Database: K8871) contains a short text that reads **AJ-ha-la CHAK cho-ko**. Given its ubiquity in the corpus, this is most likely meant to read *sajal chak chok* and the scribe may have expected the reader to understand and complete the word by filling in the missing initial 's'. Such contractions of frequently used phrases are not uncommon in the corpus; one of the simplest examples is the use of a single **ka** syllable in writing **ka-ka-wa** (for *cacaw*, chocolate), while more complex cases further shorten the reference to chocolate by omitting the traditional **ka** form entirely (see Werness 2010:fig. 22 and 216-217). Of course, it is always possible that the scribe meant to write **sa-** and instead wrote the visually similar, and more frequently used, **AJ** logograph.

[27] There are some exceptions to this general pattern. In one example (fig. 2b, blocks B4-B5), the scribe incorporated a clear *chak ch'ok bakab* string but seems to have ended the sequence with another rare (for the Cholholá corpus) title, **ba-te'**.

[28] While it has not been discussed here as it acts as a nominal modifier rather than existing as a title in its own right, the *u-yul* phrase (seemingly marking the 'polish' of the individual in question; see Grube 1990:326) is as frequently chosen as the *bakab* title it typically modifies. Indeed,

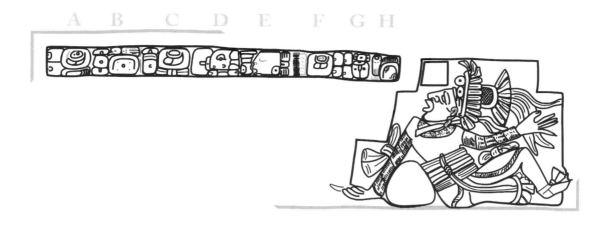

FIGURE 5. BALLPLAYER SCENE, roll-out drawing of cup. CHOCHOLÁ STYLE CERAMIC VESSEL, PUUC REGION, YUCATÁN, MEXICO, c. A.D. 700-800 (DRAWING BY MALINE WERNESS-RUDE FROM photograph © JUSTIN KERR, MAYA VASE DATABASE: K6055)

FIGURE 6. ANIMALS (BIRDS), ROLL-OUT PHOTOGRAPH. CHOCHOLÁ STYLE CERAMIC VESSEL, PUUC REGION, YUCATÁN, MEXICO, c. A.D. 700-800 (PHOTOGRAPH © JUSTIN KERR, MAYA VASE DATABASE: K508)

FIGURE 7. CALABASH SHAPED VESSEL, ROLL-OUT DRAWING. CHOCHOLÁ STYLE CERAMIC VESSEL, PUUC REGION, YUCATÁN, MEXICO, c. A.D. 700-800 (DRAWING BY MALINE WERNESS-RUDE FROM photograph © JUSTIN KERR, MAYA VASE DATABASE: K4378)

In an extension of the link between titles and imagery, specific monikers can also be connected with particular forms. In this way, the distinctive gourd shape can be connected with one of the Chocholá Dedicatory Formula iterations. In half of the examples that include clear text strings, the craftsman included *cholom* and *sajal* (Figure 7, blocks I-J), the former of which, while popular in the calabash shaped category, seems almost non-existent in the rest of the corpus.

In cases where the busts of lords emerge from misty scrolls (the largest subset of the Young Lord trope), it is also possible that the youthful figure was rendered with enough specificity to make such portraits recognizable (Boot 2006:9; Werness 2010:esp. 148-149). The idea of the portrait was certainly well developed in the Maya world and could be used to identify individual nobles as well as prisoners, as Kaylee Spencer (2007, 2015) has demonstrated. If Chocholá bust images can be seen as portraits, then they likely would have been made for (or to be given to) those whose countenances they display. At an audience level, those in the know might have been able to identify the likenesses of important political players (either as patrons or receivers) while less informed viewers would have been impressed by the emphasis on titled individuals during feasting or other social events.

Other scene categories that focus on the elite body, however, do not seem to incorporate enough visual information to encourage any identification. Particularly true of ballplayers shown in the midst of play, this may explain the greater emphasis on scene captions containing personal names in those instances. Even if portraits exist in the Chocholá style and provide more specific personal information as a result, titles occur on calabash-shaped vessels and in association with scenes showing supernatural figures. Thus, some pieces may have further modified the textual referents with identifying visual information (or vice versa, in a symbiotic relationship), yet many works did not contain such portraits and their texts mentioned titled characters rather than personal names, which may have facilitated sociopolitical interactions.

As a matter of fact, titular designations are selected much more frequently than personal names. Nikolai Grube and Maria Gaida (2006:186) have suggested that, in these cases, the title—and the political connections it offers—eclipsed any personal, individual identity. Extending this idea while keeping in mind the feasting/gifting model that partially explains the elite dissemination of such luxury goods offers further interpretive possibilities. Northern lords may have had their ceramicists create vessels that contained less specific, personal designations in order to facilitate gift giving, for instance, particularly in the case of larger feasts with multiple players, or even in anticipation of surprise visits by potential allies.[29] In this context, the variation in title selection and combination could provide a sense of individuality while still facilitating broader gift giving practices.

While the Chocholá style focuses attention on generic subsidiary titles, it would be wrong to say that no more specific references are made. Indeed, in addition to the possibility of portraits, a host of more directed allusions to people and places also occur. These ceramic texts name several sites, the most prominent being Oxkintok (two of the terms recognized as Oxkintok polity identifiers find frequent inclusion; cf. the second half of blocks A'5 and 5 in Figures 3 and 6 respectively and the first half of block P in Figure 15b).[30] Tiho (ancient Mérida), Akankeh (Acanceh), and others also receive mention. While vessels in the style have been heavily looted, Oxkintok and Mérida provide two of the few archaeologically provenienced examples, which further solidifies the connections between the corpus and these locations. Pieces archaeologically tied to these locations exhibit regionally distinct aspects of the style that do not contain glyphic references to site names. Furthermore, the unprovenienced vessel that names the Tiho location (and likely that which mentions Acanceh as well) is rendered in the sub-style connected with the Oxkintok nexus of manufacture, which then suggests an even more direct connection between the polities.[31]

Just as specific places are named in the Chocholá corpus, albeit rarely, so too are historical individuals. While many of these characters do not find further mention in other known texts, Oxkintok again makes its mark on the style. In one example rendered using a particularly calligraphic script (Figure 6), the diagonal inscription begins with the standard *u-jaay* reference (block 1) as well as the familiar *kalomte'* (block 2) designation, while a personal name (**OHL-si-?-TOK'**) and the Oxkintok site name (blocks 4-5) ends the inscription. One of the few to be granted the additional specificity of a personal name, this Oxkintok lord stands out due to his mention on multiple vessels, which likely reflects an intentional ploy. In other words, if we take into consideration the fact that most characters receive only titular mention while **OHL-si-?-TOK'** is fully, completely, and repeatedly named with titles and personal designations, this pattern serves to solidify his position relative to the rest of the *sajal'ob*, *bakab'ob* and other regional politicians named in the corpus. Given that the core expression of the Chocholá style likely originated in Oxkintok (Garciá Campillo 1992, Velázquez Valadés et al. 2005, Werness 2010, Werness-Rude 2015), it would

it either precedes *bakab* (fig. 5, blocks G-H), which then terminates the glyphic sequence, or it ends the glyphic string itself.
[29] While the northern system of government parallels that found in the south, at least at its core, there is evidence that suggests that the actual application of that governmental model looked and behaved slightly differently, with fewer 'central' sites and a larger number of directly and/ or distantly affiliated regional locations (see, for example, Ringle and Bey 2001).
[30] That this reference is meant to name the Oxkintok polity/location seems clear (García Campillo 1992). As a result, the term has been tentatively classified as the site's emblem glyph and may reflect an intentionally "archaic formula" in the presentation of the emblematic form (Graña-Behrens 2006:117)
[31] See Werness (2010) for an extensive analysis of the sub-styles identifiable in the Chocholá corpus as well as how these variants seem to be the result of regionalization in the manufacture and dissemination of the style.

make sense that one of the people responsible for driving its initial creation and dissemination would emphasize his position of power relative to those with whom he was trying to develop and/or maintain hierarchically weighted relationships.

Identifying Chocholá Dates

In addition to the historical references already established for the corpus and summarized above, the Chocholá material contains a growing body of emically dated material. As new examples have come to light, it has become clear that vessels emphasizing date cartouches form a significant sub-set within the style. Conceptual overlap occurs between many of the temporal references (e.g. Figure 2a) and one of the most frequently chosen scenes—the Isolated Bust (Figure 1a), which shows a young, lordly head and torso emerging from a watery or flowery cartouche-portal. As a matter of fact, before the most recent expansion of the Chocholá corpus, scholars identified four examples with floral or calendrical cartouches as possible substitutes for the aquatic frame from which the young figure emerges (Ardren 1996; Coe 1973; Tate 1985; Werness 2010). The diagnostic elements exhibited by the four pieces tied them to both the style and the Isolated Bust category within which it resides. In all cases, the artist set the deeply carved cartouches off through the formatting and portrayal of a single day sign, which also aligned with northern patterns of rendering dates. More specifically, the Chocholá style is identifiable in part because its vessels display a consistent visual pattern in which the main, deeply carved image is set apart not only from any textual strings but also from the lip and rim of the vessel—the image frame, which typically takes misty form, encourages this sense of separation. In the calendrical variants, the watery border transforms into a day sign cartouche but the relationships between the image and the vessel wall, text strings (when included), and even the viewer, remain consistent.[32]

Given the existence of only four known calendrical representations, these were originally seen as secondary to the main focus on misty portals. Now, however, as more works continue to come to light, the dated examples account for roughly 7% of the entire corpus when considered as a subset by themselves. As a result, they can now be classed as a distinct category, which I have descriptively named the Calendrical Group. Furthermore, when Ajaw dates are separated from the rest of the chronological references and are instead evaluated in the context of elite bust imagery, they now account for approximately 20% of that image category.

With our increasing awareness of the frequency with which Chocholá potters chose to include, and centralize, calendrical data, several key areas benefit from focused examination. To begin with, Chocholá dates provide specific anchors that support other chronological and

stylistic markers in a ceramic corpus that has largely stood outside of time. The expanded corpus of dating references allows for renewed historical analysis and each dated example can now be introduced in this light. Additionally, as already noted, the way artists rendered such information suggests ties to geographic regions in addition to the clear ideological messages of legitimization these inclusions send. Thus, after exploring what they literally say and what that suggests about the Chocholá place in history, the ideological roles fulfilled by calendrical signifiers within sociopolitical/socioeconomic spheres will be considered. Ideally, of course, the present analysis will receive further expansion and reevaluation as sampling sizes continue to grow.

It makes most sense to begin with the vessels that have already been included in the corpus and which have thus received at least passing analytic attention. The first of the four displays a clear, lone 11 Ajaw (Figure 4a). Opposite the isolated lord peeking out of his day sign cartouche, the potter incorporated a text string arranged in a T-shape (Figure 4b). This text provides an additional date, in the form of a Calendar Round that reads 6 Kawak 2 Muwan (blocks A1-B1), followed by the ubiquitous *ch'ok* title (block C1), dedication (*joy/hoy/t'ab*?, block B2), and drinking cup (*y-uk'ib*, block B3) designation. Similar youthful faces appear in other examples; a second vessel (Figure 2a) displays a 13 Ajaw (clearly identifiable as such due to the use of the Jester God headband associated with kingly power), while a third (Figure 8) seems to contain two Ajaw dates: 5 (or possibly 7) Ajaw and 1 Ajaw.

We are fortunate to have a fourth vessel (Figure 3) that adds a Long Count to the whole and partial Calendar Rounds identified above. It begins with the Initial Series Introductory Glyph, as is standard in most Long Counts, followed by **9-**[Baktun] **tu-15-ka-**[Katun]**-wa(?)/ba(?) tu-5-TUUN-ni**. The Long Count then transitions to a partial Calendar Round statement: **ti-13-AJAW**. Following the temporal notation, the scribe added dedicatory information, also truncated, including a reference to the *ch'ok* of Oxkintok (identifiable by its **7-?** site name on the right side of block A'5) that rounds out the inscription.[33]

There is some question as to how we should interpret this date. The fact that the author has ended the Long Count after the tuun period provides a range of possible readings and the Ajaw date with which he/she ended that section of the inscription causes further complications. Reconstructing the Long Count based on the information provided, with zeros filling in the missing data, results in the following Maya date: 9.15.5.[0].[0], 13 Ajaw (blocks B'1-A'3). The closest period ending that falls on a 13 Ajaw, however, should be written 9.16.5.0.0, as Boot (2008) has observed. Scribal error is one possible explanation (see Boot 2008),

---

[32] For discussion of the object-viewer relationship in the case of the Chocholá style, see Werness-Rude (2015).

[33] For consideration of the Oxkintok toponyms that appear on Chocholá style vessels, see José Miguel García Campillo (1992), and more generally, see Daniel Graña-Behrens (2006). For an analysis of this vessel specifically, see Erik Boot (2008).

FIGURE 8. CALENDRICAL GROUP, ROLL-OUT PHOTOGRAPH. CHOCHOLÁ STYLE CERAMIC VESSEL, PUUC REGION, YUCATÁN, MEXICO, C. A.D. 700-800 (PHOTOGRAPH © JUSTIN KERR, MAYA VASE DATABASE: K8853)

but there are other interpretive options. The truncated Long Count might not refer to THE period ending of 9.15.5.0.0, for example, but rather to another, micro-period ending marking the completion of a Winal cycle (Werness-Rude 2012). The educated period viewer would have been able to fill in the blanks left out by the scribe, which in this case would be 9.15.5.[6].[0], 13 Ajaw [8 Muwan], an idea that the emphasis on the preposition in this construction supports. The added preposition positions the 13 Ajaw [8 Muwan] date within each larger period of time. Regardless of the exact reading, it appears *within* the 5th Tuun, which in turn occurs *within* the 15th Katun and so on.[34] As a result, the scribe situated the 13 Ajaw date relative to the larger cycle associated with the major period ending of 9.15.5.0.0. At a broader level, this positioning is common practice throughout the Maya area and one seemingly employed in the Chocholá case, as is demonstrated by the 11 Ajaw, 6 Kawak 2 Muwan combination of (albeit partial) Calendar Rounds (Figures 4a; 4b, blocks A1-B1). The 9.15.5.0.0 period ending equates to July 20, 736 in the Gregorian calendar, and 9.15.5.6.0 falls approximately four months later, on November 17, 736. In either case, A.D. 736 coincides with the suggested period of Chocholá production in the eighth century.

Ajaw dates are not the only calendrical signs that use the temporal designation as an opportunity to focus on beautiful anthropomorphic heads. Scribes also elected to incise Ik' dates into the sides of at least two Chocholá vessels. Here the Ik' sign appears as the aristocratic profile of the Wind (Ik') God, likely to emphasize the associations with youthful power shared by that deity, young lords, and

day sign designations.[35] In the first case (Figure 9), an 8 Ik' (block A') is prominently displayed under a rim text that deviates from the standard dedication statement while incorporating another date phrase (*ti* 7 Akbal, glyph block D).

To this group of Chocholá dates, recent work in private collections and museum holdings has added several important examples. In the first (Figure 10), the artist chose to write a clear 13 Ajaw, which he then repeated two more times around the sides of the cup. Another piece mimics the form taken by dates but lacks readability—the number 8 is followed by a **lu** syllable writ large (Figure 11a), yet no known calendrical sign incorporates the **lu** syllable as its main sign. On the opposite side of the vessel, a diagonal text reads **sa-lu-la** (Figure 11b). In contrast, a third example displays heightened readability as the date is written *13 Ajaw uk'aba* (13 Ajaw is its name; Figure 12). In this case, the rounded walls of the container's standard cup form change direction to create a slightly everted rim, while tripod feet have been added at its base. This form is relatively rare in the larger corpus and the fact that the few examples to incorporate the flaring rim and feet also represent the Isolated Bust scene (see Figure 1) seems more than coincidental. Perhaps the potter selected this shape in order to create formal parallels with that scene category.

A fourth piece continues the pattern of more complex Ajaw references by including *ti 2 Ajaw* as the main image (Figure 13). A truncated form of the Dedicatory Formula runs in a diagonal line opposite the large calendrical cartouche. It

---

[34] According to Michael Carrasco (pers. comm., 2012), the *tu* phrase here likely refers to *ti+u*, which, due to its proximity to the numerical coefficient, changes the *u* to an ordinal reference (i.e. 'in/on the X-th time period' instead of the simpler 'X time period').

[35] See Taube (1992) for discussion of the conceptual parallels between the Wind God and divine kings; see Stuart (2011) for a consideration of the ways in which Ajaw day signs played into the idea of elite prerogative and duty.

FIGURE 9. CALENDRICAL GROUP. CHOCHOLÁ STYLE CERAMIC VESSEL, PUUC REGION, YUCATÁN, MEXICO, A.D. 700-800 (DRAWING BY MALINE WERNESS-RUDE FROM SOTHEBY'S, INC. [1998: SALE 7138, LOT 150])

FIGURE 10. CALENDRICAL GROUP. CHOCHOLÁ STYLE CERAMIC VESSEL, PUUC REGION, YUCATÁN, MEXICO, A.D. 700-800 (MINT MUSEUM COLLECTIONS. PHOTOGRAPH BY MALINE WERNESS-RUDE.)

begins with the by-now-familiar *u-jaay* phrase designating the vessel as a cup/bowl (see footnote 13) before focusing on an Akankeh (Acanceh) ballplayer king (NMAI 2014).

This newly expanded corpus of Chocholá dates demonstrates that temporal considerations received more attention than originally thought. The concentrated use of the Ajaw day sign also coincides with larger trends in the Maya use of dates because they mark major period endings in the Maya calendar while simultaneously focusing attention on elite abilities and responsibilities (Stuart 2011). The Chocholá interest in the Ajaw designation corresponds with the style's emphasis on the bodies of young lords, which is encoded with nuanced messages parallel to those suggested by the lord-as-date construct (Werness-Rude 2015).

At the most basic of levels, when it appears, the elite face of the Ajaw day sign peers out of his calendrical cartouche in a way that is visually similar to the Isolated Bust scene's emphasis on emergence from another kind of cartouche filled with floral and/or watery markers. In at least one case, the artist chose to emphasize the liquid nature of the calendrical frame (Figure 2a) by including dots of ascending and descending size in the scrolls typically included at the base of the Ajaw day sign. While this probably comes from the early representation of such scrolls as blood emanations on monuments such as Stela 10 from Kaminaljuyu, it also would likely have been recognized by a specific subset of northern elites as exhibiting a spatiality similar to that found in the misty portals that frame the torsos of other youthful elites in the style.[36] Other visual elements seen in the Chocholá rendition of calendrical signs seemingly emphasize their

participation in the Isolated Bust group. While the lords that lean out from their aquatic portals in the Isolated Bust Scene frequently appear empty handed, when they do hold objects, they grasp either digging sticks or plant stalks and their swirling frames can turn into strands of waterlilies.[37] In a parallel construct, the lord visible in the 2 Ajaw cartouche holds what seems to be a waterlily shoot, likely as an intentional analogue to the inclusion of such motifs in Isolated Bust imagery (Figure 13).

Two additional vessels carry date information. Rather than a single day sign or a truncated Long Count, however, both cups display three sequential day signs. The first example reads 6 Lamat, 7 Muluk, 8 Ok (Figure 14). The second vessel, possibly created by the same hand, shifts the day count by one, beginning with 6 Muluk, 7 Ok, and ending with what is likely an 8 Chuwen.[38] Using the sides of ceramic vessels to label and count sequences of days is otherwise unique in the Chocholá corpus and does not seem to have been a particularly popular practice otherwise.[39]

---

[36] For a discussion of such spatiality, see Werness-Rude (2015).

[37] The digging stick has previously been interpreted as a paddle (Ardren 1996:5). For the digging stick identification as well as comparative Chocholá examples of plant stalks held by lords emerging from misty portals, see Werness (2010:144-145, 150, figs. 63, 68).

[38] This vessel is currently on display in the Museo Regional de Cancún in Cancún, Mexico.

[39] There are several other cases that were included in the statistical analysis of Chocholá dates because they seem to include temporal notations. I have chosen not to discuss them further, however, given the uncertainty of their interpretation. One of the vessels excavated from Oxkintok, for instance, may include a 5 Chikchan(?) reference opposite the main image, but as this identification remains tentative, further interpretive analysis will be postponed until the nature of the historical marker (if it can be interpreted as such) is solidified.

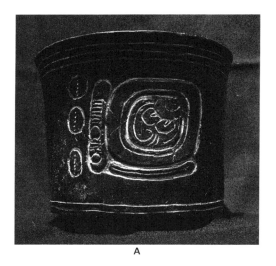

A

B

FIGURE 11 A-B. CALENDRICAL GROUP. CHOCHOLÁ STYLE CERAMIC VESSEL, PUUC REGION, YUCATÁN, MEXICO, A.D. 700-800. (A) VIEW OF 'DAY SIGN'; (B) VIEW OF DIAGONAL TEXT OPPOSITE 'DAY SIGN' (MINT MUSEUM COLLECTIONS. PHOTOGRAPH BY MALINE WERNESS-RUDE.)

FIGURE 12. CALENDRICAL GROUP. CHOCHOLÁ STYLE CERAMIC VESSEL, PUUC REGION, YUCATÁN, MEXICO, A.D. 700-800 (MINT MUSEUM COLLECTIONS. PHOTOGRAPH BY MALINE WERNESS-RUDE.)

FIGURE 13. CALENDRICAL GROUP. CHOCHOLÁ STYLE CERAMIC VESSEL, PUUC REGION, YUCATÁN, MEXICO, A.D. 700-800 (DRAWING BY MALINE WERNESS-RUDE AFTER THE NATIONAL MUSEUM OF THE AMERICAN INDIAN [NMAI 2014])

FIGURE 14. CALENDRICAL GROUP, ROLL-OUT DRAWING. CHOCHOLÁ STYLE CERAMIC VESSEL, PUUC REGION, YUCATÁN, MEXICO, A.D. 700-800 (DRAWING BY MALINE WERNESS-RUDE FROM PHOTOGRAPH © JUSTIN KERR, MAYA VASE DATABASE: K4927)

Readability and Placement

The temporal references made in the Calendrical grouping can display poetic turns of phrase, manipulate standard textual components, or may be entirely pseudoglyphic. The repeated use of 13 Ajaw makes it a particularly cogent example of this variability. The elaborate semantic reference found in the *13 Ajaw uk'aba* (13 Ajaw is its name; Figure 12) variant focuses readers' attention on the date, as does the text's scale and formatting, given that the date collocation takes up most of the vessel wall and occurs by itself. Additionally, the appearance of the more rarely used, poetic way of identifying a moment in time suggests increased engagement on the part of both the maker and the viewer. Not only does it take a higher degree of literacy to be able to write (and read) a date in this manner, doing so also signals a playful intellectualism.[40]

Another, much more common inclusion solidifies the idea that some Chocholá scribes made use of a heightened writing style involving greater use of the *ti/tu* signs (Figure 3, blocks A'2-A'3; Figure 9, block D; Figure 13). Such poetic additions, like the use of the *13 Ajaw u k'aba* phrase, provide linguistic displays that reflect an effort at greater clarity. Although it is not frequently used in dating passages, the *ti* syllable acts as a preposition meaning 'on,' 'in,' or 'at,' and can be seen leading into date phrases generally or, more specifically, attached to and preceding a Calendar Round or Day Sign elsewhere in the Maya region. More complex interpretations of its meaning suggest that it acts as a semantic flourish that complements the poetic nature of collocations such as *13 Ajaw uk'aba*. Given the preposition's more specific connotations such as "edge" and "mouth of" (Tokovinine 2013:10), the temporal marker thus modified seems to explicitly refer to the transitional nature of the time period at the same time that it is anchored to a single temporal moment.[41]

While the Chocholá style is neither uniform nor uniformly intellectual, the calendrical vessels advertise their northern point of origin. More specifically, the dates that appear on Chocholá pots reflect stylistic patterns found in Yucatán. The general dearth of extended dating information, combined with the highly truncated nature of both the Long Count and Calendar Round, parallels the brevity associated with northern inscriptions generally and dated passages specifically. The repeated *tu/ti* prepositional phrase is another semantic development with particular ties to this area of the Maya world. Similar constructions appear at Ek' Balam, for instance, and probably at Xcalumkin as well.[42] The writing of the Tuun period as **TUUN-ni** instead of the standard drum in this case also finds expression elsewhere in the north.[43]

In one case (Figure 10), the geographic tie may be even more specific. In this piece, the numbers have been reversed so that the standard relationship between bars and dots is inverted. This may reflect a slight breakdown in scribal patterns at a regional center some distance from the main node of production.[44] In this context it is perhaps noteworthy that the vessel, while it exhibits clear Chocholá traits, is also a stylistic outlier in that it atypically reduplicates the 13 Ajaw phrase three times while most Chocholá examples emphasize the correspondence between the date cartouche and the Isolated Bust imagery by isolating the calendrical sign and rendering it only once. Alternately, rather than a breakdown, we might see this inversion as another identity marker that ties the cup in question to a particular location much in the way the aforementioned **k'i** syllable functions as a regional/site-specific marker. Noticeably, Block 52 from Kabah shows a similarly inverted number (see Rubenstein and Galeev 2014 and this volume), which may reflect a relationship, either direct or indirect, between that site and the cup in question.[45]

Finally, pseudoglyphic or otherwise unreadable texts also occur in the context of the Calendrical grouping (Figure 11). While semi-readable syllables can be included, meaning remains unclear in these cases. Indeed, it is a

---

[40] Heightened literacy does not necessarily coincide with attention to visual detail or a calligraphic manner of writing; simply contrast the thickness of line usage seen in this example (fig. 12) with the thinner lines and profusion of detail evident in other works (figs. 1 and 6).

[41] Given the emphasis on the **ti/tu** prepositional phrase(s) in the reconstructed Long Count example, there is the slight chance that the 13 Ajaw date should be seen as leading into the period ending associated with 9.15.5.0.0. In this case, the prepositional reference 'at the edge of' could suggest that the exact moment indicated by the partial Long Count has not yet begun and the 13 Ajaw day verges on the 9.15.5.0.0 period ending rather than occurring just after the initiation of those nested temporal moments. If this were the case, then the intended date would be reconstructed as 9.15.[4].[11].[0], 13 Ajaw [8 Wo] (March 2, 736), instead of 9.15.5.[6].[0], 13 Ajaw [8 Muwan]. Such a reconstruction is less likely since both the 15 Katun and 5 Tun periods carry a *tu* preposition even though the 15 Katun cycle in the reconstructed Long Count would have already been entered and thus should designated as acting within the 9 Baktun cycle rather than marked as leading into it (though perhaps the preposition could carry both connotations simultaneously given its transitional nature). Furthermore, 13 Ajaw is also modified by the *ti* phrase, which in turn suggests that the whole dating sequence in this case initiates, and thus stands at the edge of, the aforementioned micro-period ending (9.15.5.[6].[0], 13 Ajaw [8 Muwan]) positioned relative to the macro-period ending (9.15.5.[0].[0], [10 Ajaw 8 Ch'en]) to which the artist also alluded.

[42] I would like to thank Michael Carrasco for calling the Ek' Balam examples (see Lacadena García-Gallo 2004) to my attention. As for Xcalumkin, note the small **ti** to the upper left of the Tuun sign on the famous vessel (see Kerr Maya Vase Database: K8017) that has long been misidentified as Chocholá (its incised lines, while skillfully rendered, are too shallow to warrant inclusion in a corpus noted for exhibiting great depth in carving).

[43] **TUUN-ni** is clearly written for the Tuun sign in the Xcalumkin vessel inscription, for example (Kerr Maya Vase Database: K8017).

[44] Less likely, the appearance of the three dots after the two bars indicating 10 may instead be a graphic misinterpretation or simplification of the **yu** knot for 10 *y-ajaw*.

[45] In the Kabah example, the dots have been further modified to take on the profile and internal details associated with the representation of eyes so that they actively look towards the date reference (a K'in sign in this case), which may explain the reversal. Another looted ceramic—this one a polychrome plate—thought to come from the northern Yucatan Peninsula shows a sequence of days signs with numbers arranged in a double column (see Kerr Maya Vase Database: K5861). The day signs on the left have numbers that appear on the left hand side of each glyph, as expected. The day signs in the right column, in an act of strict axial symmetry, reorient the associated numbers so that they appear on the right side of their respective glyphs, thus showing both number/day sign orientations simultaneously while also indicating that rigid textual ordering could be secondary to artistic considerations.

common Chocholá feature that, if readable texts could not be included, unreadable ones made up of readable or partially readable syllables often would appear. Approximately half of all vessels in the Chocholá corpus contain readable texts. Of the remaining vessels, artists chose to incorporate pseudoglyphic strings almost half of the time with the other half devoid of any suggestion of text. In this way, whether readable or not, textual passages appear in roughly three quarters of all examples, regardless of scene type, vessel form, etc.[46]

Given the strength of the desire to include text or the appearance of text, it is not surprising that pseudoglyphic sequences should appear in conjunction with calendrical notations. In the **lu** syllable example (Figure 11a), the spacing and scale differences between the bar and the three dots that would normally form an eight as the numeric coefficient call in to question such functionality. Furthermore, the main sign has been inscribed with what looks like a **lu** syllable instead of presenting Ajaw, Ik', or some other day sign, as noted above. The seeming **lu** syllable has then been used in the diagonal text on the opposite side of the vessel (Figure 11b), where **sa-lu-la** is repeated three times. As mentioned at the start, *sajal* is a common title used in the Chocholá corpus and it may be that an artist with borderline literacy tried to render that illustrious title in the diagonal glyphic string. The **lu** makes no sense as a temporal referent either (the closest option would be Muluk, which does contain the **lu** syllable), and suggests that the potter was, in this case, trying to allude to the idea of time, or rather a specific moment in time, without being able (or caring) to actually render the full word/phrase.[47] When they do not include calendrical cartouches, both these kinds of pseudoglyphic texts and their readable complements can be found in other scene groupings in the corpus, suggesting stylistic spread and multiple production centers.[48]

By now it should be clear that while Chocholá artists could choose to provide further, though still fragmentary temporal information (as demonstrated by Calendar Rounds and the truncated Long Count), they typically used the northern approach in which a single Day Sign was used

as a way of positioning the reader in time. Because this technique is relatively restricted both to the Late/Terminal Classic and to Northern Yucatán, it not only positions readers in time, it also creates a geographic anchor. The particularized dates to which the Chocholá corpus refers emphasize 13 Ajaw and 8 Ik' through repetition across vessels. These choices likely signal an even more specific set of affiliations.

In this context, the Oxkintok Ballcourt Ring is particularly important (Figure 15).[49] The Ballcourt Ring text, while fragmentary, provides enough temporal information to date the events it describes to the second decade of the 8th century, precisely at the moment when Chocholá wares were likely being created and less than two decades earlier than the Long Count vessel. A prominently displayed 8 Ik' begins the Ballcourt Ring's Calendar Round (Figure 15a, block F). Notably, it is exactly this date that is recorded multiple times even in the small number of temporal inscriptions associated with the Chocholá style. What is more, the Ballcourt Ring narrative mentions the particular Oxkintok lord, **OHL-si-?-TOK'**, who finds uniquely frequent inclusion in Chocholá texts (Figure 15b, blocks O-P). Also included are titles like *ch'ok* and *bakab* that, while by no means restricted to the Chocholá corpus, are favorite inclusions within it (Figure 15b, blocks Q-R).

Ajaw dates are a bit harder to tie to Oxkintok specifically. This is true for several reasons. First, Ajaw dates were selected more than any other day, both in the Chocholá corpus and in the body of northern hieroglyphic inscriptions. This is to be expected given that such terms were frequently used to mark ideas about kingship generally and are associated with period endings more specifically. They were commonly used, in the northern system, as a quick way of referring to the larger time period ending on/beginning after a particular Ajaw date. 5 Ajaw appears not only in the Chocholá corpus, for instance, but also at Oxkintok—where, on Hieroglyphic Stairway 2, it has been rendered as 5 Ajaw ? Muwan (García Campillo 1992: 189)—and at Itzimté (García Gallo 1987:97).[50] Similarly,

[46] When formal variation is also taken into account, these statistics develop greater skew. The shallow bowl-shaped vessels with pronounced double ridges mimicking calabashes, for instance, almost always display clearly readable sequences in contrast to the various image groups and other gourd shapes that are move cup-like and display smoothly scalloped grooves (see Werness 2010:fig. 43).
[47] In the example in question (fig. 11a), the only possible calendrical connection would be with Muluk, the sole day sign that can contain a **lu** syllable; in this unlikely scenario, the temporal reference would act as another instance of extreme contraction (see the earlier discussion of the ways in which the spelling of cacaw can be manipulated and dramatically shortened). It is also possible that rather than a date, this sign is meant to refer to the site of Oxkintok, which often gets a **7-?** name in the inscriptions; after the number, the as-yet-undeciphered visual component can appear as a head that was tentatively identified as Muluk in early investigations (García Campillo and Lacadena 1987:95 and fig. 6, Block B1).
[48] The focus on the repeated **lu** syllable in pseudoglyphic strings appears more than once, and in widely different handwriting, demonstrating just such stylistic spread.

[49] For analyses of Oxkintok inscriptions, particularly the Ballcourt Ring, see Boot (2012), García Campillo (1992, 1994), Graña-Behrens (2006), and Lacadena García-Gallo (1992).
[50] García Campillo (1992:189) has suggested that the date reads 5 Ajaw 2 Muwan, though, as he notes, numerologically, 5 Ajaw cannot typically be combined with 2 Muwan in the Calendar Round. The 5 Ajaw date that immediately precedes the 9.15.5.[6].[0] Long Count found elsewhere in the Chocholá corpus, however, is a 5 Ajaw 3 Muwan date (9.15.2.5.0). García Campillo (1992:189-190) originally proposed this same temporal identification for the Ballcourt Ring because of its closeness to the (reconstruction of the) date shown on that monument. The evidence provided by the Long Count vessel in the Chocholá style seems to support this affiliation. As mentioned, another 5 Ajaw date appears on Itzimté Stela 9, which has been positioned in the 10.0.0.0.0 to 10.1.0.0.0 range (i.e. 830-849 CE) due to the stylistic analysis of the stela upon which it was carved (García Campillo and Lacadena 1987: 97). If so, Itzimté's 5 Ajaw date was created 30-50 years after the proposed end of Chocholá production at the close of the 8th century (and approximately one hundred years after the date of the Long Count vessel). If the two 5 Ajaw dates are connected, there are several possible explanations for this discrepancy. To name just a few, production of the pottery may have lasted slightly longer, or the stela may have been made slightly earlier, than previously assumed; the 5 Ajaw event may have received subsequent mention in

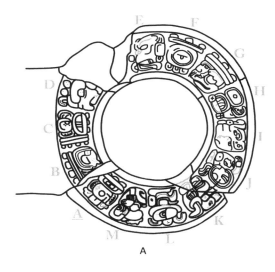 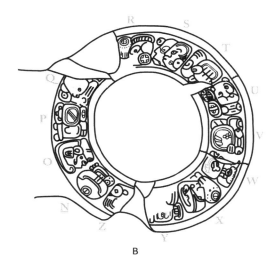

A   B

FIGURE 15 A-B. BALLCOURT RING. OXKINTOK, PUUC REGION, YUCATÁN, MEXICO. (A) SIDE 1; (B) SIDE 2. DRAWINGS BY MALINE WERNESS-RUDE.

the day 2 Ajaw was also mentioned in the monumental record at several locations, including Xcalumkin and possibly at Oxkintok and Sisila.[51] Alternately, while the number 13 frequently appears in conjunction with dates at other sites, including Oxkintok (as found inscribed on round stones at the site), the erosion of the monuments in question prevents further analysis at this time. Notably, though, the 4 Ajaw date popular at both Xcalumkin and Uxmal is absent in the Chocholá record and also seemingly at Oxkintok, at least during its Late Classic occupational phase(s).

Conclusions

The newly expanded corpus of Chocholá vessels and our awareness of the larger concentration of dates within that corpus advances our understanding of the style and the region within which it was produced in several key ways. The chronological references indicate the importance of several historical moments at Oxkintok and emphasize the tie the style has to that site. The coordination of the

Long Count and the **7-?** toponym in the Long Count example (Figure 3) solidifies a connection between these particular vessels and the site of Oxkintok, providing further evidence that the dated pots were also part of a system of ceramic manufacture focused at that site. This is significant because we still understand very little about where the style was produced. Indeed, stylistic variation within the style and even within Calendrical examples of the style suggests that it was made at several different locations; we can now add the Calendrical variant to the Oxkintok location instead of just the Oxkintok sphere of influence.

As has been suggested elsewhere (Boot 2006, Werness 2010), the Day Sign cartouche type should be included in the Chocholá corpus generally. As the corpus has expanded, it has become statistically significant enough to warrant its own category, even as it partially overlaps with one of the most represented categories in the corpus, the Isolated Bust scene (compare Figures 1 and 2). Such arguments were based on the framing similarities shared by the calendrical cartouche and the watery, misty, or flowery scrolls found in purely iconographic examples of the emergent lord category, a correlation that only becomes more visually apparent when the latest additions are taken into consideration (Figures 12 and 13).

Strong similarities in legitimizing functions can also be ascribed to each scene type. Isolated Bust and Calendrical groupings carry particularly complementary ideologies in conjunction with their similar visual appearance. In the Isolated Bust Scene, the elite individual indicates his ability to access supernatural spaces outside the viewer's domain (Werness 2010; Werness-Rude 2015). I have argued elsewhere that the use of vortex-like portal iconography to mark the location as transitional and watery exists as a way of defining the protagonists' charged place as

---

later periods; a later 5 Ajaw date may have been intentionally selected as an anniversary of the original; or Itzimté's 5 Ajaw date names a completely different temporal moment from that mentioned at Oxkintok and contained in the Chocholá style. It is worth noting in this context that the Itzimté date is treated in a way that is similar to that associated with the Chocholá style. Namely, in both cases, the 5 Ajaw is separated from any other text or text string and is given its own space. The stela is much eroded, but it seems likely that the Day Sign cartouche held the face of a young lord while an embodied king stood upon the 5 Ajaw glyph. At the very least, then, Itzimté's stela program solidifies the connection between political actors and the passage of time that is not uncommon in the Maya world and which the Chocholá style emphasizes through the Calendrical Group.

[51] See José Miguel García Campillo and Alfonso Lacadena (1987:97) for the identification of a 2 Ajaw date on Stela 20 at Oxkintok; while the text is poorly preserved, García Campillo and Lacadena initially suggested that the corresponding Long Count would have occurred in the 9.15.0.0.0 to 9.16.0.0.0 range, within which, of course, falls the 9.15.5.6.0 Chocholá Long Count date. In subsequent work, García Campillo (1992: 194) has emphasized the end of that range, focusing on the 9.16.0.0.0 period ending.

privileged while also simultaneously being separate from, yet contiguous with, the quotidian world in a seemingly natural double inversion (Werness-Rude 2015). The artists conveyed these ideas by showing a head and partial torso leaning towards viewers through a swirling ovoid frame. They also depicted the lordly bodies frequently reaching out to touch or lean against their surrounding plumes of mist (the probable agricultural objects occasionally held by these elites acted as further frame-breaking devices). The images thus demonstrated the lordly ability to engage with supernatural locations. This was not just a simple glorification of the lordly profile, however. Rather, through the occasional incorporation of agricultural references and the manipulation and constriction of the body—the figure leans forward and only the face, upper torso, and a hand or two actually fit in the scene—Chocholá artists called attention not only to lordly prerogative but also to lordly duty.

Like the Isolated Bust Scene, the Calendrical Scene presents the lord as one whose position is privileged yet entails effort. Here, the lord appears as the face of time, and as a result, time continues to move forward because of his actions.[52] Indeed, like the misty portals of the Isolated Bust Scene, the Day Sign cartouche exists in order to create a place for the illustrious actor it contains/frames. Pictorially, though, the temporal frame also provides an even more constrained, fragmented view of the elite body and such visual focusing likely added further ideological nuance.

Comparing examples from different scene groups demonstrates just how varied and conscious framing and spacing was in the corpus. The space of the ballplayer (Figure 5), for example, seems positively expansive, with the size of the ball and the full human body, dynamically arranged in play, dictating the size of the rectilinear frame. From there, artists narrowed the frame and scene in the Isolated Bust trope, likely due to the conceptual opportunities it offered, while in the Calendrical Group, they further constricted the field of vision.[53] In this context, the space of the Day Sign seems positively claustrophobic; in the Ajaw (and Wind God) Day Sign cases, the frame has tightened to the head of the lord and occasionally one of his hands. While the Isolated Bust misty portal emphasized its transitional nature by showing a lord with shoulders that might actually fit through that moving boundary, in the Day Signs, the space is no longer emphatically transitional; rather the shrinking of the cartouche means that he can only reside within/behind it. David Stuart (2011) has discussed how, in ancient Maya theory and reality, maintaining time was seen as both active and burdensome. The Chocholá case provides a nuanced view of this approach: While the elite figure appears literally as the face of time, with the accordant prestige that association offers, the pictorial

construction shows us that he must continuously embody that time and thus cannot ever shirk his role in maintaining it even as it literally and conceptually (as well as formally and ideologically) separates him from us. In addition to, and on top of, the naming of a historical date, the omission of more specific chronological information (i.e. full Calendar Rounds and Long Counts) may also indicate that the ideological message was as important as any specific historical reference.[54]

The additions presented here solidify the sense of a wider network of manufacturing centers suggested by the corpus as a whole. The variation in historical references and their stylistic appearance supports this interpretation. Several other aspects of the style are indicative of regional development. The co-occurrence of legible inscriptions and inscrutable pseudo-texts suggests that the production of the style entailed a wide range of skill sets. It is unlikely that this level of scribal and artistic diversity would simultaneously occur at any single site, especially when the sampling is further restricted to that resulting from elite patronage. The distinct variation in visual appearance despite clear use of Chocholá standards of representation further bolsters the multi-site production model.

Last, but certainly not least, the present analysis and the newly expanded corpus of vessels results in the list of Chocholá dates in Table 1.[55] These dates provide an expanded selection of moments that northern scribes deemed worthy of recording, a significant point, given their appearance on a portable medium. While the truncated Calendar Rounds do not offer much specificity regarding the exact year(s) with which they might be associated, not only would period viewers have been able to identify the specific temporal reference based on such fragmentary information, the mention of the date would have also likely called to mind a well-known event and associated actors (see Table 1, footnote a).

The fact that these vessels were only manufactured for approximately one hundred years, combined with the reconstructed Long Count date, however, allows us to suggest more specific dating possibilities for the fragmentary Calendar Rounds. This is particularly true of examples that contain multiple Calendar Round references. Returning to the vessel that included the 6 Kawak 2 Muwan Calendar Round (Figure 4b), for example, we also see a lone 11 Ajaw day sign on the opposite of the cup (Figure 4a). First, we may assume that the 11 Ajaw reference marks the temporal period beginning on that day and closest to the 6 Kawak 2 Muwan event. Indeed, the 11

---

[52] See Stuart (2011) for a discussion of the ruler as a caretaker or 'tender' of time.
[53] Indeed, the constriction seen in Figure 1a is unusual; even as the figure clearly defines his space, he can (and does) emerge from it.

[54] It is worth emphasizing that intended viewers would have recognized the contraction of the Long Counts and automatically filled in the requisite data. They would have been able to do so in part because, at the moment of creation at least (and baring further semantic devices designed to identify movement back into deeper time or forth into the future), these temporal markers related to the lived experience of many, not unlike the modern shorthand of alluding to the terrorist attacks of September 11, 2001 by simply mentioning the numbers 9-11.
[55] Reconstructions are, as always, presented in brackets, often with attendant footnotes explaining the logic behind the reconstruction.

Long Count	Day Sign	Month Sign	Vessel(s)
9.15.5.[6].[0]	13 Ajaw	[8 Muwan][a]	1. Figure 1
	13 Ajaw		2. Figure 2 3. Figure 10 4. Figure 12
	11 Ajaw	[8 K'ayab][b]	1. Figure 4
	5 Ajaw (?)		1. Figure 8[c]
	2 Ajaw		1. Figure 13
	1 Ajaw (?)		1. Figure 8
	6 Kawak	2 Muwan (?)	1. Figure 4
	6 Lamat		1. Figure 14
	6 Muluk		1. Museo Regional de Cancún
	7 Muluk		1. Figure 14
	7 Ok		1. Museo Regional de Cancún
	8 Ok		1. Figure 14
	8 Chuwen		1. Museo Regional de Cancún
	7 Ak'bal (?)		1. Figure 9
	8 Ik'		1. Figure 9 2. Sotheby's (Sale #7138, fig. 149)

(A) RECONSTRUCTED BASED ON THE PROPOSED LONG COUNT DATE, SEE ABOVE TEXT AND FOOTNOTE 41; (B) RECONSTRUCTED BASED ON ITS PROXIMITY TO THE OTHER CALENDAR ROUND NAMED ON THIS VESSEL; (C) JUSTIN KERR (MAYA VASE DATABASE: K8853) IDENTIFIES THIS AS 7 AJAW, THE BROTHER OF THE MAIZE GOD, PRESUMABLY DUE TO THE SUGGESTION OF A DIVISION FOLLOWED BY TWO CIRCLES INSIDE THE BAR ELEMENT.

TABLE 1. CHOCHOLÁ DATES. TABLE CREATED BY MALINE WERNESS-RUDE.

Ajaw inclusion is likely an effort to situate the 6 Kawak 2 Muwan Calendar Round relative to the nearest Ajaw date, which marks the conclusion of a Winal (a micro-period-ending) in contrast to the more traditional (macro-) period endings that measure the completions of major Tuun, Katun, and Baktun cycles.[56] As a result, this Calendar Round, as well as other reconstructed Calendar Rounds and Day Signs, can then be narrowed to the possibilities listed in Table 2.

What is more, several of these dates stand out. That the 13 Ajaw date is recorded without further positioning on at least four vessels (see Table 1) further supports the idea

that it was an important date for Chocholá scribes. The 8 Ik' date also seems to have been a significant one for at least one patron given that it is the only other date to be repeated in the current sample.

The current data set indicates that artists working in the Chocholá style typically chose to include text (or the appearance of text), and these inscriptions place a strong degree of emphasis on titular phrases and toponyms as well as certain personal names. Furthermore, the link between the Chocholá style and the historical record is even more evident now, as our awareness of the statistical importance of the Calendrical category grows. As both the monumental record and the Chocholá corpus continue to increase in sampling sizes, it can only be hoped that further

---

[56] Significantly, this micro-period-ending focused on the completion of a Winal cycle parallels that given in the truncated Long Count example.

Long count	Day Sign	Month Sign	Gregorian Date	Vessel(s)
9.15.5.[6].[0]	13 Ajaw	[8 Muwan]	[11/17/]736	Figure 1
[9.13.17.16.19] or [9.16.10.11.19] or [9.19.3.6.19][a]	6 Kawak	2 Muwan	[11/18/709] Or [11/5/761] Or [10/23/813]	Figure 4
[9.11.16.9.0] or [9.14.9.4.0] or [9.17.1.17.0] or [9.19.14.12.0]	11 Ajaw	[8 K'ayab][b]	[1/13/669] Or [12/31/720] Or [12/18/772] Or [12/5/824]	Figure 4
[9.15.2.5.0]	5 Ajaw	[3 (?) Muwan]	[11/13/733][c]	Figure 8
[9.16.0.0.0]	2 Ajaw		[751][d]	Figure 13
[9.14.1.8.2] or [9.14.2.3.2] or [9.14.2.16.2] or [9.14.3.11.2]	8 Ik'	[5 Sek] Or [5 Kumk'u] Or [0 Mak] Or [15 Yaxk'in]	[5/4/713] Or [1/19/714] Or [10/6/714] Or [6/23/715][e]	Figure 9 Sotheby's (Sale #7138, Fig. 149)

(A) IN CASES WHERE MULTIPLE POSSIBILITIES ARE PROVIDED, ALL RECONSTRUCTED DATES ARE GIVEN THAT COULD FALL WITHIN THE LATE CLASSIC WINDOW OF CHOCHOLÁ PRODUCTION ANCHORED BY THE LONG COUNT VESSEL.; (B) REGARDLESS OF THE EXACT YEAR, 11 AJAW 8 K'AYAB SEEMS THE MOST LIKELY RECONSTRUCTION OF THE 11 AJAW DATE, GIVEN THAT THE PERIOD OF ELAPSED TIME BETWEEN IT AND THE 6 KAWAK 2 MUWAN DATE IS SMALLER THAN THAT BETWEEN 6 KAWAK 2 MUWAN AND 11 AJAW 3 PAX. WHILE THE OTHER DAY SIGNS IN THE CORPUS LACK THE INFORMATION PROVIDED BY THE ADDITION OF MONTH SIGN HERE (FIGURE 4B), IT IS INTERESTING TO NOTE THAT THE CLOSEST 13 AJAW DATE TO EITHER THE 11 AJAW 8 K'AYAB OR THE 6 KAWAK 2 MUWAN CALENDAR ROUNDS FALLS ON 13 AJAW 3 SIP, WHICH IS ROUTINELY CONNECTED WITH EITHER MARCH OR APRIL IN OUR SYSTEM OF TELLING TIME. IF WE ARE TO SEE THESE VESSELS AS EVEN MORE CLOSELY TEMPORALLY LINKED THAN THE BROAD ONE HUNDRED YEAR RANGE ASSOCIATED WITH THE PROBABLE PRODUCTION OF THE STYLE AS A WHOLE, THEN THE REDUPLICATED 13 AJAW DATES WOULD FALL NEATLY WITHIN THE INTERVAL BETWEEN THE 11 AJAW AND 6 KAWAK 2 MUWAN CALENDAR ROUNDS. SUCH A CONNECTION IS, OF COURSE, HIGHLY SUPPOSITIONAL. CLOSER POSITIONING RELATIVE TO THE EXPLICIT LONG COUNT DATE (FIGURE 3) IS ALSO POSSIBLE; 6 LAMAT APPEARS TWICE IN THE CORPUS (SEE FIGURE 14) AND A 6 LAMAT DATE (9.15.5.2.8, 6 LAMAT 16 SAC) FALLS ON SEPT. 6TH, 736, FOR INSTANCE.; (C) THIS RECONSTRUCTION IS BASED ON THE ASSUMPTION THAT THE 5 AJAW DATE IS THE SAME ONE ALLUDED TO IN THE OXKINTOK HIEROGLYPHIC STAIRWAY 2, AND THAT GARCÍA CAMPILLO'S (1992: 189) TENTATIVE DATING OF THE STAIRWAY IS ACCURATE (SEE FOOTNOTE 50); (D) THIS RECONSTRUCTED DATE IS BASED ON THE ASSUMPTION THAT STELA 20 CONTAINS A 2 AJAW, THAT THIS DATE IS THE SAME ONE ALLUDED TO IN THE CHOCHOLÁ STYLE, AND THAT GARCÍA CAMPILLO AND LACADENA'S (1987:97; 1990: 194) TENTATIVE DATING OF THE MONUMENT IS ACCURATE (SEE FOOTNOTE 51); (E) THE RECONSTRUCTED DATE SEEN HERE IS BASED ON THE ASSUMPTION THAT THIS 8 IK' AND THE 8 IK' MENTIONED AT OXKINTOK REFER TO THE SAME DAY/EVENT. GARCÍA CAMPILLO (1992: 190) SUGGESTS THAT THE OXKINTOK BALLCOURT RING (FIGURE 15), WHICH ALSO CARRIES THE 8 IK' DESIGNATION, WAS CREATED BETWEEN 9.14.2.0.0 AND 9.14.3.0.0 (11/713 AND 11/715), AND THE RECONSTRUCTION SUGGESTED HERE PLACES THE IK' DATE WITHIN THAT TIMEFRAME.

TABLE 2. RECONSTRUCTED CHOCHOLÁ DATES WITH CORRESPONDING GREGORIAN DATES. TABLE CREATED BY MALINE WERNESS-RUDE.

comparative analysis will expand such interpretations and add additional historical ties to the tentative lists provided here.

Acknowledgements. I would like to begin by thanking Meghan Rubenstein for inviting me to contribute to this edited volume and to participate in the conference session out of which it has risen— Meghan has been a joy to work with, as an organizer, as a scholar, and as an individual. Eastern Connecticut State University also deserves recognition as the support I received while at ECSU allowed me to develop the present work. What is more, my heartfelt thanks goes to Justin Kerr for his generosity in allowing me to reproduce images of his. Maria Gaida at the Ethnologisches Museum, Staatliche Museen zu Berlin has also kindly let me include images of a vessel in the Ethnologisches collections and I am indebted to Dorie Reents-Budet and the Mint Museum for allowing me to conduct research and photograph vessels in their collections. Furthermore, many scholars have shared access to image banks and/or physical collections with me, without which I would have a much poorer contextual understanding of the style. In this regard, Traci Ardren, Sylviane Boucher, Yoly Palomo, Frederica Sodi Miranda, Blanca González, Nikolai Grube, Justin Kerr, Dorie Reents-Budet, Francis Robicsek, and Carolyn Tate as well as the Mint Museum, the Palacio Cantón, and the Ceramotca in the Centro Instituto Nacional de Antropología e Historian Yucatán have been particularly generous.

I would also like to thank other colleagues with whom I have discussed the Chocholá style as well as those who have facilitated my exploration of Chocholá dates by providing forums in which such conversations can occur. Deserving of particular mention are George Bey, III; Erik Boot; Steve Bourget; Michael Coe; Ana Díaz; Julia Guernsey; Athanasio Papalexandrou; Dorie Reents-Budet; David Stuart; and Erik Velásquez García. Michael Carrasco, Penny Steinbach, and Hope Werness also did me the honor of reading drafts of the present work and I am grateful for their thoughtful commentary. Lastly, to my family, whose support comes in myriad and innumerable forms, thank you.

References Cited

Andrews, E. Wyllys, IV, and E. Wyllys Andrews, V

1980 *Excavations at Dzibilchaltun, Yucatan, Mexico.* Publication 48. Tulane University, Middle American Research Institute, New Orleans.

Ardren, Traci

1996 The Chocholá Ceramic Style of Northern Yucatán: An Iconographic and Archaeological Study. In *Eighth Palenque Round Table, 1993*, edited by Merle Greene Robertson, Martha J. Macri, and Jan McHargue, pp. 237-246. The Pre-Columbian Art Research Institute, San Francisco.

Boot, Erik

1997 A Northern Yucatecan Origin for Kerr #4333? *Unpublished Notes on Maya Hieroglyphic Writing*: 1-7.

2006 A Chochola-Maxcanu Ceramic Vessel in a 1930's collection in Merida, Yucatan, Mexico: History and Analysis of Image and Text. Retrieved from http://www.wayeb.org/notes/wayeb_notes0024.pdf.

2008 An Oxkintok Regional Vessel: An Analysis of the Hieroglyphic Texts. Retrieved from http://www.mesoweb.com/articles/boot/Oxkintok.pdf

2012 El Calendario Maya en las Tierras Bajas del Clásico (The Calendar in the Classic Mayan Lowlands). Paper. Coloquio Internacional: "Tiempo y complejidad, Calendarios del mundo/Time and complexity, Calendars of the world." Museo Nacional de Antropología, Instituto Nacional de Antropología e Historia, México, D.F.

Brainerd, George W.

1958 *The Archaeological Ceramics of Yucatan.* Anthropological Records. University of California Press, Berkeley.

Coe, Michael D.

1973 *The Maya Scribe and His World, Exhibition Catalogue.* Grolier Club, New York.

Coe, Michael D., and Justin Kerr

1997 *The Art of the Maya Scribe.* Thames and Hudson, London.

García Campillo, José Miguel

1992 Informe Epigrafico Sobre Oxkintok y la Ceramica Chocholá. In *Oxkintok, Misión Arqueológica de España en México, Proyecto Oxkintok*, Vol. 4, pp. 185–200. Ministerio de Cultura, Dirección General de Bellas Artes y Archivos, Madrid.

1994 Comentario General Sobre la Epigrafía en Oxkintok. In *VII Simposio de Investigaciones Arqueológicas en Guatemala, 1993*, edited by Juan Pedro Laporte and Hector Escobedo, pp. 586-599. Museo Nacional de Arqueología y Etnología, Guatemala.

García Campillo, José Miguel, and Alfonso Lacadena

1987 Los Jeroglificos de Oxkintok. In *Oxkintok, Misión Arqueológica de España en México, Proyecto Oxkintok*, V. 1, pp. 91-111. Ministerio de Cultura, Dirección General de Bellas Artes y Archivos, Madrid.

Graham, Ian and colleagues

n.d. *Corpus of Maya Hieroglyphic Inscriptions.* Peabody Museum of Archaeology and Ethnology, Harvard University, Cambridge. Retrieved from http://www.peabody.harvard.edu/CMHI/about.php

Graña-Behrens, Daniel

2006 Emblem Glyphs and Political Organization in Northwestern Yucatan in the Classic Period (A.D. 300-1000). *Ancient Mesoamerica* 17:105-123.

Green, Judith Strupp

1997 A Classic Maya Lord's Atole Bowl, A Pre-Columbian Chocholá Style Vessel with Hieroglyphic Text. In *Proceedings of the 1995 and 1996 Latin American Symposia*, edited by Alana Cordy-Collins and Grace Johnson, pp. 91–99. San Diego Museum of Man, San Diego.

Grube, Nikolai

1990 The Primary Standard Sequence in Chochola Style Ceramics. In *The Maya Vase Book, A Corpus of Rollout Photographs of Maya Vases*, Vol. 2, edited by Justin Kerr, pp. 320–330. Kerr Associates, New York.

Grube, Nikolai, and Maria Gaida

2006 *Die Maya Schrift und Kunst: Der Katalog beschreibt 42 Objekte der Maya-Kultur aus der ständigen Ausstellung des Ethnologischen Museums, Staatliche Museen zu Berlin—Preussischer Kulturbesitz.* SMB DuMont, Berlin.

Grube, Nikolai and Werner Nahm

1991 Signs with the Phonetic Value *Sa*. Unpublished letter, cited in Jackson 2013 and Villela 1993.

Houston, Stephen, and Takeshi Inomata

2009 *The Classic Maya.* Cambridge University Press, Cambridge.

Houston, Stephen, and David Stuart

2001 Peopling the Classic Maya Court. In *Royal Courts of the Classic Maya, Volume One: Theory, Comparison, and Synthesis*, edited by Takeshi Inomata and Stephen Houston, pp. 54–83. Westview Press, Boulder.

Houston, Stephen D., David Stuart, and Karl A. Taube

2006 *The Memory of Bones: Body, Being, and Experience Among the Classic Maya*. University of Texas Press, Austin.

Houston, Stephen, and Karl A. Taube

1987 "Name-Tagging" in Classic Mayan Script, Implications for Native Classifications of Ceramics and Jade Ornament. *Méxicon* 9 (2):38-41.

Hull, Kerry M.

2012 Function and Form of Jaay Vessels from the Classic Period to the Modern Maya. Paper in "Precolumbian Ceramics: Form, Meaning, and Function." Organized by Michael Carrasco and Maline Werness-Rude. 77th Annual Meeting of the Society for American Archaeology, Memphis.

Jackson, Sarah

2013 *Politics of the Maya Court: Hierarchy and Change in the Late Classic Period*. University of Oklahoma Press, Norman.

Kettunen, Harri and Christophe Helmke

2014 *Introduction to Maya Hieroglyphs*. 14th ed. XIX European Maya Conference. *Wayeb*. The Slovak Archaeological and Historical Institute and Comenius University, Bratislava. Retrieved from http://www.wayeb.org/download/resources/wh2014english.pdf

Kerr, Justin

n.d. Maya Vase Database. Electronic database, http://www.mayavase.com

Lacadena García-Gallo, Alfonso

1992 El Anillo Jeroglífico del Juego de Pelota de Oxkintok. In *Oxkintok, Misión Arqueológica de España en México, Proyecto Oxkintok*, Vol. 4, pp. 177-184. Ministerio de Cultura, Dirección General de Bellas Artes y Archivos, Madrid.

2004 The glyphic corpus from Ek' Balam, Yucatán, México. Report to the Foundation for the Advancement of Mesoamerican Studies, Inc. (FAMSI). Retrieved from http://www.famsi.org/reports/01057/index.html

MacLeod, Barbara

1990 *Deciphering the Primary Standard Sequence*. Ph.D. dissertation. University of Texas, Austin.

Macri, Martha J., and Matthew G. Looper

2003 *The New Catalogue of Maya Hieroglyphs, The Classic Period Inscriptions*. University of Oklahoma Press, Norman.

Martin, Simon, and Nikolai Grube

2000 *Chronicle of the Maya Kings and Queens: Deciphering the Dynasties of the Ancient Maya*. Thames & Hudson, London.

National Museum of the American Indian, NMAI

2014 Infinity of Nations. Exhibition. NMAI, New York. Retrieved from http://nmai.si.edu/exhibitions/infinityofnations/meso-carib/248346.html.

Pollock, Harry E.D.

1980 *The Puuc: An Architectural Survey of the Hill Country of Yucatan and Northern Campeche, Mexico*. Peabody Museum of Archaeology and Ethnology, Harvard University, Cambridge.

Ringle, William M., and George J. Bey, III

2001 Post-Classic and Terminal Classic Courts of the Northern Maya Lowlands. In *Royal Courts of the Ancient Maya, Volume Two: Data and Case Studies*, edited by Takeshi Inomata and Stephen D. Houston, pp. 266-307. Westview Press, Boulder.

Rubenstein, Meghan, and Philipp Galeev

2014 The Hieroglyphic Platform at Kabah. Paper in "Recent Investigations in the Puuc Region of Yucatán." Organized by Meghan Rubenstein. 79th Annual Meeting, Society for American Archaeology, Austin.

Schele, Linda

1991 The Demotion of Chac-Zutz': Lineage Compounds and Subsidiary Lords at Palenque. In *Sixth Palenque Round Table, 1986*, edited by Merle Greene Robertson and Virginia M. Fields, pp. 6-11. University of Oklahoma Press, Norman.

Smith, Robert Eliot

1971 *The Pottery of Mayapan, Including Studies of Ceramic Material from Uxmal, Kabah, and Chichen Itza*. Papers of the Peabody Museum of Archaeology and Ethnology, V. 66. Peabody Museum of Archaeology and Ethnology, Harvard University, Cambridge.

Spencer, Kaylee Rae

2007 *Framing the Portrait: Towards an Understanding of Elite Late Classic Maya Representations at Palenque, Mexico*. Ph.D. dissertation. Department of Art and Art History, University of Texas, Austin.

2015 Locating Palenque's Captive Portraits: Space, Identity, and Spectatorship in Classic Maya Art. In *Maya Imagery, Architecture, and Activity: Space and Spatial Analysis in Art History*, edited by Maline D. Werness-Rude and Kaylee R. Spencer, pp. 229-270. University of New Mexico Press, Albuquerque.

Spinden, Herbert J.

1913 *A Study of Maya Art: Its Subject Matter and Historical Development*. Memoirs, Vol. 6. Peabody Museum of Archaeology and Ethnology, Harvard University, Cambridge.

Stephens, John Lloyd

1843 *Incidents of Travel in Yucatan*, Vol. 1. John Murray, London.

Stuart, David

1985 New Epigraphic Evidence of Late Classic Maya Political Organization. Unpublished manuscript, cited in Jackson 2013.

1987 *Ten Phonetic Syllables*. Research Reports on Ancient Maya Writing, n. 14. Center for Maya Research, Washington, D.C.

1989 Hieroglyphs on Maya Vessels. In *The Maya Vase Book*, Vol. 1, edited by Justin Kerr, pp. 149–160. Kerr Associates, New York.

2005 *Sourcebook for the 29th Maya Hieroglyph Forum*. Maya Meetings, University of Texas, Austin.

2011 *The Order of Days: The Maya World and the Truth About 2012*. Harmony Books, New York.

Tate, Carolyn E.

1985 The Carved Ceramics Called Chocholá. In *Fifth Palenque Round Table, 1983*, edited by Merle G. Robertson and Virginia M. Fields, pp. 123-133. The Pre-Columbian Art Research Institute, San Francisco.

Taube, Karl A.

1992 The Iconography of Mirrors at Teotihuacan. In *Art, Ideology, and the City of Teotihuacan*, edited by Janet C.

Berlo, pp. 169-204. Dumbarton Oaks Research Library and Collection, Washington, D.C.

Tokovinine, Alexandre

2013 *Place and Identity in Classic Maya Narratives*. Dumbarton Oaks Research Library and Collection, Washington, D.C.

Vaillant, George C.

1927 *The Chronological Significance of Maya Ceramics*. Ph.D. dissertation. Harvard University.

Velázquez Valadés, Ricardo, Raúl Morales Uh, Alfonso Lacadena García-Gallo, Ana García Barrios, and José M. Estrada Faisal

2005 Hallazgo de Fragmentos Cerámicos de Estilo Chocholá con Jeroglíficos en Oxkintok. Paper presented at the Segundo Congreso Internacional de Cultura Maya.

Villela, Khristaan

1993 *The Classic Maya Secondary Tier: Power and Prestige at Three Polities*. MA thesis, University of Texas, Austin.

Werness, Maline

2010 *Chocholá Ceramics and the Polities of Northwestern Yucatán*. Ph.D. dissertation, University of Texas, Austin.

Werness-Rude, Maline

2012 Contando el tiempo: señores y calendarios en las vasijas de estilo Chocholá/Telling Time: Calendrics and Lords in the Chocholá Style. Paper. Coloquio Internacional: "Tiempo y complejidad, Calendarios del mundo/Time and complexity, Calendars of the world." Museo Nacional de Antropología, Instituto Nacional de Antropología e Historia, México, D.F.

2015 Space Men Carving Out a Sense of Place in the Chocholá Style. In *Maya Imagery, Architecture, and Activity: Space and Spatial Analysis in Art History*, edited by Maline D. Werness-Rude and Kaylee R. Spencer, pp. 178-209. University of New Mexico, Albuquerque.

Werness-Rude, Maline D., and Kaylee R. Spencer

2015 Maya Imagery, Architecture, and Activity, an Introduction. In *Maya Imagery, Architecture, and Activity: Space and Spatial Analysis in Art History*, edited by Maline D. Werness-Rude and Kaylee R. Spencer, pp. 1-105. University of New Mexico Press, Albuquerque.

Zender, Marc

2004 A Study of Classic Maya Priesthood. Ph.D. dissertation. University of Calgary, Alberta.

The Hieroglyphic Doorway and Other Monuments from H'Wasil, Campeche

Carlos Pallán Gayol and Antonio Benavides Castillo

At the heart of the Puuc region lies the site of H'Wasil, in Campeche, a few kilometers west of Labná and south of Kabah. It was first reported in 2007 by Antonio Benavides Castillo and included in the surveys conducted by Stephan Merk. In this paper, the authors present the results of a more in-depth field documentation and epigraphic analysis of the site's carved monuments. Standing architecture at H'Wasil displays Late- to Terminal Classic features. Of special interest is a small group of monuments with hieroglyphic inscriptions. This chapter deals with their decipherment and seeks to contextualize these findings into a broader perspective encompassing regional interaction among Puuc sites as an effort toward overcoming the still prevailing lack of epigraphic documentation and analyses in this region, when compared to other parts of the Maya lowlands. This type of work, when extended to several other sites in the Puuc, could then serve as a foundation for enabling historical reconstructions of such aspects as geopolitical interaction and prevailing rulership institutions and sociopolitical conditions during the decades immediately prior to the collapse and abandonment underwent by several sites within this region.

El sitio de H'Wasil se ubica en el corazón de la región Puuc, unos cuantos kilómetros al oeste de Labná y al sur de Kabah. Fue reportado inicialmente en 2007 por Antonio Benavides Castillo e incluído también en las prospecciones efectuadas por Stephan Merk. Los autores presentan aquí resultados más detallados obtenidos a partir de una documentación in situ y análisis epigráfico e iconográfico de los monumentos esculpidos. La arquitectura en pie de H'Wasil exhibe características propias del Clásico tardío al terminal. Especialmente interesante resulta un grupo selecto de monumentos que ostentan textos jeroglíficos. El presente artículo aborda su desciframiento y busca contextualizar estos hallazgos dentro de un panorama más amplio que discute la interacción que pudo haber entre distintos sitios de la región Puuc, en un esfuerzo adicional para contribuir a paliar la todavía prevalente carencia de análisis y documentación sistemática de la epigrafía de esta región, en comparación con aquella de otras partes de las tierras bajas mayas. Trabajos de este tipo, al ser extendidos a otros sitios del Puuc, pueden entonces servir de fundamento para efectuar reconstrucciones históricas de las condiciones sociopolíticas prevalentes durante las décadas inmediatamente anteriores al colapso y abandono que afectó a un gran número de sitios en esta región.

This paper is based on the results stemming from the 2011 fieldwork season at H'Wasil carried out by Project MANZANA,[1] as well as the documentation of the monuments bearing hieroglyphs or/and iconography by the Instituto Nacional de Antropología e Historia (INAH) Ajimaya project, also in 2011.[2] The information presented here is an updated and condensed version of a previous paper presented by us in Campeche (Benavides, Pallán, and Gardner 2011), although this one focuses more on epigraphic aspects.

The site of H'Wasil is located on the heart of the Puuc region, a few kilometers southwest of Sayil, west of Labná, and south of Kabah. Four and a half kilometers southeast also lies Sabana Piletas,[3] and some kilometers to the east, Huntichmul (Figure 1). The first reports concerning H'Wasil date back to 2007, when one of us (Benavides) was informed about the existence of important architectural and sculptural vestiges at this site, which had been reported to INAH's *Consejo de Arqueología* (Archaeology Council). The *Consejo de Arqueología*, in turn, informed the National Archaeology Coordination and the Ajimaya project about the existence of undocumented hieroglyphic inscriptions in this area. Around the same time, German journalist Stephan Merk explored the site and included information gathered at H'Wasil in a publication about several Precolumbian sites close to Chunhuaymil, Campeche. This publication (Merk 2011) offers a preliminary analysis of the carved hieroglyphic blocks from H'Wasil's doorway, as does a second publication by Daniel Graña-Behrens (2011), which focused on sculpture visible on the surface.

Standing architecture at H'Wasil clearly exhibits traits usually ascribed to the Late to Terminal Classic transition (c. A.D. 800-900; cf. Andrews 1995, Pollock 1980). In certain ways paralleling Xcalumkin (Pollock 1980:418-449; Benavides 2010) or Sisilá (Benavides 2002, 2003; Pollock 1980:484), at H'Wasil exists a strong tendency towards producing public sculpture that simultaneously fulfills an architectural function. The "monuments" discovered thus far at the site actually constitute architectural elements rather than stand-alone sculptures.

---

[1] MANZANA: *Mantenimiento Menor de Zonas Arqueológicas no Abiertas al Público* (minor maintenance of archaeological sites not open to the public).
[2] Ajimaya (*Acervo de Glífica e Iconografía Maya*) is a project from INAH's *Coordinación Nacional de Arqueología* under the direction of Carlos Pallán. We are grateful to Centro INAH Campeche, Amy M. Gardner of UCL London and the Uxul Archaeological Project from the University of Bonn for their valuable assistance in making this documentation possible.
[3] For more information about Sabina Piletas see Benavides, Grube, and Pallán 2009.

Carlos Pallán Gayol - University of Bonn, Germany (s5capall@uni-bonn.de); **Antonio Benavides Castillo** - Instituto Nacional de Antropología e Historia, Centro INAH Campeche (abenavides.cam@inah.gob.mx).

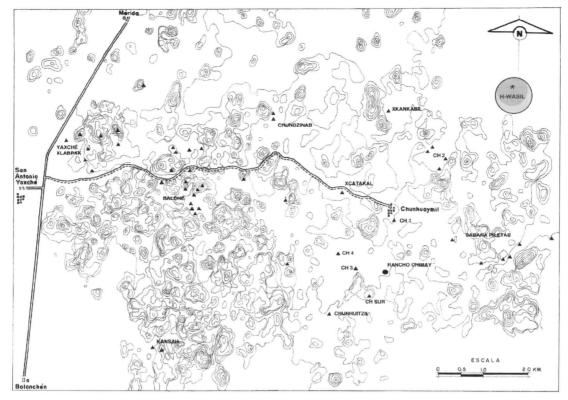

FIGURE 1. MAP SHOWING THE LOCATION OF H'WASIL (ELABORATED BY PROJECT MANZANA/INAH UNDER THE DIRECTION OF ANTONIO BENAVIDES CASTILLO).

The Sculpted Monuments from H'Wasil

The following is a brief overview of the H'Wasil sculptural corpus, after which we present more in-depth analyses of the main glyphic texts. In this section, we concentrate on items with preserved inscriptions and iconography. While some of the monuments were partially exposed on the surface previously, more complete information was recovered during the excavation of the Hieroglyphic Doorway Building, designated EPJ (*Edificio de la Portada Jeroglífica*), which originally had six paired rooms distributed along an east-west axis. All rooms opened to the south side, the three southernmost through columns and the three on the north through a single opening.

1. Hieroglyphic Doorway 1 (*Portada 1*) consists of the inner jambs and lintel, forming one doorway of a construction with six rooms (Figure 2). Doorway 1 is comprised of seven stone blocks (*sillares*), including the lintel. There are 33 associated carved glyph blocks. Due to the importance of this text, this item was documented with advanced imaging technologies (RTI and 3D photogrammetry) by one of the authors (Pallán) and Amy Gardner to maximize detail retrieval.

2. On its broad face (50 cm), the fragment of an eroded lintel contains the representation of a personage showing a circular cavity on his torso (Figure 3). Part of the waist and the upper portion of legs are visible. The narrow face (38 cm) preserves at least six glyph blocks arranged in two

FIGURE 2. H'WASIL HIEROGLYPHIC DOORWAY 1. COMPOSITE VIEW EDITED TO DISPLAY CORRECT ORIENTATION OF LINTEL. ELABORATED FROM RTI IMAGES BY CARLOS PALLÁN AND AMY GARDNER, 2011 (PROJECT AJIMAYA/INAH).

a

b

FIGURE 3 A-B. H'WASIL LINTEL 1 (BROAD SIDE) WITH THE REPRESENTATION OF A PERSONAGE SHOWING A CIRCULAR CAVITY ON HIS TORSO. (A) RTI IMAGE BY CARLOS PALLÁN AND AMY GARDNER, 2011 (PROJECT AJIMAYA/INAH); (B) PHOTOGRAPH BY ANTONIO BENAVIDES (PROJECT MANZANA, INAH).

a

b

FIGURE 4 A-B. H'WASIL LINTEL 1 (NARROW SIDE) PRESERVING SOME SIX GLYPH-BLOCKS ARRANGED IN TWO COLUMNS. (A) PHOTOGRAPH BY ANTONIO BENAVIDES (PROJECT MANZANA, INAH); (B) RTI IMAGE BY CARLOS PALLÁN AND AMY GARDNER, 2011 (PROJECT AJIMAYA/INAH).

columns (Figure 4). Its original length probably exceeded 79 cm. Unfortunately, the poor preservation prevents us from offering any in-depth analysis of the text, although it is possible that a *tzolk'in* date opens at A1 and a "carving" dedication (a possible variant of *y-uxul-il?*) could follow at A2-B2. Extant glyphic shapes and contours on this lintel are reminiscent of those at Xcalumkin.

3. A second lintel fragment was serrated on its broader face (50 cm), just before the eroded representation of what resembles a pair of legs (Figure 5a). It is possible that the stolen portion contained a well preserved depiction of the "earth" or *witz* monster. On one of the narrow sides (38 cm) at least eight glyph blocks arranged in two columns are preserved (Figure 5b). Upon analyzing both lintel fragments, we concluded that they originally belonged to

a

b

FIGURE 5 A-B. H'WASIL LINTEL 1. (A) SECOND LINTEL FRAGMENT (BROAD SIDE). PHOTOGRAPH BY ANTONIO BENAVIDES CASTILLO (PROJECT MANZANA, INAH); (B) SECOND LINTEL FRAGMENT (NARROW SIDE). RTI IMAGE BY CARLOS PALLÁN AND AMY GARDNER, 2011 (PROJECT AJIMAYA/INAH).

the same monument, which we have labeled Lintel 1. A detailed analysis of this text is offered below.

4. Capital 1, the topmost pilaster element, is carved with a glyph on one of its narrow sides (Figure 6). The item is broken. Its dimensions are 52 cm long, 49 cm wide, and 24 cm high. It was found at surface level, a few meters south of the building's rubble line (square 8P). The extant glyph seems to read horizontally and may have formed part of a calendric statement, by either providing the day name **KIMI** (T736v/SCC) or even the head variant for the number ten (T1040/SC1).

5. Capital 2 is a square column with motifs on two of its narrow sides (Figure 7). It is 47 cm long, 39-40 cm wide, and 22 cm high. Several curved lines can be seen on the side resembling "fire" scrolls. Under this motif there is a band running across the length of this face, above which

four angular signs point to the left of the viewer. On the other narrow side, there are three sculpted hieroglyphs arranged horizontally and framed by a rectangle. Although their analysis requires caution due to erosion, it is possible that they contain a date in the *tuun-ajaw* system, judging from the incomplete sequence MANIK'? **ta-u?** (on the day Manik'? from (K'atun?)...". This item was found only two meters south of the building (Layer I, square 8N).

6. A small fragment of a glyphic inscription, in which four glyph blocks are visible, was possibly part of a doorjamb (Doorjamb Fragment 1) since the glyphs read vertically (Figure 8). It measures 70 cm long, 25 cm high, and is 23 cm thick. It was found at the front entrance of the southeastern room (Layer I, square 10L). Initial analysis of the glyph blocks yields a reference to the north as *xaman* and possibly *elk'in ta' b'ih* (east of the road?).

FIGURE 6. H'WASIL CAPITAL 1 (TOPMOST PILASTER ELEMENT) SHOWING A GLYPH ON ONE OF ITS NARROW SIDES. RTI IMAGES BY CARLOS PALLÁN AND AMY GARDNER, 2011 (AJIMAYA/INAH).

FIGURE 7. H'WASIL CAPITAL 2 WITH THREE HIEROGLYPHIC CARTOUCHES. PHOTOGRAPH PROJECT MANZANA/INAH, 2011.

7. Another small fragment of a glyphic inscription (not pictured) is 23 cm long, 22 cm wide, and 15 cm thick. On one side, only a single glyph is visible. On the other, we see part of a band similar to the one described in Item 5 above (Figure 7), but with two angular motifs. It was found a few centimeters south of the previous fragment (Layer I, square 10M).

8. A relief with personage in a dynamic posture (not pictured) was found in the sector named Patio 1 in 2007, southeast of the EPJ. It shows a figure raising the right foot and holding a possible incense bag with the left hand. Part of the loincloth is visible. It measures 65 cm at its maximum height and 50 cm at its maximum width. It was found severely fragmented, although the parts could be joined.

9. Three glyphs remain on another set of fragments of glyph blocks found in the sector named Patio 2 in 2007, southeast of the EPJ. They could have been part of either a jamb or a lintel. The parts combined measure 70 cm long, 20 cm wide, and 12 cm thick.

10. Another incomplete sculpture is a column with an anthropomorphic carving (Figure 9). A human figure was carved on its front side, although only the feet, legs, and loincloth are preserved. It was found in the sector named Patio 3 in 2007. It measurements 54 cm at its maximum height, 49 cm at its maximum width, and 28 cm in diameter.

11. A cornerstone with six glyphs (Figure 10), three on each visible side, was found at surface level on the slope of a mound located some 90 m south of EPJ. This piece measures 75 cm high, 30 cm wide, and 27 cm thick. Several glyphs are damaged.

12. The final fragment of a doorjamb (Doorjamb Fragment 2) preserves at least three hieroglyphs (Figure 11), two of which are damaged. This is not a lintel, given that the glyphs are arranged vertically. The item has a length of 60 cm, a width of 47 cm, and a thickness of 21 cm. It was found at surface level on a mound some 50 m south of the EPJ.

Hieroglyphic Doorway 1

There are 33 glyphs preserved on Hieroglyphic Doorway 1, *Portada 1* (Figure 2), making it among the lengthiest and most important texts of its type within the western Puuc region. This corpus includes Panel 2 (32 glyph blocks), Miscellaneous Text 5 (26 cartouches), and Lintel 1 from Xcalumkin, although the latter once belonged to a longer text within the sculptural program of the Temple of the Initial Series. A distinctive feature of the H'Wasil Doorway 1 is that is has five round cavities distributed along the jambs and the lintel.

Epigraphically, the first issue to be resolved was to determine the proper reading order of the blocks. To help find a solution, comparative analyses with similar texts

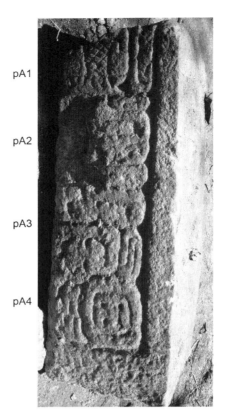

pA1
pA2
pA3
pA4

FIGURE 8. H'WASIL DOORJAMB FRAGMENT 1 WITH FOUR GLYPH BLOCKS. PHOTOGRAPH PROJECT MANZANA/INAH, 2011.

FIGURE 9. H'WASIL COLUMN WITH ANTHROPOMORPHIC REPRESENTATION. PHOTOGRAPH PROJECT MANZANA/INAH, 2011.

FIGURE 10. H'WASIL CORNERSTONE 1 WITH SIX GLYPH BLOCKS (THREE ON EACH SIDE). PHOTOGRAPH PROJECT MANZANA/INAH, 2011 .

FIGURE 11. H'WASIL DOORJAMB FRAGMENT 2 WITH THREE GLYPH BLOCKS. PHOTOGRAPH PROJECT MANZANA/INAH, 2011.

CLAUSE 1: DATE			
Pos.	Transcription	Transliteration	Translation (preliminary)
A1	4?-KIB'?	*Chan Kib?*	"on the day 4 Kib(?)"
B1	K'IN-ni	*k'in*	
C1	ta-3-su?-tz'i?	*ta ux suutz'?*	"on (the) 3rd of Suutz'(?)"
D1	ni-* CAVITY(??)	*ni-...?*	"my ?..."(round cavity)
CLAUSE 2: DEDICATION			
E1	K'AL? yu-JAGUAR.GOD ta (HAAB':FLAT.HAND)	*k'al? yu.... ta'*	"it was finished, the...? for"
F1	ya-xa-*la?	*Yaxal Ha'al? Chaahk*	"Yaxal? Hal? Chaahk"
G1	ha-la cha-ki		
TEXT (SECOND PART)			
A2	NAH-ki-ti	*Naah Kit*	"First/great Father"
A3	a?-AJAW?-wa	*Ajaw?*	"(the) Ruler?"
A4	u-KIT?	*u-kit*	"Ukit (Father of)...."
A5	*CAVITY(??)	*?...*	?...(inlay?)
A6	yu-xu-lu-li	*y-uxulil*	"It is his carving,"
A7	TAL?-ki ta	*talik? ta'*	"it was touched(?) by..."
A8	??-T533	*?...??*	"??.. Flower?"
A9	ka?-b'i	*kaab'?*	Earth?
A10	* CAVITY (??)		?...(inlay?)
A11	4-TE'	*chante'*	"four..."
A12	??-T533	*?....??*	??Flower(s)/Son(s)...
A13	AJ-K'IN	*ajk'in*	"Calendar priest(s)"
A14	i-tz'a-ti	*itz'at-tul?*	Wise ?...
B2	tu-lu?		
B3	??-T533	*?...?*	??Flower(s)/Son(s)...
B4	AJ-tz'i-b'a	*ajtz'ihb'*	"the scribe"
B5	* CAVITY (??)		(inlay?)
B6	i-tz'a-ti	*itz'aat*	"the wise man"
B7	wi-WINIK-ki	*winik*	
B8-B9	AJ-K'UH-b'a	*Aj k'uh b'a(ah)*	"he of the holy image?"
B10	* CAVITY (??)		(inlay?)
B11	u-XUKUB'?-OL-la	*u-xukuub' ohl* (sign AV5)	"it is his "antler" doorway"
B12	tu-B'AH?/ -hi?	*tu-b'aah?*	"for the first(?)... "
B13	sa-ja-la	*sajal*	The Sajal (subordinate dignatary)

Table 1. A running transcription, transliteration and translation of the text of the Hieroglyphic Doorway 1 (*Portada 1*) at H'Wasil.

were performed, including Xcalumkin Miscellaneous Text 1 (Graham and Von Euw 1992:195), the Hieroglyphic Doorway of Sisila Building 35 (Graña-Behrens 2002:plate 142) and Halakal Lintel 1. Table 1 is a running transcription, transliteration, and translation of the text from Doorway 1, based on the reading order we have determined is most likely.

Hieroglyphic Doorway 1 Text

After considering at length the various possibilities, with the valuable help of Nikolai Grube, we concluded that position A1 should be the leftmost collocation on the Doorway's lintel (Figure 12a) and the reading order should continue from there horizontally across the lintel,

given that it opens with a rather formulaic date expressed on the *Tuun Ajaw* "Short Count" system, widely used at the western Puuc region (cf. Graña-Behrens 2002).[4] The *tzolk'in* coefficient appears to be four (or alternatively three), and the *haab'* coefficient is clearly three, followed by a possible *Sotz'* month written phonetically as **su-tz'i** (C1). The second sign of this collocation (**tz'i**) can be readily compared to the **tz'i** syllable at position B4. Taking this into account, along with the +1 day shift in the *haab'* coefficients between Puuc texts and their southern lowlands counterparts (Edmonson 1976; Pallán 2009:60 note 24; Vail and Aveni 2004:134-35), only the days Imix,

---

[4] Grube's observations were very helpful for us to narrow down the dating alternatives.

A1   B1   C1   D1   (E1)   F1   G1   H1   I1

a

b

FIGURE 12 A-B. H'WASIL HIEROGLYPHIC DOORWAY 1. (A) DETAIL OF GLYPHS ACROSS LINTEL (POSITIONS A1-I1); (B) DETAIL OF POSITIONS H1-I1 SHOWING POSSIBLE *YAX HA'AL CHAAHK* THEONYM. RTI IMAGES BY CARLOS PALLÁN AND AMY GARDNER, 2011 (AJIMAYA/INAH).

Kimi, Chuwen, and Kib' are possible with a 3 coefficient. From these, the very few preserved details of the main sign at A1 favor Kib' (T525), although an unusual variant for the day Kimi cannot be completely ruled out.[5] Given the general archaeological setting and the "late" paleographic features of the site inscriptions, it seems safe to attribute a general Late to Terminal Classic date for the placement of the Calendar Round herein recorded. Thus, the three more likely possibilities in our view are:

10.01.10.07.16	4 Kib' 3(4) Sotz'	March 13th, 860
09.18.17.12.16	4 Kib' 3(4) Sotz'	March 26th, 808
09.16.04.07.16	4 Kib' 3(4) Sotz'	April 8th, 756

From the above alternatives, the general similarity to the Temple of the Initial Series at Xcalumkin (A.D. 744) and Building 35 at Sisila (dated to A.D. 755, Graña-Behrens 2002:365) ought to be considered. The lintel provides some indication that the carved glyphs could conceivably have "interacted" with something embedded into the cavities in antiquity, given that a sign T116 **ni** attaches in position D1 to the central Lintel cavity in a manner similar to a glyphic prefix in relation to a (now missing) main-sign, perhaps even as a first person ergative pronoun, thus providing a "possessed noun"-type construction so common in dedicatory texts (cf. Stuart 2005:48). It can therefore only be speculated that these "niches" held valuable inlays (possibly incised with motifs), which due to their intrinsic

value were removed or stolen in ancient times; no signs of them were found, even in the two lowermost ones hidden under the surface. The two signs at E1 provide a common dedicatory compound not uncommon on Chocholá ceramics, formed by the "flat-hand" verb with the "tun/year" sign on top (T548:713). The whole might read **K'AL**(?), with the sense of "finishing" or "completing" (cf. Grube 1990:324, Fig. 5; Stuart 1989:Fig. 5). The next block presents the head variant of the Jaguar God of the Underworld prefixed by **yu** and suffixed possibly by **ki**, although the reading remains uncertain. Then a possible theonym or anthroponym follows through H1-I1 (Figure 12b), which might read **ya-xa-?-ha?-la-cha-ki**, thus perhaps providing a variation on *Yax Ha'al Chaahk*, "Chaahk of the first rains." This phrase appears in Classic period inscriptions from Copan and Piedras Negras (cf. Looper 2003:78; Pallán 2009b:22; Robiscek and Hales 1981:40), the Chilam Balam of Chumayel (Roys 1973), and Diego de Landa's *Relación de las cosas de Yucatán* (1966). The phonetic spelling of *yax* as **ya-xa** is widely attested in the mid 8th century inscriptions of Chichén Itzá, which could provide grounds for the later possible date, A.D. 860.

The text likely continues at A2 on the left doorjamb (Figure 13a) with the expresion *Ukit*, "first/great father," followed by what might be an *ajaw* title for "lord," although the first sign has an uncertain reading. Between A4 and A5 appears another plausible term **u-KIT**. The reverential form *kit* "father" embedded into personal names is widely attested

---

[5] This possibility was suggested to us by David Stuart upon examination of the authors' field images.

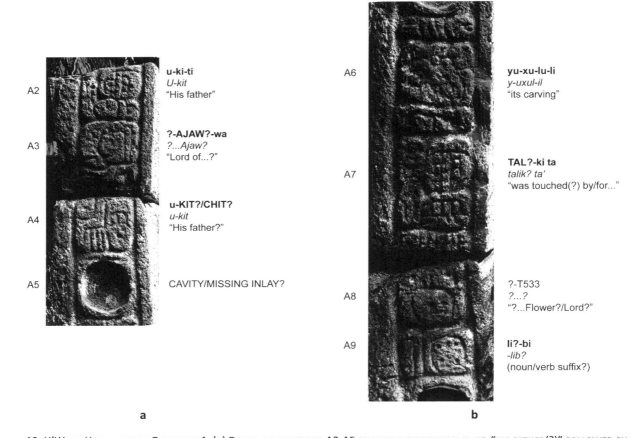

A2 — **u-ki-ti** / *U-kit* / "His father"

A3 — **?-AJAW?-wa** / *?...Ajaw?* / "Lord of...?"

A4 — **u-KIT?/CHIT?** / *u-kit* / "His father?"

A5 — CAVITY/MISSING INLAY?

A6 — **yu-xu-lu-li** / *y-uxul-il* / "its carving"

A7 — **TAL?-ki ta** / *talik? ta'* / "was touched(?) by/for..."

A8 — ?-T533 / *?...?* / "?...Flower?/Lord?"

A9 — **li?-bi** / *-lib?* / (noun/verb suffix?)

a   b

FIGURE 13. H'WASIL HIEROGLYPHIC DOORWAY 1. (A) DETAIL OF POSITIONS A2-A5 SHOWING EXPRESSION *U-KIT*, "HIS FATHER(?)" FOLLOWED BY PERSONAL NAME/RANK. RTI IMAGES BY CARLOS PALLÁN AND AMY GARDNER, 2011 (PROJECT AJIMAYA/INAH); (B) CONTINUATION THROUGH POSITIONS A6-A9 SHOWING CARVING DEDICATION (*Y-UXULIL*) FOLLOWED BY SEQUENCE **TAL?-KI-TA** AND THE FIRST OF TWO CONSTRUCTIONS INVOLVING SIGN T533 (PROBABLY NOT TO BE READ AS **AJAW** IN THESE CONTEXTS). RTI IMAGES BY CARLOS PALLÁN AND AMY GARDNER, 2011 (PROJECT AJIMAYA/INAH)

in the Puuc region, particularly at Xcalumkin and Sabana Piletas (Benavides, Grube, and Pallán 2009), as well as in Ek' Balam (Lacadena 2004). The way into which the sign T211/HE6 **u** is depicted at H'Wasil is also reminiscent of mid 9th century inscriptions at Chichén Itzá, providing additional grounds for considering the A.D 860 dating (Figure 13b). This is followed in A7 by a sign, which could correspond to either one of the **TAL?** variants suggested by Schele and Grube (1997:175) and Davoust (1995:574), or an undeciphered "rope" sign, as explained by Stuart (2005:30). The first alternative could imply a transitive verb construction followed by a preposition *talik*(?) *ta'*, "it was touched by....", according to lexical entries for **TAL** as "to touch" (Barrera Vásquez 1980:764; Yoshida 2009:87). The following glyphs specifying the possessor (or agent) of the carving remain difficult to fully decipher, although reference to four "learned" or "wise" calendar priests is made between A11-A14 (*chante' ?-T533 ajk'in itz'aat*), as could be ascertained once the excavations by Project INAH/MANZANA reached the base of the jambs at floor level (Figure 14).

As for the right jamb of the doorway (Figure 15), evidence suggests that the correct reading order should connect both jambs (from A12-A14 to B2-B6), as in this way a semantic couplet results as follows:

A12: ?-T533
A13: **AJ-K'IN-ni**
A14: **i-tz'a-ti**
B2: **tu-lu?**
B3: ?-T533
B4: **AJ-tz'i-ba**
B5: * CAVITY (??)
B6: **i-tz'a-ti**

?...ajk'in Itz'aat ??... ajtz'ihb' itz'aat winik would mean "?....the wise one(s) of days, the wise person(s) of writing," alluding at once to (a) priest(s) versed in calendrics and writing (Figure 16). A similar couplet appears at Xcalumkin Panel 4 (A1a, A1b; Graham and Von Euw 1992:182). Then follows another agentive-type title, likely written as **AJ-K'UH-b'a**, "he of the holy image(s)?".[6] The last part of the inscription (Figure 17), after the fifth cavity, seems to reiterate and complement the dedicatory clause at the beginning: *u-xukuub'(?) ohl*, "his deer-antler portal/doorway," which seems to employ the so-called "deer-antler" sign for which a decipherment

---

[6] In the past we have read this collocation as **AJ-K'AB'A?-b'a**, "he of K'ab'a'?" (Benavides, Grube, and Pallán 2009), but more careful examination favors the possibility that the main sign involved is simply T1016c/AMC **K'UH** (God C), without the **K'AB'A'** distinctive "elbow"-like element.

FIGURE 14. H'WASIL HIEROGLYPHIC DOORWAY 1 AFTER RESTORATION. NOTE BOTTOM LEFT COLLOCATION **I-TZ'A-TI** AT GROUND LEVEL NOT PREVIOUSLY VISIBLE. PHOTOGRAPH PROJECT MANZANA, INAH.

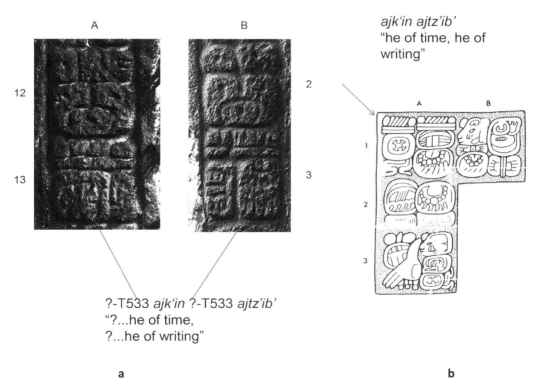

FIGURE 15 A-B. H'WASIL HIEROGLYPHIC DOORWAY 1. (A) DETAIL OF PARALLEL COUPLET AT POSITIONS A12-13 (LEFT JAMB) AND B2-B3 (RIGHT JAMB), WHICH SERVES TO CONFIRM THE CORRECT READING ORDER OF THE OVERALL TEXT. RTI IMAGES BY CARLOS PALLÁN AND AMY GARDNER, 2011 (PROJECT AJIMAYA/INAH); (B) XCALUMKIN PANEL 4. DETAIL OF SIMILAR PARALLEL COUPLET AT POSITION A1 READING **AJ-K'IN-NI AJ-TZ'I-B'A**, "HE OF DAYS, HE OF WRITING." DRAWING BY ERIC VON EUW IN GRAHAM AND VON EUW (1992:4:182) © PRESIDENT AND FELLOWS OF HARVARD COLLEGE.

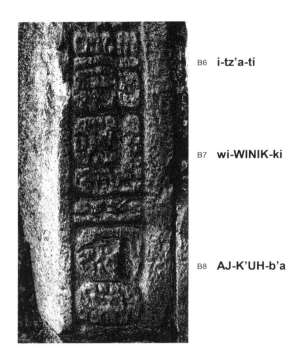

B6 **i-tz'a-ti**

B7 **wi-WINIK-ki**

B8 **AJ-K'UH-b'a**

FIGURE 16. H'WASIL HIEROGLYPHIC DOORWAY 1. DETAIL OF POSITIONS A12-13. RTI IMAGE BY CARLOS PALLÁN AND AMY GARDNER, 2011 (PROJECT AJIMAYA/INAH).

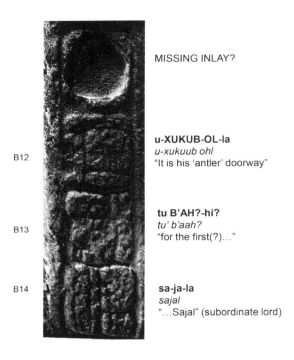

MISSING INLAY?

B12 **u-XUKUB-OL-la**
u-xukuub ohl
"It is his 'antler' doorway"

B13 **tu B'AH?-hi?**
tu' b'aah?
"for the first(?)…"

B14 **sa-ja-la**
sajal
"…Sajal" (subordinate lord)

FIGURE 17. H'WASIL HIEROGLYPHIC DOORWAY 1. DETAIL OF POSITIONS B12-B14. RTI IMAGE BY CARLOS PALLÁN AND AMY GARDNER, 2011 (PROJECT AJIMAYA/INAH).

as *xukuub'?* has been proposed by Luis Lopes and Albert Davletshin (2004). The glyphic term *ohl* has been related to the meaning "doorway" by several authors (i.e. Boot 2002:34). The last two blocks provide possibly **tu-B'AAH?-hi** followed by a clear **sa-ja-la**. Either *tu' ?… sajal* "for the ?… sajal" or *tu' b'aah sajal* "for the first sajal." From Classic period inscriptions, the term *sajal* (probably "he who fears") denotes lesser-rank dignitaries, subordinate to a *k'uhul ajaw* or "holy lord." Although, after the Terminal Classic transition several *sajalo'b'* seem to be in control of sites within the northern lowlands, often without any overlords being mentioned on the texts, which suggests political transformations affecting former rulership systems were taking place.

Lintel 1

Unfortunately, the site of H'Wasil was looted prior to the beginning of the archaeological work by Project MANZANA/INAH. This lead to a loss in significant portions of the texts and iconography of Lintel 1 (Figure 3). Presumably some of the best preserved portions were taken. The upper portion of Lintel 1 contains the representation of a personage on its front side, attired in such a way to suggest he is a local ruler or high ranking dignitary. Most conspicuous is a round cavity on his chest, similar to the ones described on the doorway itself, which could likewise have contained an inlay of some kind. The figure also carries a rounded headdress (Figure 3b), which often appears in connection with specific groups depicted on Terminal Classic art at northern sites such as Chichén Itzá, Uxmal, and Labná, as well as southern ones such

as Caracol, Ucanal, and Seibal. This type of headdress is also prominently featured in the Pabellon molded-carved ceramics, which parallel representations on the Rio Blanco Veracruz ceramics, thereby suggesting a Terminal Classic trait that again favors the A.D. 808 or the A.D. 860 dating as proposed above.

What we take to be the lower portion of Lintel 1 contains a text showing ten extant glyph blocks running along its left side (Figure 4). In Table 2 we offer an epigraphic analysis of this text, which greatly benefitted from observations made by Nikolai Grube and David Stuart.[7]

The first preserved glyph (pA1) possibly reads *ohl?*, combined with other, now lost, signs. If correct, this could refer again to a "heart" or a "doorway." Unfortunately, all of block pB1 is missing. Whatever was recorded here, it was followed at pA2 by **9-?-ki?**. One way to read the eroded head-variant is *b'uluk winik?*,[8] "nine persons"; although, this is difficult to establish as it occurs with the next badly damaged sign. The text becomes clearer at pA3, where a reference to the "north" (*xaman*) is made, seemingly to end this incomplete clause. There follows at pB3 what Houston and Stuart (1996) have termed a deity impersonation formula (see also Nehammer, Thun, and Helmke 2009), which is not uncommon at Puuc region sites, notably Xcalumkin (Grube 1994) and Sabana Piletas

---

[7] The impersonation statement and the related supernatural's name were pointed out to me first by Stuart (pers. comm. Mexico City, ca. 2007).
[8] We prefer here the Yukatekan *b'uluk* over the Ch'olan *b'uluch* form, because of the geographic/cultural setting and also of its attestation as **b'u-lu-ku** on the Madrid Codex.

Position (provisional)	Transliteration	Transcription	Translation (preliminary)
(pA1)	***OL?-la?**	*ohl?	"heart?/doorway?"
(pB1)	(missing)	(missing)	(missing)
(pA2)	**11-WINIK?-ki**	b'uluk winik?	"nine persons?"
(pB2)	**b'a?/ma?-?**	-----	----
(pA3)	**xa-MAN-na**	xaman	"north"
(pB3)	**u-B'AH-hi-AHN-li**	u-b'aah-ahn-il	"he is the impersonation of"
(pA4)	**TIL? -CHAN-na**	Tihl? Chan K'awiil	"K'awiil who lightens the sky"
(pB4)	**K'AWIL**		
(pA5)	**OK?/TIL?-CHAN?**	Ok?/Tihl? Chan?	"Jewel who Lights?/Enters?
(pB5)	**UH-la**	Uhal	the Sky"

TABLE 2. A RUNNING TRANSCRIPTION, TRANSLITERATION, AND TRANSLATION OF THE TEXT OF LINTEL 1 AT H'WASIL.

(Benavides, Grube, and Pallán 2009). Such formulae imply that a theonym follows after the opening statement *u-b'aah-ahn-il* ("he is the impersonation of," as in pB4), in this case possibly *Tihl Chan K'awiil* or "K'awiil who lightens the sky."[9] Lastly, there is an anthroponym belonging to the historical personage impersonating the supernatural, in this case either *Ok? Chan Uhal* ("Jewel who enters the Sky") or a partially repeated name *Tihl? Chan Uhal* ("Jewel? who lightens the Sky"). Although no preserved titles are connected to it, this could well have been the name of a local ruler or dignitary, perhaps even the *sajal* mentioned earlier in the Hieroglyphic Doorway 1 text, his overlord or one of his subordinates.

Conclusions

Puuc texts from the Late/Terminal Classic very often fail to offer a richness of historical detail. They do, however, occasionally provide important insight into the realm of priesthood and scribal practices, non-royal elites, and the role that both newly introduced and also carefully preserved religious cults continued to play during these turbulent political times. The now relatively well documented textual corpus of H'Wasil is no exception to this general pattern. It is medium to moderately sized site with a level of preservation typical of the region. However, the concentration of glyphic texts found scattered around the EPJ building—even after severe looting had taken place—suggests that this building once contained an extensive sculptural program with texts and iconography along its columns, jambs, and lintels comparable to those found at Xcalumkin, Sisila, and other Puuc sites. Based on its geographic location, characteristics, and overall architectural and sculptural discourse, it seems safe to say that H'Wasil was secondary in importance to the larger Sabana Piletas close by, where far longer texts and more imposing architecture have been documented (Benavides,

Grube, and Pallán 2009). The historical figure(s) identified thus far seemingly bear no clear rank higher than *sajal*, which together with the overall discourse of H'Wasil monuments reinforces our hypothesis that the site was subordinate to a larger polity. Whether the latter could have been Sabana Piletas, Itzimte Bolonchén (Von Euw 1977), Xcalumkin, Kabah, Sayil, or even a larger regional capital, such as the political entity of *Ka'an* or *Chan* mentioned at Jaina, Xcalumkin and other sites (cf. Pallán 2009a:288 and Figs. 6.11e; Graña Behrens 2006:110), or Uxmal during the early to mid 9th century (cf. Kowalski 2003), depends to a large extent on the correct dating of the H'wasil Doorway 1, for which we currently hesitate to favor one of the three dates that fall within a period from A.D 756 to A.D 860. At any rate, such a question appears to require further data to be addressed properly. It is probable that more centralized modes of rulership from the Late Classic lowlands cannot be readily extrapolated into this time, as comparative evidence suggests that processes implying a significant degree of political fragmentation into small and relatively locally-autonomous polities were taking place within the Puuc during the Late to Terminal Classic transition, before the advent of more focused control was exerted by the rise of hegemony at metropolises like Chichén Itzá and Uxmal.

Acknowledgments. We want to thank INAH's National Archaeology Coordination for providing both the required authorizations and funding from which the research presented here stems; Centro INAH Campeche and Sara Novelo Osorno for their support in greatly assisting collaboration between the two INAH Projects MANZANA and AJIMAYA; the University of Bonn, Germany (*Abteilung für Altamerikanistik und Ethnologie*); the Uxul Archaeological Project (Nikolai Grube and Kai Delvendahl) for kindly facilitating an all-terrain vehicle which enabled us to reach locations difficult to access otherwise; Nikolai Grube again for his always helpful comments and insights which helped us to solve important aspects of H'Wasil inscriptions; David Stuart who also helped us to understand aspects of the inscription on Lintel 1; and special thanks to Amy Maitland Gardner from UCL London for her valuable help in the RTI and 3D photogrammetric documentation of the H'Wasil sculpture.

---

[9] Collocations reading *tihl* with the probable sense of "burn, lighten" (Kaufman 2003:524) were recorded at Itsimte-Sakluk Stela 17, Motul de San José Stela 3, incised bones from Burial 116 at Tikal, and in the name of Naranjo ruler *K'ahk' Tiliw Chan Chaahk* (Boot 2007:154, Martin and Grube 2008:74).

References Cited

Andrews, George F.
1995 *Pyramids and Palaces, Monsters and Masks. Vol. 1: Architecture of the Puuc Region.* Labyrinthos, Lancaster, CA.

Barrera Vásquez, Alfredo, and Silvia Rendón (editors)
1980 *Diccionario Maya Cordemex.* Ediciones Cordemex, Mérida, Yucatán.

Benavides Castillo, Antonio
2002 Informe de labores de mantenimiento menor, Proyecto MANZANA, Temporada 2002 en Sisilá, Campeche. Centro INAH Campeche. *Archivo Técnico,* National Archaeology Coordination, INAH, México, D.F.
2003 Labores de conservación arquitectónica en Sisilá, Campeche. *Mexicon,* XXIV (6):161-164.
2007 Informe de labores del Proyecto MANZANA. Temporada 2007: Sabana Piletas, Chundsinab, Kansah. Centro INAH Campeche. México. 164 pp. (Document at the *Archivo Técnico* (Archive) from the National Archaeology Coordination, INAH, México).
2010 *Xcalumkín. Un sitio Puuc de Campeche.* Colección Bicentenario Campeche Solidario, State Government of Campeche. Campeche, Mexico.

Benavides Castillo, Antonio, Sara Novelo Osorno, Nikolai Grube, and Carlos Pallán Gayol
2009 Nuevos hallazgos en la región puuc: Sabana Piletas y su escalinata jeroglífica. *Arqueología Mexicana* 97:77-83.

Benavides Castillo, Antonio; Nikolai Grube, and Carlos Pallán Gayol
2009 "La escalinata jeroglífica 1 de Sabana Piletas: nuevos datos sobre el Epiclásico en la región Puuc". Proceedings of the *XVIII Encuentro Internacional Los Investigadores de la Cultura Maya,* t. 1. Universidad Autónoma de Campeche, Campeche 2009.

Boot, Erik
2002 A Preliminary Classic Maya - English/English - Classic Maya Vocabulary of Hieroglyphic Readings. Available online at Mesoweb. URL: http://www.mesoweb.com/resources/vocabulary/Vocabulary.pdf
2007 *The Updated Preliminary Classic Maya-English, English-Classic Maya Vocabulary of Hieroglyphic Readings;* Mesoweb Resources. Available online at Mesoweb, URL: http://www.mesoweb.com/resources/updated-vocabulary/index.html

Davoust, Michel
1995 *L'Écriture Maya: et Son Déchiffrement,* CNRS Editions, Paris.

García Barrios, Ana
2008 Chaahk, el dios de la lluvia, en el periodo Clásico maya: aspectos religiosos y políticos. Doctoral Dissertation. *Universidad Complutense de Madrid. Departamento de Historia de América II.*

Graham, Ian and Eric Von Euw
1992 *Corpus of Maya Hieroglyphic Inscriptions. Vol. 4, Part 3; Uxmal, Xcalumkin.* Peabody Museum of Archaeology and Ethnology. Harvard University Press, Cambridge, Mass.

Graña-Behrens, Daniel
2002 *Die Maya Inschriften aus Nordwestyukatan, Mexiko.* Unpublished doctoral dissertation. Rheinische Friedrich-Wilhems-Universität, Bonn, Germany.
2006 Emblem Glyphs and Political Organization in Northwestern Yucatán in The Classic Period (A.D. 300–1000). *Ancient Mesoamerica* 17:1:105-123.

2011 Reconstructing the Inscription on a Building in H-Wasil and Remembering an Ancient Noble Yucatec Family of "Wise Men" and "Scribes." In *The Long Silence. Sabana Piletas and its Neighbors: An Architectural Survey of Maya Puuc Ruins in Northeastern Campeche, Mexico.* Acta Mesoamericana, Vol. 21, edited by Stephan Merk, pp. 263-274. Verlag Anton Saurwein, Markt Schwaben, Germany.

Grube, Nikolai
1990 "The Primary Standard Sequence in Chocholá Style Ceramics". In: *The Maya Vase Book Vol. 2: A corpus of Rollout Photographs of Mayan Vases* pp.320-330. New York: Kerr Associates.
1994 "Hieroglyphic sources for the history of northwest Yucatan" in *Hidden among the Hills.* Acta Mesoamericana 7: 316-358. H.J. Prem (ed.) Verlag von Flemming. Möckmühl.
2005 "Toponyms, Emblem Glyphs, and the Political Geography of Southern Campeche". *Anthropological Notebooks* 11: 89–102. Slovene Anthropological Society 2005
2007 "The birth of the wayoob - a narrative on Codex style ceramics". Conference presented at the 12th European Maya Conference (EMC), Geneva, Switzerland, Wayeb (Asociación Europea de Mayistas); 7 de diciembre de 2007.

Grube, Nikolai, Alfonso Lacadena, and Simon Martin
2003 Chichen Itza and Ek Balam. In Notebook for the XXVIIth Maya Hieroglyphic Forum at Texas, March, 2003:II-1 – II-84. Maya Workshop Foundation, Austin.

Houston, Stephen D. and David Stuart
1996 "Of gods, glyphs, and kings: divinity and rulership among the Classic Maya." In: *Antiquity 70(268):289-312.* Cambridge, England.

Kaufman, Terrence S.
2003 *A Preliminary Mayan Ethimological Dictionary.* Available online at Famsi, URL: http://www.famsi.org/reports/01051/pmed.pdf

Nehammer Knub, Julie; Simone Thun, and Christopher Helmke
2009 "The Divine Rite of Kings: An Analysis of Classic Maya Impersonation Statements". In: Le Fort, Geneviève, Raphael Gardiol, Sebastian Matteo and Christopher Helmke (eds.) The Maya and their Sacred Narratives. Text and Context in Maya Mythologies. Acta Mesoamericana, vol. 20, Anton Saurwein, Markt Schwaben, pp. 177-195.

Kowalski, Jeff Karl
2003 "Collaboration and conflict: an interpretation of the relationship between Uxmal and Chichen Itza during the terminal Classic/Early Posclassic periods". In: *Escondido en la selva: arqueologia en el norte de Yucatan. Hanns J. Prem, ed. pp. 235-272.* Instituto Nacional de Antropologia e Historia; University of Bonn, Germany-México.

Lacadena García-Gallo, Alfonso
2004 "The Glyphic Corpus of Ek" Balam, Yucatán, México". *Report submitted to FAMSI,* available online at URL: http://www.famsi.org/reports/01057/section10.htm

Landa, Diego de
1966 *Relación de las cosas de Yucatán.* Editorial Porrúa. México.

Looper, Matthew G.
2003 *Lightning Warrior: Maya Art and Kingship at Quirigua.* Austin: University of Texas Press.

Macri, Martha and Gabrielle Vail
2009 *The new catalog of Maya hieroglyphs; Volume two: The codical texts.* University of Oklahoma Press

Martin, Simon and Nikolai Grube

2008 *Chronicle of the Maya Kings and Queens: Deciphering the Dynasties of the Ancient Maya* (2nd revised ed.). London and New York: Thames & Hudson

Maldonado C. Rubén, Ángel Góngora S. and Alexander W. Voss
2002 Kalom Uk'uw, señor de Dzibilchaltún. In *La organización social entre los mayas prehispánicos, coloniales y modernos. Memoria de la Tercera Mesa Redonda de Palenque*, edited by Vera Tiesler Blos, Rafael Cobos and Merle Greene Robertson: 79–100. México, D.F. and Mérida: INAH y UADY

Lopes, Luís and Albert Davletshin.
2004 "The Glyph for Antler in the Mayan Script". *Wayeb Notes*, No. 11. <http://www.wayeb.org/notes/wayeb_notes0011.pdf>

Merk, Stephan
2007 "Two Maya sites with hieroglyphic inscriptions in northern Campeche en *Mexicon*, XXX(3):67-68. Möckmühl.
2011 *The Long Silence. Sabana Piletas and its neighbours*. Acta Mesoamericana 21. Verlag Anton Sauerwein. Markt Schwaben, Germany.

Pallán Gayol, Carlos
2009a Secuencia dinástica, glifos emblema y topónimos en las inscripciones jeroglíficas de Edzná, Campeche, (600-900 d.C.): implicaciones históricas. M.A. Thesis. Estudios Mesoamericanos. Facultad de Filosofía y Letras. UNAM. México.
2009b "The Many Faces of Chaahk" in: The Maya and their Sacred Narratives: Text and Context in Maya Mythologies, Memorias de la 12va. Conferencia Maya Europea, Ginebra. Editado por Geneviève Le Fort, Raphaël Gardiol, Sebastian Matteo and Christophe Helmke, pp. 17-40. Acta Mesoamericana, Vol. 20. Verlag Anton Saurwein, Markt Schwaben.
in press "Statements of Identity in the Archaeological and Textual Record. Discerning the Protagonists of Terminal Classic Culture Contact in Mesoamerica" Conference presented at the 16th European Maya Conference (EMC) Wayeb. Copenhaguen, Denmark, Dic. 2011.

Pollock, Harry E. D.
1980 *The Puuc. An architectural survey of the hill country of Yucatan and northern Campeche, Mexico*. Memoirs of the Peabody Museum of Archaeology & Ethnology. Harvard University. Cambridge, Mass.

Robicsek, Francis, and Donald Hales
1981 *The Maya Book of the Dead: The Ceramic Codex*. Charlottesville: University of Virginia Art Museum.

Roys, Ralph L.
1973 *The Book of Chilam Balam of Chumayel*. University of Oklahoma Press. Norman.

Schele, Linda and Nikolai Grube
1997 *Notebook for the XXIst Maya Hieroglyphic Workshop*, "The Dresden Codex," Department of Art and Art History, The College of Fine Arts, and The Institute of the Latin American Studies, University of Texas, Austin.

Schele, Linda, Nikolai Grube and Erik Boot
1997 "Some suggestions on the k'atun prophecies in the Books of Chilam Balam in light of Classic-period history". In *Tercer Congreso Internacional de Mayistas*, pp. 399-432. Universidad Nacional Autónoma de México.

Stuart, David
1998 "Hieroglyphs on Maya Vessels", in Kerr, Justin, 1989, *The Maya Vase Book, a Corpus of Maya Rollout Photographs on Maya Vessels,* edited by Justin Kerr.
2005 *Glyphs on Pots: Sourcebook for the XXXIst Maya Hieroglyph Forum at Texas.* University of Texas at Austin

2008 Unusual Signs 1: A Possible Co Syllable. Published online at Sep. 13 2008 at URL: http://decipherment.wordpress.com/2008/09/13/unusual-signs-1-a-possible-co-syllable/

Tokovinine, Alexandre
2007 "Classic Maya Place Name Database Project, Mesoamerica", report submitted to FAMSI; Available online at: http://www.famsi.org/reports/06054/index.html

Vail, Gabrielle and Anthony Aveni.
2004 "Research Methodologies and New Approaches to Interpreting the Madrid Codex. In *The Madrid Codex: New Approaches to Understanding an Ancient Maya Manuscript*, ed. Gabrielle Vail and Anthony Aveni, 1-30. Boulder: University Press of Colorado.

Von Euw, Eric
1977 *Corpus of Maya Hieroglyphic Inscriptions. Vol. 4, Part 1: Itzimté, Pixoy, Tzum.* Peabody Museum. Cambridge.

Wyllie, Cherra
2002 Signs, Symbols, and Hieroglyphs of Ancient Veracruz: Classic to Postclassic Transition. Doctoral Dissertation. Yale University, Department of Anthropology. 385 leaves, New Haven.

Yoshida, Shigeto
2009 *Diccionario de la conjugacion de verbos en el maya yucateco actual*. Graduate School of International Cultural Studies, Tohoku University.